HOW JAMES JOYCE
MADE HIS NAME

HOW JAMES JOYCE MADE HIS NAME

A READING OF
THE FINAL LACAN

ROBERTO HARARI

TRANSLATED BY LUKE THURSTON

OTHER

Other Press
New York

Originally published in Spanish as *¿Cómo se llama James Joyce?*

Copyright © 1995 Roberto Harari. Translation copyright © 2002 Luke Thurston.

Production Editor: Robert D. Hack

This book was set in 11 pt. Berkeley by Alpha Graphics of Pittsfield, NH.

10 9 8 7 6 5 4 3 2 1

Library of Congress Cataloging-in-Publication Data

Harari, Roberto.
    How James Joyce made his name : a reading of the final Lacan / by Roberto Harari ; translated by Luke Thurston.
      p. cm.
    Includes index.
    ISBN 1-892746-51-4 (pbk.)
    1. Joyce, James, 1882–1941—Criticism and interpretation—History—20th century. 2. Lacan, Jacques, 1901—Contributions in criticism. I. Title. II. Series.

PR6019.O9 Z574 2002
823'.912—dc21   2001036649

For my wife Diana,
who with her love, her patience,
and her clear-headed encouragement
accompanies all of my psychoanalytic endeavors.

(bababadalgharaghtakamminarronnkonnbronnton-
nerronntuonnthunntrovarrhounawnskawntoohoo-
hoordenenthurnuk!)

J. Joyce, *Finnegans Wake*

I wish for blankness, emptiness, the absence of words. But
it is always words that speak inside my head, speak without ceasing.

M. Didier, *Contrevisite*

Contents

Prologue

Great bows on her slim bronze shoes: spurs of a pampered fowl.

J. Joyce, *Giacomo Joyce*

Yo to doró
To doró ñoño hormoso
To doró ono coso
Ono coso co yo solo so
COFO

Cabrera Infante, *Tres tristes tigres*

Exile is a kind of living apart, a feeling of being limitless like a man without body or emotion, anonymous and without biography.

H. Tizon, *Experiencia y lenguaje*

I

In the present work I pursue the pathway opened by my introductory studies of Lacan's Seminars 11 and 10 (Buenos Aires: Nueva Vision, 1987; Buenos Aires: Amorrortu editores, 1993). The subject of the work is Seminar 23, *Le sinthome*, which was delivered by the French psychoanalyst in 1975–1976. In my opinion, the intent, significance, relevance, and context of this choice are sufficiently explained and developed by the work itself for me to dispense with discussing them here. The fundamental ingredient of my books is the text transcribed from recordings of my classes, given at the Centro de Extension Psicoanalitica in the General San Martin Cultural Center at Buenos Aires. I followed the same procedure here, even if I was amiably requested to do so by the Secteur d'Etudes et Recherche en Sciences, Cultur, et Société of the Center, directed by Adriana Zaffaroni. I am therefore profoundly grateful to her, and also to the audience at San Martin, which once again in 1993 packed the lecture hall to accompany, with interest and with a striking degree of receptivity and discussion, a topic that was completely new for very many of those present, regarding both its psychoanalytic-topological and its literary aspects. On this occasion, I have respected the breaks set by each of the ten classes, in order not to efface the productive traces of the book's origin. Despite this, as can be seen from the publication dates of a section of my bibliography, my growing interest in those chapters dealing with the seminar caused me to extend the initial text by including themes and approaches that did not form part of my classes at San Martin, nor indeed were addressed in the seminar itself. In this sense, I have observed in myself a certain retreat, with full admiration and respect, from Lacan's text, in particular when I have turned to his own sources. As will be seen, I do not always share the same conclusions as Lacan; this "Introduction," therefore, seeks to enable the development of a judgment governed by reason, not by acritical fascination. On the other hand, I have not refrained from using schemas, comparative tables, and drawings when—in my own view, naturally—the argument requires them. It is in this sense that I would stress the guiding thread of my work: to attain the maximum clarity of exposition without making any illegitimate concessions. Rigor does not equate with obscurity, just as one should not confuse didactic verve with the proverbial jargon of psychoanalysis.

II

I would also like to express my gratitude to Lorena Reiss, for her meticulous and devoted labors with the word processor. The many "corrections" of the original text have also benefited from her comments on the writing itself.

III

As the epilogue of this Prologue, we might introduce immediately one of the book's principal subjects, if only as an indication. If there is indeed—or perhaps there only should be—a "post-Joycean" psychoanalysis and literature, and given that my text deals more with the first of these, I would like to include here a few references to post-Joycean writing as seen in Spanish. This is bound up with the difficulty of reading Joyce's *Finnegans Wake*, which obviously requires, first, a great mastery of the English language. Since it is radically untranslatable—a point that my book duly acknowledges—it is good to know that in Spanish there are works of great significance able to arouse the jouissance of a post-Joycean act of writing. "Post" here, of course, does not define a chronological time but a subjective position before "the letter." This is why Gongora, and to a lesser extent Quevedo, form part of this lineage. As does Julio Cortazar's *Rayuela*, G. Cabrera Infante's *Tres tristes tigres* (see above epigraph), L. Marechal's *Adan Buenosayres*, and J. Rios's *Larva*. Let us leave the final word here to this last author (a contemporary, at last), in a kind of wreath or emblem that serves as an ideal hinge for the reader to begin immersing him- or herself in what my pages set forth: "Hourra, Mr. Joyce! The animator again straddles the microphone. He rejoyces in the name of Freud. May the joy continue!"

1

Joyce and Lacan: A Quadruple Borromean Heresy

Seminar 23, *Le sinthome* (1975–1976), is probably the last moment in the whole of Lacan's teaching where a rigorous internal unity is emphasized. What emerges there is a coherent reconceptualization of many themes that relate not only to the clinical practice of psychoanalysis—although they have a considerable bearing on it, and we will see how—but also form part of a sort of tradition: the psychoanalytic turn to art, in particular to literature, the aesthetic domain that is closest to the analytic experience. Psychoanalysis is connected to literature through its work with spoken language; as analysts, we are inevitably located on the borders of the literary field. In this sense, in the seminar we are to explore, Lacan uses his engagement with Joyce to set in motion transformations that are *without precedent* in any writer—and that, in the first place, put in question certain prior phases of his own teaching.

At various points in our study we will invoke puns and wordplay, in a way necessarily entailed by Lacan's thought. Some people might find that, as such, these *jeux de mots* are trivial, gratuitous, embarrassing. There is indeed some justification for this feeling: by rupturing the limits of our lexicon, wordplay is an affront to common sense, thus the unavoidable awkwardness. Yet there is nothing trivial about these puns: on the contrary, they enrich Lacan's discourse, making it a worthy successor of the Joycean endeavor. Lacan's wordplay, his verbal figurations and disfigurations, bear witness to an extraordinary encounter—beyond their actual meeting in 1921—between two theoreticians, two practitioners of the letter who were remarkably akin. Thus, as we follow the unfolding of the seminar, we will be working with the same kind of effects. In this sense, and so as to accompany our trajectory, we will sometimes have to ask the reader to suspend his linguistic common sense.

In addition, we should repeat our initial warning [made in the Preface]: we will not seek to tackle every topic raised by the seminar, as this would be impossible in ten chapters. We will attempt, rather, to understand—as we read, sometimes moving back and forth to situate differences—the fundamental lines of thought, the driving concepts that will let us realize our single aim: to grasp what Lacan was aiming at. There is clearly no question here of our substituting a reading of Seminar 23; on the contrary, it is a question of pushing the reader toward that reading.

One question remains to be cleared up, before we start. It is well known that Lacan's unpublished seminars are not freely available for legal reasons, due essentially to financial issues relating to Lacan's family. Faced with such a situation, we will use transcripts of recordings in various versions, both in French and Spanish.[1] This implies our establishing a text,

---

1. Translator's note: English versions of the texts used by the author will be given, with indications of any problems or dilemmas in translation.

one that can be debated and reworked. These different versions are not on sale commercially, but their existence has given rise to conflicts, even to judicial persecution, which will one day have to be opened up to public debate. Meanwhile, we must be content with the material to be found in the libraries of psychoanalytic institutions, those which are attempting to keep Lacan's work alive—despite every effort to imprison that work or produce a "stuffed" version of it, on the part of his so-called testamentary executor, whose true aim is to pass over that work in silence, as we see from the series of delayed publications and the numerous conceptual errors that can be spotted in the "official" versions of the seminars. Our choice of Seminar 23 thus represents a clear decision: to respond to this attempt to silence and distort Lacan's work, one which centers particularly on its final period—the period, precisely, that presents additional difficulties because of its complex topological elaborations.

Having formulated these opening thoughts, one has to shed some light on the following issue. Topology is, precisely, a distinct field, one which we will have to consider if we are to follow the thread (a word in no sense innocent here—it takes on more than one sense in the following text) that is a feature of our seminar. Topology is a branch of geometry defined by the existence of nonmetric relations. What counts in this discipline is not the function of measurement but the relation at work between, for instance, the elements making up a particular surface amenable to constant deformation. Properly speaking, "surfaces" constitute one of the branches of that discipline.

This point, actually, leads us into some introductory classifications. Lacan's interest in topology began by approaching the theme of surfaces before it moved over to a separate approach, the one that is explored in Seminar 23 and that had been worked on in the preceding period. We will specify the moment this approach is initiated and what precisely it consists in. It is evidently a matter of questions about knots.

In Lacan's first reference to topology, in Seminar 9, *Identification* (1961–1962),[2] his interest bears on surfaces because, precisely, identification is a psychical phenomenon immediately entailing a fundamental problem of "inside" and "outside." A very basic, crude definition of identification would be that it comprises a psychical process that transforms the external into the internal. This is not, to be sure, the most precise way of approaching the subject—yet right away it gives us an indication of how *space* is in question here. The concept of space at stake here is, of course, radically transformed by Lacan, insofar as he shows that "inside" and "outside" cannot be given obvious definitions. That well-known division between "I" and "not-I" (or internal and external worlds, for that matter), dear to so many psychologists and psychoanalysts, is not so self-evident after all. Or better still: if it seems so transparent, that would be a good reason for us to problematize it, not out of sheer delight in making things more complicated but in order to set out from the fact that the experience here may be deceptive—or, in Lacan's terms, *imaginary*. What does Lacan mean by describing space as imaginary? Simply that it is only from within a space where we can immediately recognize ourselves that we are ready to believe that we have—and can master—an

2. This seminar immediately precedes the one we studied in a recent work: cf. R. Harari, *El Seminario, "La angustia" de Lacan: una introduccion.* Buenos Aires: Amorrortu editores, 1993.

interiority; and it is on this basis that we can easily posit a matching exteriority.

A whole series of surfaces (we will refer to them only in passing) is studied by Lacan in Seminar 9—the Moebius strip, the interior eight, and the cross-cap, among others— that allow him to explore some crucial problems relating to identification. Several years later, however, as we have already noted, Lacan will reach another logical point in his topological elaboration, that of knots. And it turns out that the knots in question are not simple knots. Lacan introduces the topic with a highly particular form of knotting: the Borromean knot.

Before we proceed with this point, the reader should consider the following question. As we have indicated, when we tackle topology, geometry also comes into the account. When we refer to knots, our first image is almost inevitably that of a sailor's knot or a knot of a similar kind. It would be a matter of taking several pieces of rope and manipulating them in some way; here effectively, as we said, we are referring to threads. Yet they only form representations of lines, characterized above all by a series of properties, of relations. We could represent them with strings, with chains, with rings from a binder—given that the definition of the knot is not empirical but relates to the system of formal relations at work.

Lacan introduces the problem of relations in the Borromean knot in the seminar given in 1971–1972, entitled . . . *ou pire*, "or worse," which means simply, "that's it, or else it's worse." In classical psychoanalytic terms, he is referring here to castration, that condition where we assume that either we stick with it or else there'll be something worse. In the session of . . . *ou pire* on February 9, 1972,

Lacan touches on the matter lightly, in passing, almost in what our Joycean perspective might consider a *joke*,[3] when he mentions what somebody had told him the day before about the Borromean knot. Thus, since this had struck him as very interesting, he had decided the following day to include it in his seminar. Such a pretense of randomness masked, for sure, many years of work, to be brought in as the chance discovery of an idea. If we go back to the seminar on *Identification*, where Lacan had already shown clear evidence of his work with the basic knot known as the *trefoil*, it becomes obvious that we are dealing with a joke. But is from . . . *ou pire* onward that the recourse to knots becomes more and more intensive, continuing throughout the subsequent years. Even in the final phases of Lacan's teaching, those of the most difficult seminars and the most complex topology—for instance Seminar 25, *Le moment de conclure*, or Seminar 26, *La topologie et le temps*—he appeals to a combination of the topology of surfaces and knots. Lacan makes use above all of a surface we have deliberately refrained from mentioning so far: the torus. A rudimentary example of a torus is the inflatable section of a tire. As an object, a torus is just as problematic as it is every day, if we compare it to a straightforward spherical ball. We are used to thinking of ourselves—perhaps because of the circular movements we can make with our hands—as spherical entities, with a sharply defined inside and outside. But the torus has the quality of being a sphere with a hole in it, where the interior can be transformed into the exterior and vice versa, something that is possible if one passes through it. Furthermore, this surface can be covered with threads, making things more

---

3. In English in the original.

complex and calling for a convergence of the topological domains that we mentioned above.

Lacan approaches his work with the triple (three-ring)
Borromean knot starting out from elaborations by a mathematician to whom he often refers, Georges Th. Guilbaud, who had
first introduced him to the problems this object involves. In
this way, he arrived at the basis for an innovative rearticulation
of what we could term the central or nodal point of all his previous teaching: the imbrication of the three registers of experience, Real, Symbolic, and Imaginary. In a very preliminary way,
we could say that if the Symbolic refers to the place of speech
and language, the Imaginary is that which relates to the experience of the mirror: in other words, to self-recognition in a
captivating and fascinating image, before which the ego remains
caught in a phenomenon of equivocal "sameness"—equivocal
because it is only an effect of alienation in and by the other. As
for the Real, the last of the registers explored by Lacan and the
most difficult to define, we will indicate only that it entails that
which is located outside of any law. Not in the sense of juridical law, but outside of any regulation, any determined order,
either manifest or latent. It is a register without organization,
whose essential quality is to provoke anxiety, and which Lacan
wishes absolutely to separate from what is called reality. Reality is centered on what is collective, what is codified somewhere
between the Symbolic and the Imaginary, what allows us to
establish forms of agreement and consensus. In this sense,
reality is asleep—it keeps us in a sort of comfortable haze, from
which we are torn by the Real, which wakes us screaming. It
is precisely this register, as crucial as it is difficult, that Lacan
tackles in his last seminars.

Let us return to the elaboration of the triple Borromean
knot. Due to its pictorial layout, it constitutes an ideal tool

for offering a hierarchy that corresponds to the three registers. Taking its place within this structure, no single register
prevails over the others: there is no register more important
than, or determinant of, the others. This is a decisive point,
which when the moment comes will allow the psychical problematic of Joyce to be posited.

The seminar *R.S.I.* (1974–1975) is where Lacan begins
to deploy persistently his problematic of the knot. *R.S.I.* stands
for Real, Symbolic, and Imaginary, in English as well as in
French—except that in French, these letters can be spoken
to rhyme with *hérésie* (heresy). Lacan considers himself a
heretic in the domains of culture and psychoanalysis; and he
is to say the same of Joyce, to call him another remarkable
heretic who, like Lacan himself, submitted to the Other's
confirmation the means by which he attained his real. In *R.S.I.*,
Lacan works on the triple Borromean knot, allowing him to
articulate the three registers as in Figure 1:

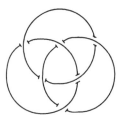

Figure 1

At this point, we should observe that the discovery of knots
does not indicate an appeal to a didactic methodology. Lacan
gives this discovery a status outside of methodology, beyond
that of a mere theoretical mode. Here, Lacan found himself
confronting something that has been lucidly described by an
American, Jonathan Scott Lee, in a valuable study of Lacan

dealing with these late seminars: ". . . the challenge for the inter-preter of this final work by Lacan is precisely to determine how he constructs this extraordinary blend of formal mathematical proof (or at least construction), psychoanalytic theory, and even poetry, which makes these last seminars into something unique in the history not only of psychoanalytic theory but also of theoretical writing in general."[4] This interesting comment is made, not by an analyst, but by a historian of ideas. We can keep close to this quotation, even as we note that the intellec-tual adventure produced by the introduction of the knot goes beyond formalization, just as the recourse to Joyce goes beyond mere allusion, in grasping the work of a poet—we use the term in a broad, nongeneric sense, given that Joyce's poetic output was rather limited, and not a fundamental element of his work—to develop a new adventure of thought.

The Borromean knot is often shown by means of three circles. But is it necessary to present it in this circular way? We shall see that far from being what defines the knot, this presentation is simply conventional. The decisive property of the triple knot is something else—precisely what causes any-one eagerly trying to draw it, or tie it, to make boo-boos, as Lacan puts it, alluding to the awkwardness attending any at-tempt by a speaker to produce a Borromean. He becomes a booboo-rromean,[5] because of the ineptitude revealed in our capacity to imagine and in the way we handle our bodies.

---

4. J. S. Lee, *Jacques Lacan*. Amherst: University of Massachusetts Press, 1990, p. 197.

5. Translator's note: *bobo-rroméen*: Lacan's wordplay tropes "Bor-romean" with something *bobo*, the childish babble for a sick or bad feeling (*Ça te fait bobo?* [Do you feel poorly?]); the English slang "boo-boo," while not exactly an equivalent, preserves the homophony, and conveys a sense of the clumsy or awkward feelings, the *maladresse*, generated by the knot.

What is the property privileged by Lacan in this triple articulation? It is what allows, when all three are tied together, for the unknotting of one to entail the separation of the others. One may deduce from this that it is a matter of a definition *a posteriori*. How am I able to prove whether or not a knot is Borromean? If, when we are presented with it, we cut one of the rings, and the others are automatically released. Let us try to draw it (Figure 2) in an unusual way in order to verify that it is just as Borromean as the previous knot:

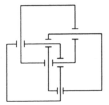

Figure 2

Due to the topological principle already mentioned, that of continual deformation, we can see that even if it looks completely different, we are still dealing with the same knot. Whether there are circles, squares, and/or any other "aform," what is essential is the invariance of the relations. Here, it is important to distinguish between phenomenon and structure—in other words, what appears before our eyes and what concerns the details, the definition of properties. As long as there are identical points of crossing, they will be equivalent bo-knots, despite appearing so different.

Let us continue with the above experiment. If we observe the articulations, we will see that none of the rings that are included are placed in such a relation right away (Figure 3):

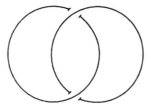

Figure 3

Here, each ring is knotted simply by passing through the hole of the adjacent ring: it is a Hopf's chain.[6] In Borromean-knotting, on the other hand, the relation of the initial pair is one of simple superimposition; they are not tied together (Figure 4):

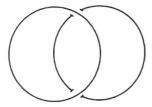

Figure 4

It is precisely the introduction of a third, passing successively above and below the first two rings, that allows for a triadic relation that cannot be reduced to a group brought about and supported by pairs. In its trajectory, the third ring passes underneath the bottom ring and above the top ring, in an alternating sequence (Figure 5):

---

6. Cf. C. C. Adams, *The Knot Book*. New York: W. H. Freeman, 1994, p.18.

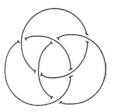

Figure 5

One will observe that once the three rings are together, each one supports an identical relation with its neighbors, and thus they are all equivalent. Structurally, the links all pass through the same points, from whichever position the Borromean knot is observed and whichever ring is examined. It is evidently necessary to pay attention to these crossing-points during the actual process of drawing, which doesn't stop us from regularly making mistakes.[7]

Once this triple schema has been presented, we might wonder where Lacan wishes to lead us by introducing it. Here, we reach a decisive question that is addressed at the end of Seminar 22, *R.S.I.*: that of the name. The three rings are exactly the same until we mark the picture in some way, even if the mark is only a small letter. If we do this in such a way as to name each type of consistency, it is only then that an identity emerges. If we write, for instance, the following (Figure 6):

---

7. In order not to overload our presentation, we have omitted here any reference to the construction of Borromean chains through the deployment of false holes—a topic we explore in Chapters 3, 7, and 9.

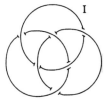

Figure 6

This allows us to situate the topmost ring as the representative of the Imaginary register. From what does the condition for something to have an identity arise? From the possession of a name; without a name it is impossible to distinguish between one existing being and all others. Once the letters are put in place, the rings become entities, and are moreover given the advantage, we might say, of being included in a list. The incorporation of the name is a crucial way into what interests us, making visible to us what is entailed in being named—and naming—in people's lives. In fact, this is not simply a question about knots: we should pause over the metaphorical slant of each of these points in Lacan's teaching, which cannot be reduced to what is strictly topological. These points are relevant, in fact, to the way we constitute ourselves, to our mode of existing in the midst of difference.

Why have we begun with this reference to the triple bo-knot, something that comes earlier than the seminar that interests us? Because during the period of *R.S.I.*, Lacan had very many occasions to reflect on the principle theme of Seminar 23—namely, the quadruple bo, in other words a form of knotting where the detachment of one of the rings would undo the other three. When Lacan first contemplates this alternative kind of knot, he is to approach it very critically. We can point to these first mentions of the quadruple knot in *R.S.I.*, another "forbidden" seminar. In the session of January 14, 1975, Lacan explains that if Freud required four terms, it was due to an inability to complete the theoretical reduction that has allowed him, for his part, to posit only three. To that extent, even if not explicitly, Lacan adheres to the traditional scientific principle of parsimony. According to the latter, one should dispense with unnecessary hypotheses by reducing them to the minimum number. In *La science et la vérité*, Lacan had already referred—implicitly—to that notion, terming it the principle of reduction and considering it the foundation of science.[8] The reference to Freud in *R.S.I.* marks a need to bring theory to completion: to dispense with the fourth term needed by the master—which was, according to Lacan, the concept of psychical reality (*Realität*).

This is not, of course, the only reference to Freud in that seminar. In an earlier session, Lacan had related his three rings to a Freudian triptych that is profoundly linked to our theme. It concerns three of Freud's concepts that deserve to be labeled as the principle material of our daily analytic work, as they return us to the neuroses. It is these concepts that are captured, as will have been guessed, in Freud's classic title *Inhibitions, Symptoms, and Anxiety* of 1925. Nor is this the first time that Freud produced categories in triadic phrases—we find, for instance, the famous "Remembering, Repeating, and Working-Through" (1914). We observe a certain tripartite structure in Freudian epistemology, which makes us doubly attentive when Lacan describes it as notoriously quadripartite.

---

8. "La science et la vérité" ("Science and truth," 1965), *Écrits*. Paris: Seuil, 1966, pp. 855–877.

A Freudian trinity, then, within a Lacanian trinity—
which Lacan will take to be progressions or intrusions of one
register into another, zones where one register invades another alongside it. It may happen that "something" of the
Imaginary is displaced toward the Symbolic, that a "part" of
the latter is oriented toward the Real, or even that a sector
of the Real gives onto the Imaginary. As we may see, such
situations can only be approached on the basis of the triple
Borromean schema, in other words by converting the strings
into zones on a diagram. It is by "freezing" the knot that this
schematization acquires its meaning and opens up new perspectives. In addition, Lacan places that which hitherto he has
termed "his invention"—the object *a*—in the central zone, a
sort of half-moon opened by the intersection of the three rings
that reduces to a single point when the knot is pulled tight. It
is an irreducible point of intersection, wedged in between the
three strings. However, here we are faced with the deployment
of a sort of fiction: it is not, strictly speaking, a question of
the Borromean knot, but of a flattened version of it, *mise à
plat*; such is the reduction to two dimensions of a mobile three-
dimensional structure. Let us now examine more closely these
"progressions" or immixtures.

An advance by the Symbolic into the Real will be what
characterizes the traditional analytic symptom (in Freud's
sense—not the *sinthome* that Lacan will define a year later,
indicating the difference). It is crucial from the outset to
differentiate this from the medical symptom. In psychoanalysis, the symptom does not designate anything: we are
far away from nosology, because we do not conceive it as a
sign referring in a fixed manner to any particular disease.
Therefore, we place the Freudian symptom at this point of
"invasion" in the triple-Borromean. As for anxiety, it is situ-

ated in the zone where the Real invades the Imaginary, while the overflowing of the Imaginary into the Symbolic will be the area belonging to inhibition. These compound inter-relations were schematized by Lacan in the following manner (Figure 7):

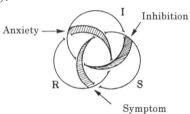

Figure 7

Here, we can see to what point Lacan had brought his elaboration of Freud's teaching. For purely informative purposes, and so that the triple-Borromean in our diagram is not left unfinished, we will add four Lacanian concepts that have not been mentioned so far, but that are given crucial places in the schema. These are the object *a* that we have already mentioned, phallic jouissance (JΦ), the jouissance of the Other (JÁ), and meaning (Figure 8):

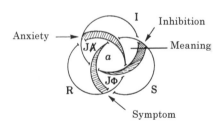

Figure 8

Having reached this point in our exposition, to give a detailed account of these concepts would take too long and be unnecessary. Regarding jouissance, we will come back to it in our discussion of Joyce and of what he brings about through his writing. However, including these concepts allows us to observe that they not only entail the invasion of the registers R, S, and I, but that the jouissance of the Other projects into anxiety, while meaning projects into inhibition and phallic jouissance does so in relation to the symptom. These are complex interrelations. We may thus wonder what our work as analysts amounts to, according to *R.S.I.* Well, it is to cause the real symptom—which is inscribed in the register we could also define as that which always returns to the same place—to be displaced once more in the direction of the Symbolic. The subject is unable to resolve the situation on his own: the real of the symptom makes it something recurrent. He can only be confronted by what persists in not functioning. Analytic treatment thus seeks to recycle this element. We can say, as did Freud, that by means of analytic treatment it comes to reenter collective circulation. What was split off, hidden away, reemerges into exchange.

We have reached the session of *R.S.I.* of December 10, 1974. As with the session of January 14, 1975, we can pick out a critique of Freud. The debate with Freud, it should be remarked, has gone on right through the seminar. Lacan seeks, effectively, to establish whether or not Freud's theses are valid, or at what point he got stuck halfway; or again, whether or not he fell into what epistemologists term a superfluity—that is to say, the production of more hypotheses than necessary, adding them on in an extrapolatory way. According to Lacan, one can do without the fourth ring since psychical reality, he argues, possesses the same mechanisms as religion. The connection is a strange one, very close to the conceptualism of a Quevedo, with its extraordinary, unpredictable leaps between

disciplines and semantic fields. Lacan himself provides us with
authority for making this connection, when he names that
other conceptualist, Baltasar Gracián.

Such leaps paralyze the reader, leaving him flabbergasted,
wondering what it can mean. In the present, almost laughable
case, the question is unavoidable: Why religion? Our reading,
which we consider to be pertinent—although it is purely con-
jectural, as Lacan sheds no light on the question—indicates that
this psychical reality calls for just as much faith as does the
existence of God. The latter exists because I believe in him. What
is known as the ontological proof is absolute, going beyond the
various arguments that can be put forward (and that, we know,
can easily be used with success to prove the opposite case).
Briefly, it is enough to be able to predict his existence for there
to result a proof that cannot be countered. The same thing happens with psychical reality. I assert the existence of a fantasmatic
internal world, and I take possession of it in the same gesture.
Hence, I conclude that I am the master of that psychical reality;
here we have one of the most radical criticisms of Freud formulated by Lacan. In place of the concept that he rejects, Lacan
will insist on another term that can also be picked out in Freud's
texts: *Wirchlichkeit*, which could be translated as functional reality, effective reality, or practical reality. We will see further
on how these questions return in Seminar 23. *Wirchlichkeit* is a
kind of reality that is linked to "doing," to the Latin *facere*; it is
linked, in the end, to the realization of effects. The term *Realität*,
so dear to psychology, refers to something quite different from
this, as it presupposes an internal world bound up with the
domain of religion. We repeat: the debate is not about whether
or not this psychical reality exists empirically, but about its being
posited as indisputable and "proper." To accept such a notion
is to invite being duped. It is, in fact, absolutely incapable of

accounting for that which concerns us as analysts. The notion is actually fairly close to the function of the dream. There is undoubtedly a dreamlike component to be found in this Freudian *Realität* that is so acceptable.

The third reference comes in the session of February 18, 1975. Lacan begins at this point to develop what he terms the "quadric," in other words what relates to the quadruple-Borromean. It is striking that he does not seem especially critical here; he simply comments that such a form of knot seems to him a plausible one, without going into too much detail. A little later, on March 11, when he speaks of what is superfluous, what is excessive—still regarding Freud's elaborations—he says such an "excess" would be the Name-of-the-Father, which makes possible another return of the fourth ring. We should pause over this concept, with its unavoidably religious echoes (the inevitable association is with "the name of the Father, the Son, and the Holy Ghost"); it is a psychical agency that, above all, serves to separate the Desire of the Mother from the phallicized son. In this sense, it is a question of the introduction of a Law—not that of any juridical normativity, as it bears on a fundamental order, that of sexual difference. According to Lacan, Freud appears to have been obliged to use the Name-of-the-Father in order to knot together the three registers; failing which, they would break apart. Lacan's implication here is that there is no need for this agency as a fourth strand to knot the other three; he thus leaves it to one side, but not before remarking on what characterizes it—the act of "giving things their name." The Father as the one who names: a subject that we will return to repeatedly.

In the eleventh and final session of the series, on May 13, 1975—we might say periphrastically that, like Joyce's *Finnegans Wake*, Lacan's seminars are a "work in progress"—we are able to verify that when Lacan began a new seminar, he did not know exactly where or how it would finish. In this session, in fact, he affirms: "It is thus that, however complete the simplicity of the triple Borromean knot, it is by starting from four—and I emphasize this—by engaging with this four, that we can find a way forward, a particular way which only goes as far as six." Thus the whole course of his elaboration is overturned. What was hitherto criticized in relation to the fourth element becomes—with the support of the topologists, naturally—something of indisputable significance.

Now, what is striking is that Lacan ascribes to Freud, in a critical manner, the number four (as we have already shown in several texts), whereas in fact it is undeniably a feature of his own work. In a recurrent manner, when Lacan theorizes the analytic experience (at moments that can easily be outlined), the number four is present. We do not wish to pause over this point here, but we can affirm that four is "Lacan's number."[9] His criticisms of the number four, first of all ascribed to Freud, are thus rather intriguing, since Lacan nevertheless considers that number more than useful in his own theorization. We can start from this point to distinguish between the registers, with Lacan introducing *nomination* as a fourth term that could be at once real, symbolic, and/or imaginary. The final session of *R.S.I.* is precisely what serves as a hinge between that seminar and the one we will be exploring from now on. It initiates, we might say, the breakdown of the epistemic insistence on the three registers.

9. Cf. R. Harari, "No hay desenlace sin reanudación," in ¿*De qué trata la clínica lacaniana?* Buenos Aires: Catálogos, 1994, pp.191–211; and "4 = 3+1," *Esquisses Psychanalytiques* n° 22, C.F.R.P, May 1995, pp. 9–18.

Nomination is quite different from the Name-of-the-Father, which now consists, as we have said, in the act of naming as understood in a creationist mode. Nomination is not an agency [*instance*] but, as we will see, it entails—inexorable—suppletions when the latter agency is lacking. What could be better than to turn to a man of letters in order to approach the way such processes work? What could be better, at the same time, than to construct in this respect a place for the creation of the literary characters to be named?

Once again in this Lacanian alignment, we have a quadruple structure. It is a question of different kinds of nomination, posited as a new concept to be taken into consideration. These different nominations are linked to the three registers, but at the same time they exceed them by doubling each of them in turn. This notion cannot be encompassed by any of the three registers, which when doubled are written as adjectives alongside the nomination (N). This takes place in the following way: each kind of nomination is *not* connected directly to its adjectival register, but indirectly across or via the other two registers; as is shown in the Figure 9 schema:

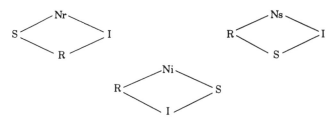

Figure 9

It is on this basis that Lacan poses the problem to be explored the following year in the seminar whose title he announces to be "4, 5, 6." We should understand these figures according to the thematic opened by the Borromean knots and their development. The reader should try to imagine the extent to which the claim to have arrived at a sextuple Borromean knot would complicate matters. The attention required by the over- and undercrossings, by the mode of work, by the need to respect a certain kind of construction, is already demanding in the quadruple version. Lacan does not attempt to arrive at a knot of six; he admits that four is enough. He even goes so far as to delight in this, and performs a pirouette when he tells the story, at the beginning of Seminar 23, of how a well-known Joyce specialist, Jacques Aubert, invited him to give the opening address at a James Joyce Symposium—which had taken place in June that year, 1975—thus diverting his attention from "4, 5, 6" to direct it once again (one detects again here the tone of a *joke*) toward a study of the work of the Irish writer. This invitation led him, above all, to read numerous texts written on Joyce, in order to prepare for his paper at the Paris Symposium.

Was it thus really a matter of a detour? Quite the opposite, one suspects. Lacan took advantage of the opportunity to re-affirm the move to the quadruple Borromean knot, on the basis of a consideration of the author of *Dubliners*. The title of the seminar had been conceived in this perspective: Lacan called it *Le sinthome*, a term that resembles, but remains distinct from, the word *symptom*. At any rate, Lacan's contribution to the symposium was still entitled *Joyce le symptôme*, to be read as a single unit, like a name—the result of a symbolic nomination, as if the terms could not be separated from one another. *Sinthome* relates to the emergence of a new concept. Now, we could wonder innocently, since Joyce's first name was James, why should he be called Joyce-the-symptom? Lacan's joke is centered on the importance of the establishment, on Joyce's part, of a—his—name. This is one of the fundamental threads of the whole seminar; it is a question, as the everyday expression has it, of "making a name." The phrase occurs frequently—and not by accident—in the language of everyday life.

The *sinthome* takes us back to the spelling of Old French, which in this context Lacan prefers to modern French. We shall see how this is justified, and wonder whether something else is at stake. The reason given by Lacan is that this is how the word is spelled in the incunabula, the earliest printed books that appeared around the end of the 15th century and the beginning of the 16th. This spelling is indeed to be found there, to be replaced eventually by the modern spelling, *symptôme*. But what is behind this allusion to the incunabula? We must once again lend an ear to the metaphorical effects in Lacan's teaching. He himself gives us the answer, not in that seminar but during a series of lectures given in the United States in parallel with these developments in his work. To be precise, Lacan's visit to America occurred between the first and the second session of the *Sinthome*.

A reading of these lectures in America is necessary because Lacan pursues his *Work in Progress* in them. On November 24, 1975, at Yale University, he observes that the change of spelling was not a simple product of an enthusiasm for etymology, the term being constantly caught up in "remaking" [*refection*]. What does this remaking consist in? Beginning to restore, to reconstruct the self. One could even use the term to describe a refreshing drink, intended to give back your energy. In other words, it was not a question of fishing out some old word that is dead and buried, in the course of a scholarly excursus into the 15th century, in order to reveal one's sophistication. On the contrary, Lacan sought in this way to revitalize an open pathway: in sum, to move from the symptom to the *sinthome*. Thus, Lacan tells us, he is employing a different nomination in order to account for different constellations. They should not be confused, they are two quite distinct concepts; and this is why, if we were to call this seminar *The Symptom*, we would alter its object. Lacan speaks to us of a distinct psychical formation, in connection with which Joyce and his work will serve to outline a new structure in psychoanalysis, where the number four will be decisive.

During his lecture at Yale, Lacan will signal—something particularly revealing—that which the writer testifies to:

> When I take an interest in Joyce [. . .] it is because Joyce tries to go beyond [. . . .] How does one end up stuck in this job of being a writer? To explain art with the unconscious seems to me most dubious, yet it is what analysts do. To explain art with the symptom [or the *sinthome*?] seems to me more serious.[10]

This already amounts, then, to a fundamental explanation (although not one that excludes others) of Lacan's new approach to art. It will not be a question of the usual procedure adopted by psychoanalysts, which Lacan calls at one point "a clownish psychoanalytic aberration": what is known as "applied psychoanalysis." This is a very common game, which consists in taking any work of art whatsoever in order

---

10. J. Lacan, "Conférences et entretiens dans des universitaires nord-américaines," *Scilicet* 6/7. Paris: Seuil, 1976, pp. 33–36 [our translation]. N.B. Given the provenance of this material, it is not certain that we are dealing with written texts; thus the indispensable interpretative work, and the proposed transcription given.

to discover what was already known there, by means of a not very subtle trick of generalization. Everything becomes explicable in this way—a clear sign of the gratuitous, empty quality of such efforts. Moreover, the task in question is a very simple one, since it allows one to link whatever one pleases to the well-known motifs involving childhood, family problems, the Oedipus complex, castration, and so on.

Lacan attempts to do something quite different: to engage with Joyce's work, with the deployment of that work and its role in the author's life. This entailed the sweeping away of the subject's constitution in language; and if this was so, it entailed a consideration of how the subject had been undone, and how it was refounded, in language. Or indeed, an exploration of the viability of an undertaking as revolutionary as Joyce's (in the formulation Lacan borrows from Sollers[11]): the attempt to liquidate the English language, as something self-contained or self-identical, which *Finnegans Wake* implies. Such a cyclopean labor would correspond, indeed, to Joyce's desire for the university professors to talk of him, in their struggle to understand, for the next three centuries. In his case, what a mighty effort to make a name for yourself! Joyce was in fact driven by a need for recognition—as we could express it in generic terms—that was remarkably strong.

Lacan does not plunge into the details of Joyce's biography. He does not seek to discover the relation between the life and the work in a kind of guaranteed specular game of *fort/da* projections. In this type of operation—which is some-

---

11. Philippe Sollers, "Joyce & Co," in D. Hayman and E. Anderson, *In the Wake of the Wake*. London: University of Wisconsin Press, 1978, p. 107.

what perverse, given the absence of anybody to respond to our shrewd "interpretations"—one tends, as we have already observed, to find more of the same thing. This was not, of course, the intention of Freud. When he studied a work of art, it was in an attempt to advance, and not merely to apply, psychoanalysis. The *desideratum* was always some new element; it was precisely by producing applied psychoanalysis that Freud failed. As we have noted, there is a special case here, one that is mentioned by Lacan: Jensen's *Gradiva*.[12] In the analysis of this work, Freud could offer only that which concerned things already known. But this was an exception; more frequently, Freud's efforts met with success—as when he tackled "The Uncanny" (1919) and, on the basis of Hoffmann's work, proposed a new theorization of anxiety that made his article on that topic indispensable.

The *sinthome* is, therefore, in another of its aspects, a new way for Lacan to approach phenomena that had attracted him from the outset; we refer to the period of his relations with the Surrealist movement, or much earlier, with Dadaism. It is well known that Lacan was involved with artists and thinkers such as Breton, Tzara, or Dali; above all with the latter, whose method of "critical paranoia" he converted into the "controlled paranoia" of psychoanalytic method. Lacan's earliest engagements with art showed him to be extremely sensitive to its thematics.

Due to Seminar 23's elaboration of the name (a far more decisive elaboration than that of the previous seminar), we can clarify the way in which Lacan introduces the question

---

12. S. Freud, "Delusions and Dreams in Jensen's *Gradiva*" (1907), *Standard Edition* 9, pp. 1–95.

of the letter there. In putting forward the term *sinthome*, he states, he is returning, like Joyce at the beginning of *Ulysses*, to the moment when language is "hellenized." From the very first words of the seminar, it is clear that it will deal not only with *sinthome* but with Joyce; indeed, the two will be linked throughout Lacan's teaching.

Having drawn attention to "hellenization," we should get used to Lacan's *jokes*, as well as to the *puns* by which he also goes along with the Irishman.[13] And, thanks to a metaphor, this comes down, through Joyce, to the one who *seems* to have been the first to give things names: Adam, whose name means "he who was born of the soil." We should note, however, that according to the biblical myth before Adam, God had already given things names. Effectively, for God, to name and to create were the same thing: he says *Fiat lux!* and there was light. Thus, when God offers the animals to Adam so that he can name them, He clearly locates him in a relation of impotent dependence, masked as some kind of foundational naming. The language of Adam, in sum, is nothing but an occurrence regulated, supervised, and supported by an incontestable and imperious judge, in a situation of implied examination. Here it is a question of speaking with signs, as it represents something for someone.

Joyce also brings in the character of Adam, choosing to dub him *M'Adam*, punning on the French *madame*. What does this name imply? That in the end the *monsieur* in the fable does not have all the gifts ascribed to him, in the same way that in our clinical work we see the scars left on a boy by the eternal love of a father. Lacan defined this very well: we boys

---

13. Translator's note: The words in italics are in English in the original.

are in fact the weaker sex, confronted by perversion. The Joycean Adam, as M'adam, encounters the one Lacan calls Evie, incorporating the French *vie*, "life": Eve is thus connected with life. In a more singular manner, she is connected with speech: Lacan remarks that Evie, distinguished by her loquacity, would seem to have been the complete mistress of the language used in the *m'adamish*—mocking, abject—procedure of "giving" names to the animals presented by God the Creator. Bound up with this gossip, Evie is linked to another character, the serpent. She generates life, but in the same act she comes out with bullshit [*conneries*], to use a phrase often used by Lacan. The only language recognized by Evie and the serpent, in brief, is bullshit: speaking in order to name, rather than naming in order to appease a judgmental God.

In this Lacanian version of the Joycean Eden, we can already discern certain questions, certain thematic kernels, without wishing to give rein to free association. The subject of the serpent will slide us toward another point concerning the word *sinthome*, which will constantly return (appropriately enough, in a version of Paradise): that of *sin*. This is what leads to the expulsion: M'Adam and Evie fall because of sin, "the first fault." The notion of sin that is constantly present in Joyce's work—let us not forget that it is the work that we are analyzing, not the speculative biography of its author—begins precisely with an idea of the fault, of something lacking, according to Lacan. This goes back directly to the problematic of castration, which means that a valid approach to it is to attend to what does not function. Let us begin on the side of sin, and not that of the idyllic, "paradisical" situation where everything is enclosed by perfection. Through Joyce, Lacan marks a certain inflection in the story of the Bible: the point that highlights how a site of castration or lack is linked to a certain knowledge. This is why Evie bites the apple and falls into the serpent's trap.

This combination will make Lacan remark that the alliance between speech and a mark, namely the end of a prick, is precisely the Phallus. This phallic mark is lacking or in the wrong place for Joyce, says Lacan, and so he tries to compensate for this through his writing. Here, we confront one of the fundamental terms of the seminar: that of suppletion [*suppléance*] or "making up for." Thanks to his work, Joyce strives to make up or find suppletion for what he lacks; his art serves as the guarantee of his Phallus. This observation immediately implies our abandoning any temptation to do "applied psychoanalysis": it is not a matter of giving "illustrations" of some alleged Joycean psychopathology. By contrast, the task consists in emphasizing the function of the work, including how it implicates its author. Joyce himself suggested this when he claimed to have sacrificed his life to his work; and of course he "demanded" that we do likewise and sacrifice our lives to reading his work. The reader may wonder whether Lacan himself is very far from such a sacrifice and such a demand. All those who have labored on his work for almost thirty years would answer no; and in a virtual sense, Lacan also demands that we sacrifice our entire lives to him.

Evie, M'Adam's Eve, bears the mark of completeness, according to Lacan. This is a decisive moment in his work, for he has taught that woman is not-all, being divided, barred: thus he could write *La femme*. In order to support this idea, we recall, he refers to Freud: specifically to the latter's claim that there was a split between two libidinal tendencies, one marked by the clitoris and the other vaginal. Lacan concludes from this that what has been isolated is the division of woman, caused by the absence of a controlling zone that man, for his part, possesses: the Phallus, situated and symbolized by the penis. This condition of *La*, of not-all, leads Lacan to contend that Woman, taken as a totality, the set of all women, does not exist. This is a particularly offensive statement: How can it be that she doesn't exist? It is yet another example of an aphorism designed to shock, and thus, having a certain impact, make waves and generate work and reflection. Lacan now adds: Woman does not exist as whole, apart from Evie. She was unique in that she entailed another name of God; all the rest are already something else. All of this, in our view, amounts to a joke by Lacan—a cryptic one—referring to the opening line of *Finnegans Wake*: "riverrun, past Eve and Adam's . . ." Lacan later claims that this Evie shows another characteristic—here we begin to make out one of the foremost and most radical features of the *sinthome*: that of "singularity." It is crucial to take this into account, as this could be termed the constitutive value of analysis as treatment in terms of its direction: the respect given to, the demand for, singularity. It is of course important not to confuse this with particularity: Lacan greatly stressed this difference, arguing that what is particular is only an illustration of some generality, each implying the other as mutual reference; whereas singularity, as the term indicates, is what singles out something as distinct. We are thus dealing with a category that lies outside the dialectic of general and particular: the *sinthome* is singular. Lacan points out that it is precisely here that Aristotle goes wrong. Another surprise: How has the philosopher gone wrong? To quote him allegorically, referring to his famous syllogism of the general and the particular: "All men are mortal/ Socrates is a man/ Socrates is mortal." Lacan's joke here is a serious one: Aristotle is wrong, because Socrates is not a man. This may seem rather abstruse, but it turns out that he is not a man precisely because he prefers to die.

Although Socrates could certainly have won a pardon when it came to the famous verdict (as narrated in the *Phaedo*, the *Apology*, and other Platonic dialogues) if he had defended himself—for his defense would certainly have carried more weight than the arguments of his accusers—he chose to drink the hemlock in order to save his own honor and that of the *polis*. Thus, by subordinating a common value—the defense of one's own life—to the defense of a supreme value, Socrates becomes no longer a particular man in the general set of all men. This is the point where in Lacan's view Aristotle goes wrong with his famous syllogism, the one we all learned at school as a paradigmatic deduction from a major to a minor premise. Such a conclusion would be wrong, for it is not his condition as a man that makes Socrates decide to accept his sentence with resignation, due to his powerful desire to die, together with a parallel desire that the *polis* should live. There are several texts we would recommend concerning the trial of Socrates and the decision he takes in this extreme situation.[14] The choice of Socrates to die was governed not by a suicidal melancholia, but by a wish that the act should inspire horror in the living after his death. Thus, confronted by the allegation of having been a corrupter of standards, customs, and values, his position remains unchanged; he does not regret the course of his life, nor does he seek to justify its "carnality." This is why with Socrates we are not dealing with a man. He is not the particular case of a generality, but some-

---

14. Cf. I. F. Stone, *The Trial of Socrates*, London: Jonathan Cape, 1988, and C. Mossé, *O precerpo de Sócrates*, Rio de Janeiro: Jorge Zahar, 1987.

one singular; he therefore has the same value, the same outline, as Lacan will isolate with his notion of the *sinthome*.

Let us return to another singularity—that of Evie, of the
woman. Lacan states that the belief in a complete Woman is
made possible by a particular slant, that of equivocation. It is
this that occurs, for instance, in the situation of a sexual advance, when, if a woman is faced with a rather bold, uncon-
ventional proposition, she declares, "Yes, it's true that I'll do
all sorts of things with you—but not that." This decisive "but
not that" is what allows a belief in totality to be maintained.
If the woman had said "and that as well," it could easily be
shown that after "that" there would be something else. Here
we see a mode of singularity emerging: the "but not that" is a
way of putting down a mark—"I don't do that sort of thing;
I'm not that kind of woman (or: one of those women)." This
is the point where the question is no longer confined to so-
ciocultural considerations, those of rules and prohibitions; it
bears on a domain that is difficult to define empirically. "But
not that" does not refer to any predetermined or identifiable
thing, but to a domain of secrets, of a privacy necessarily kept
apart from a phallic logic. To continue with our scenario, the
woman's negative response might carry on with: "How dare
you demand something like that of me!" The reader has certainly noticed how the "demand" invoked here is manifestly
related to the demand of the Other, to the extent that the "but
not that" is a *confrontation with demand*. What does this mean?
It refers to Lacan's notion of the fundamental structure of neurosis, which amounts to an almost uncritical effort to conform
to the demand of the Other; a position that might be given the
following standard form: "I did it, but . . . did I do it for myself? Was it due to my own desire or due to his demand? He
didn't force me . . . but I don't know." In the face of this domi-

nance, "but not that" indicates, precisely, a reaction, the beginning of an escape from the subjection to the neurotic symptom—regarding which the *sinthome*, in its singularity, would entail a break from these subjective positions.

The problem is thus a crucial one; to the extent that Lacan can state: "This 'but not that' is what I am introducing in this year's title as the *sinthome*." In other words, what he is seeking as singularity and therefore maintaining as a nonexchangeable, non-negotiable value. Lacan comments that it is a question precisely of Socrates' act: he accepted some things, but not that. There is something that cannot be shifted, which forces him to accept the death sentence. This *but not that* is not, we can easily deduce, linked to any typical symptom of obsessional neurosis, hysteria, or phobia; it bears, ultimately, on an ethical dimension. Shortly before this, Lacan makes reference to the *Not-I*; not in a psychological sense, as that which differs from the ego in an imaginary mode, but as the response to a certain demand. Let us give this a detailed formula: "If you claim that about me, I will not accept it." In such a position, the argument that is maintained constitutes the decisive weight of singularity.

If, in the domain of analysis, there has been a singular figure, this is indeed Lacan. Yet his triple Borromean knot remains, in our view, too balanced, too oriented toward the general–particular dialectic; and in fact he did not wish to see his clinical work give rise to subjects of, and through, such a condition. Let us clarify this point. At a certain moment, Lacan remarked that he was sorry not to have been more psychotic; his implication was that if he had been he would have been more logical. What he had in mind—with a great deal of insight—was what is termed "rational madness" or paranoia. One of the greatest problems of a paranoiac is an *excess* of logic, and this is what Lacan is referring to; but he also alludes to the fact that for the most part being balanced, being "normal," to the extent that this indicates lack of passion, so to speak, is linked to the position of not wishing to get too involved in maintaining one's "but not that." It is our view that the introduction of the quadruple Borromean knot overturns the firm balance between the three Borromean registers by breaking up the system as conceived in an Apollonian, harmonious manner with a quasi-aesthetic quality. With the fourth register, a point of discordance is introduced through the singularity of the *sinthome*, of the "but not that," discussed above.

With the eruption of singularity, we come back to the question of heresy. Joyce, declares Lacan, "is like me: a heretic." The author, he continues, "chooses" the way to take hold of truth, but "he does it well": by "rightly grasping the nature of the *sinthome*." On this point, Lacan plays on the word *hère*, which means "wretch," "poor chap." The *hère* that forms part of "heretic" [*hérétique*] is also fairly close to another Lacanian reference, which we can relate to what may be considered one of Joyce's preparatory works. We describe it as such because it was to be the origin of another work that came to absorb it, so to speak, and that we know better: it is entitled *Stephen Hero*, and Lacan forgets (?) to bring his copy with him to the seminar. *Stephen Hero*: perhaps the somewhat ironic title is close, in a Joycean, translinguistic manner, to *hère*; the narrative that follows it is a draft of what will become *A Portrait of the Artist as a Young Man*. The original title gives more emphasis to the singular character of the text. At the same time, this *Hero* captures perfectly the character that the writer aspires to embody in his life throughout the work. *A Portrait* itself recalls a ballad entitled *Turpin Hero*; the novel forms part of the *Bildungsroman* genre, that of the coming-of-age novel;

at stake is the constitution of a young man's personality and his eventual choice of a literary destiny. This takes place in accordance with the alleged views of Saint Thomas on the aesthetic (by mentioning his name, we launch one of the *jeux de mots* we will come back to later); and concludes that exile is the best means of achieving such a destiny. The theme of exile will be fundamental for Joyce, not only in a geographical but also in a linguistic sense. He will struggle to exile himself from the imprisonment of language; such an undertaking is not alien to Lacan. But let us pause over what Joyce writes through his young protagonist named Stephen Dedalus (referring to Daedalus, a mythological figure of the utmost significance, even if Lacan seems not to have taken much note of its place in Joyce—nor in his own work, around the problematic of the end of analysis).

Stephen is chatting with a friend, and we begin to make out signs of an emerging "man of letters"; he talks of genres, of the lyrical, the epic, and finally the narrative. Concerning this, he states: "The narrative is no longer purely personal. The personality of the artist passes into the narration itself [note how Lacan takes this seriously, by not concentrating on the individual but on the work], flowing round and round the persons and the action like a vital sea. This progress you will see easily in that old English ballad *Turpin Hero* which begins in the first person and ends in the third person" (P, 214). Let us note the importance of what is already in play in the "young" Joyce, when he indicates an acceptance of the incidence of other voices within him. He therefore does not write in the first person after the lyrical manner, pouring his personality into the text, without allowing other voices to begin to take effect in his writing, not in the embodied form of new characters—as in a multiplication of personalities—but by means of the interaction of a multiplicity of languages. He is to pursue this manner of working, powerfully bringing together different languages, and with a humorous reading of them in his speaking being, to the point of practically generating a *lingua franca*. In *A Portrait* he begins to express his own reflections, which we will explore in the next chapter as they expose, in particular, a somewhat free interpretation of Saint Thomas. The latter's name gives rise to yet another Lacanian pun: *St. Thome* is of course a *saint homme*, both puns on *sinthome*. As for St. Thomas Aquinas, Lacan writes this *sinthome-madaquin*. In fact, the little aesthetic breviary sketched out by Joyce in *A Portrait* takes a course that it is not so easy to describe as specifically Thomist. But this aesthetic attempt will give rise to a crucial aspect of Joyce's work, which Lacan takes up in order to outline (if only by implication) a privileged Joycean mode of grasping the real: the *epiphany*. On this point we would do well to add to our reading the famous story from *Dubliners*, "The Dead," which has been made into a remarkable film by John Huston. Toward the end, when the main actors are leaving the family gathering, the epiphanic moment takes place—a character hears, in hopeless rapture, a traditional song—which is marked by what in Joyce's version of Thomist aesthetics is termed *claritas*. We will return to this notion, given that it implies an aspect that allows us to focus on a concept of the Real that Lacan struggled to articulate in his last years.

2

Eve in the Labyrinth of Daedalus

One of the first things to strike a reader of Joyce's work is its humor. We could link the ironic Eden mentioned in the previous chapter to another kind of irony, given fuller expression a few years earlier by that distinguished thinker and comic writer much admired by Joyce, Mark Twain. Freud, of course, had already told us how men of letters preempted psychoanalysts, hence our constant, fertile preoccupation with them. In his *Eve's Diary* (1906), the American writer deals with a theme that is crucial not only for Lacan's Seminar 23, and more broadly for psychoanalysis in general, but also for life itself (*la vie*: we recall Lacan's pun linking Eve to "life," *Evie*).

Our journey with Twain's book will be both enjoyable and intellectually rewarding. We find there precisely what Lacan is getting at when he talks about Eve the chatterbox— the one who relishes tittle-tattle, piles up silly gossip, talks without saying anything—who, in telling her tales, constantly strings words together. In Twain's novel, these words also have the function of giving things names, without making the names bestowed by God superfluous. Lacan insisted many times—it was a constant feature of his work up to *R.S.I.*—that without the signifier, there could be no creation. This was Lacan's position, which he called—in terms that were not original, but placed him in a tradition—a "creationism" of the signifier. In *R.S.I.*, however, something arises to prefigure a new concept of nomination: so-called "divine" creation. In this, the Symbolic makes the Real "surge up," relegating nomination to a secondary moment. Thus, at this point Lacan distinguishes between creation and nomination.

Let us then, before we begin our exploration of Twain's text, return briefly to something relating to the theme of nomination. In this, Lacan's debate with Freud—in particular, around the Freudian trio of inhibition, symptom, and anxiety—will be illustrated. Naming is defined by Lacan, in the seminar *R.S.I.*, in terms of its Imaginary, Symbolic, and Real versions or features, each of these names corresponding to one of the terms in the Freudian trio. We examine below how the concept of nomination will later come to be given a different sense, which will require the exploration of new elements in Lacan's teaching; but for the time being, we can present these relations as follows:

Ni: inhibition
Ns: symptom
Nr: anxiety

In other words, for Lacan, imaginary nomination corresponds to Freud's concept of inhibition. In order to establish the interrelation of the three terms, we should bear in mind Lacan's comment in Seminar 10, *Anxiety* (1962–1963), that "an inhibition is a symptom put in a museum." This remarkably acute, aphoristic phrase is a reference to the emergence of an inhibition when a symptom has been "overcome," leaving behind clear aftereffects. This is not in fact a matter of getting rid of the symptom, but of transforming it into a character trait; and imaginary naming, incontestably, accounts for such a transformation. Why should this be so? Because the change bears the stamp of a narcissistic identity, being profoundly marked by the notion of "I'm like that." In this sense, the act of naming amounts to isolating and identifying the libidinal or enjoyable aspect of a character trait, which allows the passage from "what I'm suffering from" to "I'm like that, that's how I'm staying, leave me alone." Furthermore—to the despair of any psychology of hedonism—this remains so when the person saying "leave me alone" happens to be the subject himself. We could put it like this: "Let's make a pact. If you don't question my Imaginary nomination—which is often inhibition—I won't question yours." We could even justify this by invoking a certain democratic or liberalizing value in naming. Why not? All of this testifies to the effect of the signifying bar, which is presented in topology by means of the infinite line; we will return to this below.

When we come to Symbolic naming, the table of correspondences shows the symptom. This is the symptom as traditionally conceived in psychoanalysis, not the *sinthome*. Concerning the latter term, we should point the reader to the Brazilian edition of a book by the Slovenian Lacanian Slavoj Žižek: when this author makes use of Lacan's *sinthome*, the Portuguese translation has *sinthomem*.[1] The word *homem*,

---

1. S. Žižek, *Eles não sabem o que fazem*. Rio de Janeiro: Jorge Zahar, 1990, p. 169 ff.

meaning "man," has a special significance in this condensed term, echoing the *homme* that Lacan reintroduces at the end of his teaching, alongside the concept of subject. The latter, already considered "classical," emerges as divided between what it says and what it knows.

In order not to fall into the widespread confusion deriving from the nearly identical sounds of "symptom" and *sinthome* (along with some of those responsible for the transcription and translation of the seminar, it should be added), we must carry out a process of refinement, of intratextual and intertextual criticism, to determine with conceptual rigor whether or not, when we read *sinthome* in a text, it is really that, and not in fact the classical symptom, which is in question. We cannot at present have complete confidence in any of the versions of Seminar 23 that are in circulation, each one of them containing its own set of contradictions and obscurities. These errors are not simply Lacan's: he was attempting to introduce, as rigorously and consistently as possible, a new signifier, in the manner of Evie. One would be wrong to think that what we read was indubitably said by him; in fact, it is what was heard by those responsible for the transcription (and very often repeated unquestioningly by translators). There is thus no single version, and we all have the task of putting forward readings, attempting to "establish" the text. We do not possess a "canonical" version like that of the *Écrits*. Hence, some of our interpretations may produce a text that is different from the other available versions: it is quite possible, for instance, that we would argue for *sinthome* in certain passages where the transcription reads "symptom," and vice versa. But let us not imagine these claims to be arbitrary; they must be grounded in a reading that goes along with a coherent conceptualization.

Let us return to Symbolic nomination. At this stage in our exploration, we can take this to be the conceptual description of symptomatic formations. Eventually, we will be confronted by Real nomination, which corresponds to Freud's notion of anxiety—once again, a Lacanian trio for a Freudian trio.

We will now, with the help of Mark Twain, examine the encounter of Adam and Eve. In this, everything turns around language, names and naming: in particular, it concerns the way each person seeks to give things a name. We should emphasize that it is precisely this term that Lacan uses, refusing any notion of "creativity" (a term dear to contemporary pop-psychology). Once more: it is Creation that is divine, and naming comes afterward; in other words, gossip, with its inventiveness, obliquely doubles Creation.

This pair, Adam and Eve—they aren't very sure who is who. Twain tells the story in Eve's words. Having caught sight of the male creature, she thinks "it" must be a reptile, and tries to attract its attention by throwing clods of earth:

> One of the clods took it back of the ear, and it used language. It gave me a thrill, for it was the first time I had ever heard speech, except my own. I did not understand the words, but they seemed expressive. When I found it could talk, I felt a new interest in it, for I love to talk; I talk all day, and in my sleep, too, and I am very interesting, but if I had another to talk to I could be twice as interesting, and would never stop, if desired.[2]

---

2. M. Twain, *Eve's Diary: Translated from the Original MS* (1906), in *The Diaries of Adam and Eve*. New York: Oxford University Press, 1996, pp. 23–25.

The narrative posits the existence of a language "naturally" without any place for communication, but subsequently, at a second moment, another appears to open the possibility of dialogue. Twain's fiction, then, implicitly assigns an idealist, monadic origin to language. Eve continues: "If this reptile is a man, it isn't an *it*, is it? That wouldn't be grammatical, would it?" Note that her discrimination passes strictly through grammar, not through any "thinglike" quality. She goes on: "I think it would be *he*. I think so. In that case, one would parse it thus: nominative, *he*; dative, *him*; possessive, *his'n*. Well, I will consider it a man and call it he until it turns out to be something else."[3]

Eve now goes on to the subject of nomination. "I have taken all the work of naming things off his hands, and this has been a great relief to him, for he has no gift in that line, and is evidently very grateful."[4] Once again, then, it seems that for Twain the question of the jouissance of speech is very close to that of femininity: the woman—we can say with Lacan—talks and talks, because she is searching for what she doesn't have, and keeps on talking as she finds nothing at all. Thus, Eve is shown to be a real gossip—without that having any pejorative connotations, on the contrary, indeed, given her ability to speak (about) things and make them speak back to her.

Concerning her power of naming, Eve comments that "the right name comes out instantly, just as if it were an inspiration."[5] She describes how the animals appear before her; she gives them the name she "knows" to be correct. More-

---

3. Ibid., p. 25.
4. Ibid., p. 29.
5. Ibid., p. 31.

over, a very interesting detail of Twain's text recalls *La guerre du feu*, the brilliant film by Jean-Jacques Annaud: it is Eve who discovers fire, while Adam remains dumbfounded by it. We should pay close attention to the text here, as it links up with Joyce and his aesthetic credo: "I had created," says Eve, "something that didn't exist before; I had added a new thing to the world's uncountable properties; I realized this, and was proud of my achievement. . . ."[6] Eve guesses that the pragmatic Adam will ask her what the new discovery can be used for; and her response would be that "it was not *good* for something, but only beautiful."[7] Note that what she has made is primarily an artistic object: fire is "useless" and beautiful, like a true work of art. The description that follows evokes the beauty of the rising flames, of the glowing ashes and the drifting smoke. And, of course, Eve gives all this a name, because they were "the very first flames that had ever been seen in the world."[8] At the end of this naming process, Adam appears, and, standing stupefied before the fire, asks: "How did it come?" Eve responds: "I made it. . . . Fire is beautiful; some day it will be useful, I think."[9]

Where is this long description leading us? Toward revealing, precisely, the connections between inventing something, naming it, and making an artistic object. This is a crucial theme for us, which gives rise to something different from the classical definitions of Man. It is not *Homo sapiens* that interests us here; the notion of the "rational animal" is of no more use to us than that of the "political animal." Rather, a

---

6. Ibid., p. 55.
7. Ibid., p. 57.
8. Ibid., p. 59.
9. Ibid., p. 65.

dimension emerges around *Homo faber*, man as "maker" or artisan; and what he makes, of course, is not useless.

A philosopher rarely cited by analysts, Henri Bergson, writes something in his 1907 work *Creative Evolution* that is highly relevant here: "Intelligence, considered in terms of what seems to be its originary task, is the faculty of creating artificial objects, above all tools, and to endlessly vary such a production."[10] The point can be wholly assimilated to the aesthetic credo of *A Portrait of the Artist as a Young Man*, with its emphasis on the figure of the "artificer." It was not hard for Lacan to follow Joyce's lead in highlighting the function of the artisan, the producer of artifice. Here, we will underline the difference between such an artificer and the factory worker by a conveyor belt; we will thus be able to illuminate Joyce's "Thomist" aesthetic credo—such is the principle aim of this chapter. But let us first explore another aspect of the Joycean *sinthome*.

Lacan remarks that Joyce's manner of working, of forging linguistic artifice, is well captured by Philippe Sollers when he coins the term *l'élangues*.[11] The pun on *les langues* ("languages") also connotes "elongation," "stretching-out." Just like Evie—that is, by naming—we invent a new concept, filling up the ineluctable deficit of names left by the Father of Creation. The elongation of one language toward another results in a fertile mixture of composite linguistic extensions. No doubt, although Lacan does not emphasize this, the pun also echoes a kind of energy or vital *élan*—a Bergsonian idea.

---

10. H. Bergson, *Creative Evolution*, trans. A. Mitchell. London: 1919, n.p.

11. P. Sollers, "Joyce & Co," op. cit., p. 114. The article links this term to Lacan's notion of *la langue*, which we will explore below.

And why not, adds Lacan, see here a reference to "elation"? This would be that condition of mental excitement, of constant, extreme lightheartedness, which is linked in psychopathology to mania. Clearly, elation must be considered manic if it constitutes a state of unlimited, continual, and irrational high spirits. Is the Joycean engagement with *l'élangues* thus to be considered a product of mania? Does Joyce suffer from manic symptoms? The answer is no.

In psychoanalytic terms, it would be wrong to consider Joyce's writing to be a symptom of any kind. The only person to suffer from a symptom for us, as analysts, is the one who says that he or she does. A symptom is of course what causes suffering, indicating something amiss in the Real; but to note it as an observer is quite different from acknowledging it as a sufferer. If a symptom cannot be formulated as such, the conditions for analytic treatment have not been fulfilled. Operating in an "outside" beyond transference, we might be able— perhaps very astutely—to isolate, classify, and describe certain psychopathological signs; but in doing so we do not in any way involve the subjective position of the other. Freud, for instance, in the famous case of the "young homosexual," gave views on a series of technical questions in a way that is absolutely still valid today, concerning the results of trying to "bring" somebody to analysis, and how such an undertaking necessarily fails, even if an analytic situation seems to have developed. This is largely because the alleged analysand is not implicated in the transference. Ultimately, this kind of procedure is—as Lacan concludes in his reading of the Freudian case study— like throwing a stone into the sea. Nothing happens, even if the external signs of a psychoanalytic event appear.

What happens, then, with Joyce? The answer raises something crucial for our understanding of Lacan's approach. It is that Joyce does not admit to any symptoms, but strictly speaking has a *sinthome*. Better still, rather than having it, he is one with his *sinthome*. This question must be explored and worked through, which will be one of the nodal projects of the seminar. But Joyce does not suffer from symptoms; we are unable to assign him any without immediately sliding into applied psychoanalysis—by "diagnosing," for instance, a Joycean mania. All those suffering from mania, very obviously, start to mix up and play with words. They link up words, or parts of words, in the most wayward manner; and they do so not only playfully but also irrationally, according to a secret logic, a logic of homophony that gives rise to associations without restraint and is devoid of surface meaning. Again, if we were to bring all this to bear concerning Joyce, we would be merely approaching his work from the "outside," for, to our astonishment, we discover that the writer kept rigorously and carefully to a program of work, developed at length with great precision, and through reflecting on *l'élangues*. Effectively, as David Hayman puts it, Joyce's writing is innovative in the way it "knots things together" in new groupings. Here, of course, we note the coincidence (clearly an intuitive one, but not therefore groundless) with Lacan's views: for Hayman, *Finnegans Wake* is organized through "knots of allusion or meaning, clusters or strips which make up topographies and serve as ways of structuring the text rather than as integral parts of its argument."[12]

In this chapter, we seek to understand the beginnings of Joyce's literary project in two closely linked texts, *Stephen Hero*

---

12. D. Hayman, "Some Writers in the Wake of the *Wake*," in *In the Wake of the Wake*, op. cit., p. 22.

and *A Portrait of the Artist as a Young Man*. The hero of these works, who is to reappear in *Ulysses*, is Stephen Dedalus. It is worth pausing over the mythological allusion this name entails, in order to outline some of what is at stake concerning the question of *artifice*. Drawing on several studies of mythology, we can pinpoint certain features of Daedalus, and his "protector," in other words the ancestral figure he is referred back to: Hephaestos. The lineage has little to do with *Homo sapiens*, but rather evokes *Homo faber*. The *Dictionary of Classical Mythology* indicates, concerning Daedalus—the provocation of a mythical outpouring of desire on Joyce's part—that he excelled in sculpture and architecture.[13] We could describe Daedalus as the inventor par excellence; and this will be precisely one of the major points that Lacan will seek to bring out concerning Joyce: that he was the inventor of a new kind of practice with letters.

Furthermore, after Daedalus has constructed the famous labyrinth—which we should remember has a connection with Ariadne's thread, for this will constitute another avatar of Daedalus—he ends up as the prisoner of his own creation, sentenced to remain there by King Minos, whom he has tricked. Finally, being such a talented inventor, Daedalus manages to escape with his son Icarus, by making artificial wings. He gives his son precise instructions about the flight from the labyrinth: "If you fly too high, your wings might melt in the sun; but if you fly too low, you risk falling into the sea and thus also dying." Icarus, of course, ostensibly disobeys his father, but what kind of care does this father show to his

---

13. C. Falcón Martínez, E. Fernández-Galiano, and R. López Melero, *Diccionario de la mitología clásica*. Madrid: Alianza, 1980, pp. 160–168.

son? What the father gives are manifestly instructions, but they can be read as a handbook for disobedience, in which Icarus can detect signs of denial. What does he do? He flies so high that his wings, stuck onto his body with wax, melt and fall away—and so he falls into the sea and drowns. The extremes defined by Daedalus as opposing dangers ultimately cooperate in the destruction of Icarus.

The *Dictionary of Classical Mythology* states: "Daedalus is in later tradition the inventor through autonomasia—the name given to every excellence in architecture and ancient sculpture, whose origin had become unknown." Moreover, he was called the "ingenious artificer"[14]; this was his principle characteristic. And what is an artificer, if not the inventor of things, one at a time? The very opposite of someone who produces objects in series, it is a matter of inventing something for each occasion, for each addressee. Hephaestos, the ancestor of Daedalus, is the god of fire and of blacksmiths, the one who tends and controls the forge. Our interest in these mythological figures will be understood when we read the closing lines of *A Portrait*.

What we have outlined is the nodal point through which passes a network that allows *A Portrait of the Artist as a Young Man* to finish with its hero "forging" himself—Hephaestos is present—as an artist, in an account of his experiences up to the moment when he sets off to begin his exile. It is more a linguistic than a geographical exile, which consists in Joyce seeking elsewhere a support for his subjective position. But at what risk! As most commentators agree, Joyce breathes Ireland through every pore of his skin. There are indeed cer-

---

14. Ibid., pp. 160–168.

tain parts of Dublin that one could practically recreate on the basis of journeys that appear in *Ulysses*. The precision of Joyce's descriptions—he makes extensive use of maps and Thom's Directory—allows him to reconstruct his native city; it is very likely that this was his way of reconstructing his patrimony: his only work for the theater is entitled *Exiles*.

Patrimony, of course, is what belongs to the *pater*; unlike matrimony, which derives from *mater*.[15] The opposition is crucial, for us, in any account of the relation between homeland and marriage. But let us return to the Motherland or Fatherland (which in the end amounts to a bond between man and woman); it is that which makes Stephen exclaim at the end of the *Portrait*: "Old father, old artificer, stand me now and ever in good stead."[16] Just before this invocation, comes: "I go to encounter for the millionth time the reality of experience and to forge in the smithy of my soul the uncreated conscience of my race."[17] Lacan will return several times to this quotation—to a "conscience" that can be neither ascribed to an author nor situated precisely in time, and a "race" that is to be understood not in terms of biology but of lineage. Next, "old father" is linked to "old artificer": the young artist, setting off to find his destiny in the world, simultaneously seeks protection from a father who can defend him. It is well known, of course, that Joyce accumulated an extraordinary number of addresses, continually on the move from one place

---

15. Translator's note: In Spanish, the opposing terms are *matrimonio* ("marriage," from the Latin *mater*, "mother") and *patrimonio* (lit. "fatherland," "homeland," from the Latin *pater*, "father.")

16. J. Joyce, *A Portrait of the Artist as a Young Man* (1916). New York: Viking, 1964, p. 253.

17. Ibid.

to another. This astonishingly nomadic life reveals the impossibility of Joyce ever finding the place where the "old father," the ancestral artificer, would be able to protect him. Thus, Joyce's life reveals his failure to find satisfaction for the exclamatory demand made at the beginning of his career.

Having touched on the problem of exile, let us turn to another central Joycean theme marked out by Lacan with wordplay: St. Thomas Aquinas, an important reference in Joyce's early writings, will be written as *sinthome-madaquin*.[18] As we will see, the pun on Aquinas' name refers to another current, deriving from his presence in the text where Joyce first posits himself as a writer.

Lacan makes some radical observations about St. Thomas Aquinas, which we will trace *à la lettre*. This is one of the rare occasions where Lacan affirms something with refreshing bluntness. Concerning Aquinas, he states: "We should put things clearly: when it comes to philosophy, [Aquinas] has never been bettered. That's all the truth there is." The judgment leaves no room for doubt: "that's all the truth there is." Here, however, we think one should discern the subtle effect of a metaphor. Is Lacan not alluding to the need to take very literally how St. Thomas deals with the question of truth? In this sense, Lacan is a Thomist: he follows Aquinas in his criteria of truth.

Concerning this, we could take from the *Summa Theologica* an idea relating to the cognitive subject. St. Thomas, believing man to be a finite being, sets out from concrete, sensory experience; he does not ally himself with any kind of spiritualism, theorizing only on the basis of what is perceived. But the

---

18. Translator's note: Lacan puns on *Saint Thomas d'Aquin*, St. Thomas Aquinas.

cognitive subject actively collaborates with knowledge, for it is received through the intermediary of the recipient, or the "recipiend" (perhaps a better term, implying an active process of reception). In other words, the question begins with sensory experience, but I receive it according to the way that I am. Here, we are not dealing with an empiricism, if that means I am presented with something from the outside, already printed as such. Nothing is copied or reflected, but what is perceived is produced by its own articulation—ultimately, by its own constellation. Such a theory, as the reader will have seen, is emphatically opposed to the Platonic theory of "reminiscence," according to which we know something because we remember a timeless self-identical essence, which returns in the act of cognition. In the latter theory, the subject of knowledge had to be bracketed off for there to be an effective connection to the reminiscence. In the Platonic dialogue *Meno*, Socrates claims to prove that the ignorant slave can eventually manage to discover that he knew about geometry, ostensibly revealing through his guiding questions the presence of an eternal knowledge, inscribed as an Idea beyond the contingency of any particular speaker.

Thus, here we are faced with a theory of knowledge based on a spiritual or innate essence, which completely bypasses the recipient, as it does not account for any subjectivity whatsoever. Such a theory is not to be found in Lacan: rather than Platonic, his thought is Aristotelian-Thomist. Thus—in our reading—"that's all the truth there is." For Thomas Aquinas, it is difficult to gain access to knowledge, because one does so not by direct vision but by necessary labor: an indispensable methodical work, on a systematic task, is required, and even this does not deliver a full, complete truth. Can we not locate such a conception on the borders of the Lacanian no-

tion that truth can only be half-said or is not-all, and thus
cannot be fully known? Because, in the same line of thought,
we recall that truth has the structure of a fiction. It is in this
understanding that, for us, there is nothing more than that of
the truth: this is the teaching of St. Thomas.

Here, we reach a fascinating question (especially concerning what we have already noted about the "establishment" of
Lacan's text). It concerns a reflection on the Beautiful. Lacan
comments: "In *sinthomadaquin* [i.e., Aquinas], there is something he terms *claritas*, for which Joyce substitutes something
like the splendor of being, which is certainly the weak point
in question." Lacan thus points to a failing of some kind,
with a corollary critique. His next statement is even more uncompromising: "It's a personal weakness, the splendor of being
is not something that strikes me." The latter, strictly speaking,
is the third characteristic required by beauty, according to the
reading of Aquinas that Joyce outlines in the *Portrait*: in order
to be beautiful, an object must conform to three conditions:
(1) *integritas*, (2) *consonantia*, and (3) *claritas*. "Wholeness,
harmony, and radiance," as Stephen translates the terms.[19]

Lacan takes up the third term, indicating playfully that
he is not struck by the splendor of being (radiance, it goes
without saying, would be striking). He thus sees it as a term
that could be left aside, since it entails nothing meaningful.

---

19. *A Portrait of the Artist as a Young Man*, op. cit., p. 211. As Father
Noon shows, Joyce's Thomist aesthetic is founded on a pun—St. Thomas
never wrote on aesthetics or claimed to have invented one (the very term
"aesthetic" had not been coined in his period). Thus, for purist Thomists,
integritas, consonantia, and *claritas* are only steps toward the cognitive grasp
of the external, thinglike object. Cf. W. T. Noon, *Joyce and Aquinas*. New
Haven, CT: Yale University Press, 1957, pp. 53–57.

The concept, Lacan emphasizes, is mistaken; we will see, for our part, where that takes us.

Toward the end of the *Portrait*, Stephen raises the three terms in his discussions with schoolfellows; in addition, he brings in the term *pulcher*, "the beautiful." Here, we should note something crucial: aesthetics is not a discipline concerned with beauty. From its outset and by definition, aesthetics bears on *aesthesia*, sense-experience or feeling: thus, the aesthetic is closer semantically to terms like "anesthetic" than to any notion of beauty. Of course, one might object that all the same it is common for a work on aesthetics to refer to the beautiful; but this is not necessarily so. It may refer to beauty, but it may also evoke directly or implicitly something addressed by Freud with unparalleled insight: the uncanny.[20] By forging the notion of *Das Unheimliche* in his famous article of 1919, Freud overturned the whole field of aesthetics.

But let us return to St. Thomas and his *pulcher*. As Joyce indicates, its presence requires the triptych of wholeness, harmony, and radiance. Let us briefly examine what we are told about each of the terms in the *Portrait*; we will see how Lacan gradually makes use of them. By "wholeness," Stephen explains, is meant simply the perception that allows us to separate an object that interests us from the universe. "You see it as one whole. You apprehend its wholeness. That is *integritas*."[21] He goes on:

---

20. On the uncanny, we strongly recommend the work of a Spanish philosopher, Eugenio Trías, *Lo Bello y Lo Siniestro*, where the author balances a chapter on beauty with another on the uncanny, dealing in particular with Freud's fundamental contribution, as well as with the anxiety and enjoyment provoked by works of art.

21. *A Portrait of the Artist as a Young Man*, op. cit., p. 212.

> . . . the synthesis of immediate perception is followed by
> the analysis of apprehension. Having first felt that it is *one*
> thing, you feel now that it is a *thing*. You apprehend it as
> complex, multiple, divisible, separable, made up of its
> parts, the result of its parts and their sum, harmonious.
> That is *consonantia*.[22]

Lacan takes this concept as a starting point for one of his
characteristic meditations, where an ostensibly "manic" association is shown to have an underlying, strictly Joycean
logic. *Consonantia* gives him an opportunity to criticize "those
English philosophers," so-called at least because "they are not
psychoanalysts": for they persist in referring to "instincts."
Unlike them, Lacan states, we psychoanalysts talk of *Triebe*:
"drives." How can this be related to *consonantia*? Through the
effects of speech on the body: its "resonance" or *consonance*
there. Speech transforms the orifices of the body (mouth, anus,
urethra) into holes that open onto drives. Thus, *consonantia*
becomes a way for Lacan to talk of the impossibility of aesthetic
jouissance without the concept of the drive. We cannot speak
of the aesthetic, for Lacan, without invoking a jouissance that
resonates (or con-sonates) due to effects of language. And a
detail is added to this linguistic jouissance here: someone has
pointed out to Lacan, he says, that in talking of language [*la
langue*], we should not forget the "so-called taste-buds."[23]
Doesn't *Homo sapiens* mean precisely that, in the true sense
of the name?[24] We note the apparent link between knowledge

---

22. Ibid.
23. Translator's note: *La langue* literally meaning "tongue" as well
as "language."
24. Translator's note: Punning on the Latin *sapere*, which can mean
both "to be wise" and "to taste."

[*savoir*] and taste [*saveur*]. Once again, we see how a single term can be grist to Lacan's mill.

What happens with tongues or languages? Lacan makes a reference to seasoning or "condiment": it is only due to the tongue that we can experience its tasty effects; and then another pun transforms *ce condiment* into *ce qu'on dit ment* ["what one says is a lie"]. This is a very radical claim: when someone speaks, he's lying. It means that we should be very careful when we imagine truth and lies to be two essentially distinct moments; even popular wisdom says that *la mentira tiene patas cortas*—effectively, when someone lies, he tells the (half-) truth in a thousand ways.[25]

With his *ce qu'on dit ment*, Lacan uses *ment* in conjugating the verb *mentir*, but let us recall that it is also very often used as the last syllable of French adverbs of manner or degree. Thus, we could write *franchement* as *franche ment*, making "frankly" into "frank lie." If such an adverb might be said to end in a lie, as it were, we should pay attention to another adverb of manner: the equivocal "as" in Joyce's *A Portrait of the Artist as a Young Man*. We will return to this equivocal title, and the question of equivocation and analytic interpretation.

But let us continue our discussion of drives. We can see how Lacan's deployment of *consonantia* gives rise to a line of thinking, which may not be exhaustively dealt with in Seminar 23 but which links up with other moments in his work. Lacan isolates two drives, which can properly be termed Lacanian because they are not present in Freud's writing. In the first place, Freud had highlighted oral and anal drives; here

---

25. Translator's note: The Argentine proverb means "a lie has short legs"; thus, it doesn't get very far—truth will always sooner or later catch up with it.

we can situate demands, neediness, complaints, either "you don't give me enough" or "that's too much" (it is frequently thought that people fall ill because they are given too much, overprotected; or given too little, frustrated). Such drives strongly tend to produce fantasies, as these relate to the mouth or the anus. It is "all" very clear; and that is the problem—there's too much *claritas*. In fact, since "everything" can be very easily understood, one must take great precautions vis-à-vis the dimension of the *ment* (the potential deceptiveness of "as") as a possible factor in this high-speed understanding.

Lacan seeks to go beyond Freud in isolating two new drives, in such a way as to produce an object that is not "obviously" incorporated or expelled, but encircled by a movement looping back to a bodily orifice that has become a hole. The objects of these drives are the gaze and the voice. The table below summarizes the drives Lacan deals with in Seminar 11 (1964):

Drive	Object	
oral	breast	} demand
anal	feces	
scopic	gaze	} desire
invocatory	voice	

We would emphasize here that the drive is linked to a notion that is Lacan's own "artifice" (in the true sense of the word: something produced skillfully); throughout his teaching, right up to Seminar 23, he claims that it is the only *discovery* he has contributed to psychoanalysis. Even if the latter point is highly debatable in a body of work so rich with important discoveries, it shows the value Lacan attributes to this concept. It is, of course, the object *a*—which is the object of the drive, among other ways of understanding it. In this context, it will be identified as follows: the breast, the feces, the gaze, and the voice are the different objects *a* of the respective drives. Later on, we will discuss the decisive weight given to the voice in Joyce's *sinthome*, through a singularity dubbed by Lacan "imposed speech." The voice bound up with the drive is not, of course, the voice we hear when we talk: it is a voice that can be isolated or outlined in a way that is exemplary—but not exclusive—in the psychoses. Thus, schizophrenics describe the hallucinated, polyphonic voices they hear, in a paradigmatic manner: "they're telling me that. . . ." Voices commanding, scandalous, or seductive; voices impossible to escape from, with all the suffering that entails, for they leave a subject defenseless before them. The gaze and the voice, the two objects introduced by Lacan, are precisely the most infamous features of the psychoses. It is here that we can see a theoretical advance, in which the Freudian objects (those relating to demand: breast and feces) occupy a different position than the Lacanian objects, which relate to desire. We should view these claims cautiously, but they seem to us valuable. Every object is object-cause of desire, indicates Lacan, but differentiating between them through stages—as Lacan does in Seminar 10, *Anxiety*—will give us a guiding thread in our explorations.

Why, the reader will be wondering, are we getting sidetracked into drives? Above all, due to the way Lacan addresses the pathology of the obsessional neurotic, and in particular because of his emphasis on the question of the gaze there. This is not an easy domain to comprehend; it is not linked to the simple matter of lines of sight. It is not a question of someone looking at us or vice versa; such a tendency is what in fact defines the pair voyeurism/exhibitionism. The gaze is more evanescent, harder to grasp—it is what occurs, for instance, Lacan tells us, when I look through a keyhole and hear a noise behind me. At that precise moment—I see no one, I'm only looking through the keyhole, and I hear something—I am gaze. The object is thrown upon me, I am identified with the gaze, I *am* the gaze. Is this, we might ask, because I am seeing, or seeing myself seen? No—it is because I've been caught: through the gaze thrown upon me, in the shame it arouses in me, I become the gaze completely. It is also a question of the gaze at work when we look at a picture. The picture looks at me because I have laid down my gaze there, as one lays down arms. If such statements seem almost deranged, they convey, in their very strangeness, the difficulty of grasping these objects in immediate experience. These phenomena occur in a very different manner from the objects examined by Freud: their scope is far wider, they are more "scandalous." No doubt, the frustrations and gratifications of the oral and anal zones can be detected with greater "clarity" through hearing the analysand tell his mythical history.

The gaze "holds" the obsessional neurotic because the latter is above all constantly undergoing tests, performing pirouettes and death-defying leaps with no safety net, always thinking (unconsciously, of course) of an eventual "onlooker," the implicit motivator of such exploits. Thus, there is an omnipresent eye, everywhere and nowhere, always seeing but never seen by the subject. Sometimes this eye is named God, but there is no reason why this should be so; it could just as easily be a matter of the subject's dead father, as in the Freudian case of the Rat Man. But to a large extent the prowess and all the activities of the obsessional subject make him a *nullibist*—that is to say, not an "ubiquist" but someone whose very ubiquity, whose striving to be everywhere, results in his being nowhere. In his hyperactivity, his efforts to always supposedly obtain a little bit more, the obsessional offers himself as sacrifice before what we have termed "the scatological spectator."[26] It is anal—but nonetheless scopic—domination that leads so many "nullible" exploits to be aimed at an Other who cannot be seen.

Using a well-known fable, Lacan illustrates how the obsessional tries to swell up like the frog who wanted to make himself as big as an ox, with the results you'd expect. On the basis of this trope, we could imagine the obsessional compulsion as an empty, inflatable sack, its volume capable of expanding; it is a question here, without doubt, of the sphere. The obsessional inflates himself more and more, striving— and this is what interests us—to become like one of the formal objects that Lacan extracts from set theory: ultimately, he states, this self-inflation leads to an empty set. What is an empty set? Precisely a set possessing, paradoxically, no elements. It can be drawn in the following way (Figure 10):

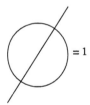

Figure 10

The empty set allows Lacan, following the work of Cantor and Peano, to maintain that the question resides—and this

26. Cf. R. Harari, *De qué trata la clínica lacaniana?*, op. cit., pp. 115– 127.

is precisely the problem—in the number. This void does not imply any possibility of counting; precisely to the contrary: logical enumeration begins with 1. Even though it is empty, the set is nevertheless 1, the first set; this is the only element of the empty set, which makes it a set with one element.[27] This is the paradox: How do we begin to add to this? We are familiar with the well-known theory of the successor, which states that it is the product of adding 1 to n: after 1 comes 1 + 1, then 2 + 1, and so on. We thus obtain each number by adding the empty set to the preceding one, by adding a kind of nothing, a void, to a number. It is by adding nothing that we advance: Lacan will link this to the domain of creation, which he conceives as *creatio ex nihilo*, a creation that begins from nothing, like that attributed to God.

Now we come to a problem. We have traced, in the seminar *R.S.I.*, Lacan's move from the triple to the quadruple Borromean knot; we should now examine more rigorously this passage from 3 to 4. To begin with, we recall, Lacan stipulated that Freud had gone one beyond him, but that for his part, three was enough. Subsequently, though, he maintains that without this fourth term, the Borromean knot can offer nothing to analysis. It is without doubt this last position that Lacan ends up adopting; but it allows us to observe something very surprising—that, in effect, to move from the knot of three orders to that of four, a procedure that does not form part of the numerical sequence of the successor becomes necessary. The knot of three must completely come undone—for this, we recall, it only requires one ring to slip, as this is the only

---

27. Cf. J. Lacan, *Le savoir du psychanalyste*, seminar of May 4, 1972 (unpublished).

way to form the quadruple knot. In other words: it is not a matter of adding one to the triple knot, but rather of undoing it and retying it as the "successive" knot. The result is the quadruple Borromean knot, which we can present as follows (Figure 11):

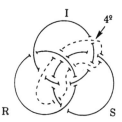

Figure 11

If one looks closely, it can be seen that the three rings drawn with an unbroken line remain detached from one another, the fourth ring (drawn with a dotted line) being what constitutes the knot. The three are superimposed: the S at the bottom, then the R on top of the S, and lastly the I on top of the two others. It was necessary to undo the triple knot—which had six crossing-points—in order to include one more order, which now serves to tie together the resulting quadruple figure. Referring back to the article mentioned in Chapter 1, its title could just as easily be inverted: there is no retying without untying.[28]

At this point, we can link the knot up with what happens at the end of analysis. Bringing about the quadruple knot corresponds exactly to the end of analysis; it is only possible if, in a concrete sense, the triple knot comes apart. The pas-

28. R. Harari, "No hay desenlace. . . ," op. cit.

sage from the triple to the quadruple knot, therefore, rather than merely resulting from the addition of a ring, completely transforms the status of what governs it. It was this, in our view, that Lacan problematized, leading to his initial criticisms of Freud's requirement of four terms. For the difference, of course, does not reside in one more or less. In the third session of Seminar 23, Lacan emphasizes that in the triple knot, the consistent orders—as these words imply—are equivalent, harmonious, or analogous. But the fourth term introduces an asymmetry or asynchronism: the same ring now crosses one of the others, no matter which one, no less than four times. In Figure 11, we have made this privileged ring the Imaginary, but we could have made it either of the other orders, as the terms are not in any way fixed. One ring is privileged by being crossed four times by the fourth ring, while it only crosses each of the other two rings twice. In total, the two-dimensional image of the quadruple knot's structure requires fourteen crossing points, while the triple knot has only six. It is precisely in this respect that the new knot's asymmetry implies a far greater degree of complexity. The "discovery" of the fourth order we have termed the *sinthome* amounts to one of the most difficult of Lacan's topological interventions, and one that has a radically subversive effect on his teaching.

What, then, did Joyce carry out by means of his writing, according to Lacan? Nothing less than a *mise en scène* of this quadruple knot. However, he was not alone in carrying this out—and this point is crucial. Regarding this question, there are two currents of thought: let us explain why we choose to support only one of these. In our view, the fourth order accounts for a habitual psychical structure. According to the alternative view, it entails a sort of forced addition, a supplementary ring whose function is to make up for a fault; it would therefore only emerge in cases where a specific event (for instance, the presence of a father) failed to occur. Thus, one might say—clinging to Lacan's teaching without reflecting on it—that a work like that of Joyce is governed by the lack of a paternal presence; and thus the emergence of the fourth order would be something sporadic, even quite exceptional.

One might think that Lacan's allusion in *R.S.I.* to the Name-of-the-Father as superfluous might be taken as support for the above hypothesis. But let us go farther. Lacan will claim that the three separate rings do not define perversion, because the latter is a matter of *père-version*, a pun that combines a "version of the father" with a "turning toward the father." One only turns to the father due to a specific version of "father," and there can of course be many of these, even mutually contradictory ones. In general, as clinical treatment shows, the father fails—for one reason or another, he is structurally inadequate in fulfilling the ideal function corresponding to his place. This is very clear in hysteria, with its impotent father, the fantasmatic victim of a mother who, so to speak, wears the trousers. In the case of the obsessional neurotic, we have the son who is supposed ("sub-posed," kept under) to keep to a very strict set of rules, derisory in its empty formalism. The father is always deficient or excessive, provoking such assertions as "so he thought he could get me that way," "he gave me money but no love," or "he loved me in his way, but not in the way I wanted," and so on. Thus, each "version" of the father is a poor one, something set apart from the Name-of-the-Father in that the latter, like everything connected with the Symbolic, implies a calming effect.

Such a calming effect is produced by a good number of self-styled "brief psychotherapies"—but later on the symptom returns, as such therapies are not up to dealing with the repetition compulsion. Confined to the Symbolic, the Name-of-the-Father entails an agency of order and the reduction of stress; this is not the case with *père-version*. It is not an accident that Lacan's pun here evokes "perversion": it occupies a disturbing, transgressive position, bound up with drives, far removed from some supposed peace offered by the collective code.

The transition from the triple to the quadruple knot constitutes, we insist, a qualitative shift. And here we should also take into account something very important, implied by Lacan when he states that the three separate rings do not correspond to perversion. As soon as we topologize this question, as we have seen, it becomes clear that the move from three to four orders requires the breakup of the triple knot. Yet, as Lacan states, the three rings are "already separate"—indeed so, but precisely as a knot "pending," awaiting the fourth ring to produce it. Such a structure shares with perversion a pattern of negation: the effect of the fourth ring is both affirmed and denied simultaneously, emerging as a virtual potential and not—yet—something actually effective. In other words, then, there is no way of turning toward the father except by means of a version of the Symbolic, which is doubtless imaginary and which thus brings specular rivalry with it.

This is why the version usually encountered gives rise to complaints and dissatisfaction (we refer to a typical situation in clinical analysis, not something peculiar to the metaphysics of the father). In truth, what our Western societies reveal is a certain weakening, a humiliating interrogation of the place of the *père-version* that supports the father. It is subjected to criticisms, dwelling on various inadequacies and shortcomings. Thus, one's singularity, what is specific to each subject, does not depend exclusively on the mythical pattern of one's *père-version*, but also on what one expects from the coming fourth order. Even *père-version*, for example, can occur without the three rings being detached—in other words, two of them can already form a chain, as in the Hopf chain (Figure 12):

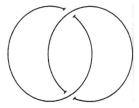

Figure 12

This of course leads to overall modifications of what is "expected" of the fourth term. Lacan proposes that in one of the knots that define Joyce, Real and Symbolic remain together; this is why, as we shall see, in another kind of quadruple knot (not Borromean), one ring passes through another, unlike what appears in Figure 11. Later, we will examine a diagram that will show the discrepancy between what Lacan terms Joyce's *ego* and the quadruple Borromean knot, which we could describe as the "general" quadruple knot. To argue the contrary would be to imagine that Seminar 23 is exclusively devoted to Joyce, to his artistic work, without taking any note of the broad and various implications of what reveals itself to be a major theoretical advance, the culminating point of Lacan's unparalleled journey: namely, the move from the triple to the quadruple Borromean knot, with all its vital consequences for clinical treatment.

After these remarks that took off, associatively, from our consideration of *consonantia*, let us now explore some aspects of the Thomist notion of *claritas*, which Lacan declared he did not find particularly "striking." In truth, the notion is absolutely decisive in Joyce's thinking. It seems to us especially important to pursue our own critical reading, without necessarily subscribing without reflection to every claim made by the French master. Joyce wrote that the radiance or *claritas* spoken of by St. Thomas is an equivalent of the scholastic term *quidditas*, the "whatness" or essence of being. Lacan reads this as though Joyce were offering a philosophical, ontological hypothesis: he thus misses something that is not without importance. We recall in the previous chapter mentioning how Lacan makes an analytic comment about forgetting his copy of *Stephen Hero* one day: the slip is revealing, for it concerns precisely the work in which Joyce privileges the concept of *claritas*, making it the equivalent of a fundamental motif of his aesthetic thought: the epiphany. What is an epiphany? A revelation of being, but in the guise of a moment of brilliance having nothing to do with any ontological theory; it corresponds, rather, to what theologians have named *parousia*: presence, appearance, advent—a revelation that precisely exceeds theorization. St. Paul, in the First Epistle to Timothy, speaks of the "manifestation" of Jesus Christ: this is an epiphany, an unexpected manifestation, a sudden glimmer revealing something essential. It is given great importance in Joyce's work, since the young artist conceives it his first literary task to become a collector of epiphanies.

Lacan's slip, then, is a significant one. On this topic, it is worth reporting a brief exchange between Lacan and Jacques Aubert in the seminar of January 20, 1976. In his presentation to the seminar, Aubert mentions a little "playlet" in *A Portrait of the Artist as a Young Man*, adding that it is written "according to the Epiphany model"; at which point Lacan, visibly surprised, asks, "Is that a term of Joyce's?"[29] Aubert seems somewhat perturbed by Lacan's question, and gives a short explanation of the term "epiphany." Now, by the end of one of the last sessions in Seminar 23, May 11, 1976, Lacan himself is referring to "the famous epiphany," something that "can be found all over the place in Joyce." There is clearly a movement here on Lacan's part, from an initial unfamiliarity with the Joycean epiphany to the development by the end of the seminar, as we will see, of a potentially very rich conceptualization around it. Only a desire to idealize the master could lead to a suppression of the earlier moment.

We have mentioned the points in *Stephen Hero* where we can see the emergence of the epiphany. This is something very much bound up with the quadruple knot, which is not necessarily a Borromean knot, in Joyce. It concerns an event— this is what is most surprising—that is absolutely banal, something insignificant. The first example offered could be a slip or a joke (there's no need to spell out how much half-truth it may contain):

> Young Lady (drawling discreetly) . . . Oh, yes . . . I was . . . at the . . . cha . . . pel. . . .
> Young Gentleman (inaudibly) . . . I . . . (again inaudibly) . . . I. . . .
> Young Lady (softly) . . . Oh . . . but you're . . . ve . . . ry . . . wick . . . ed. . . .[30]

---

29. J. Lacan, Seminar 23: *Le sinthome*, January 20, 1976 (A.F.I. Edition), p. 80. Translator's note: Note that the exchange Harari refers to does not appear in the version edited by Aubert in *Joyce avec Lacan*.

30. J. Joyce, *Stephen Hero* (1944). London: Paladin, 1991, p. 216.

Joyce hears this, nothing but these murmurs, and then adds:

> This triviality made him think of collecting many such moments together in a book of epiphanies. By an epiphany he meant a sudden spiritual manifestation, whether in the vulgarity of speech or of gesture or in a memorable phase of the mind itself. He believed that it was for the man of letters to record these epiphanies with extreme care, seeing that they themselves are the most delicate and evanescent of moments.[31]

The *claritas* invoked by Joyce is related to a paradoxical moment at which an episode gives rise to a certain "radiance" on the part of the perceiving subject. Here, we are dealing with a coincidence of opposites: the triviality of the event, stripped of any epic connotations, comes to be linked to what it triggers off for the man of letters, whose distinguishing characteristic is to turn these empty incidents into, precisely, letters. These moments consist of interrupted fragments of speech, and we recall Lacan's work on Freud's Schreber "case": in rereading *Memoirs of My Nervous Illness*, Lacan showed how the broken phrases in Schreber's text open up onto something causal, become messages to be deciphered. In Schreber, we find the following fragments: "now I will. . . ," "as for you, you ought to . . . ," "I will certainly. . . ."[32] To sum up, it is

---

31. Ibid.

32. Cf. J. Lacan, "On a Question Preliminary to Any Possible Treatment of Psychosis," *E: S*, 186. As Sollers shows convincingly, when Schreber writes his *Memoirs* he adopts a classical judicial style: he writes on every topic, except his linguistic fantasies, since they derive from the Real. Thus, his writing is "readerly," even if not necessarily comprehensible. In this perspective, Joyce is an "anti-Schreber." Cf. Sollers, "Joyce & Co," op. cit., p. 118.

not a question of messages that do not fail but succeed; only insofar as there is a listener capable of making them into letters can there be a successful moment, an epiphany.

Claritas emerges, then, as an element of unique importance in Joyce's aesthetic theory. Lacan's abrupt comment that he "is not struck" (by the splendor of being) seems to relate more to the doctrine of Thomism than to Joyce's own reinscription of it. As we have indicated, it is only at the end of Seminar 23 that Lacan develops a precise theorization of the Joycean epiphany that, although it is very brief, opens a pathway that allows us to explore further. However, we do not take this late reference to the epiphany to be the only valid way of approaching it, as some of the questions raised earlier in the seminar allow us to envision other ways of theorizing the epiphanic moment. We should emphasize, again, Lacan's surprise when he comes across this word, with its popular association with the three Magi, the feast of the Epiphany, and so on.

In the epiphany, Lacan declares, we can detect an articulation, a bond between the Unconscious (in other words, the Symbolic) and the Real. The two orders are linked, as we have seen, like a Hopf chain. The moment of the epiphany: an unexpected flash of luminous *claritas*, which is something to be made into letters. Let us put it in a formula: the occurrence of the lived epiphany follows the pattern of the symptom; its writing turns this symptom into a *sinthome*. The attempt to elaborate the symptomatic event—hearing in the street a fragment of dialogue that is banal, almost ridiculous, in its appearance of everyday meaninglessness—becomes something pathognomic, a paradigmatic epiphany. It can be considered, in one reading, as a revelation, provided that this is not understood as divine, but as a revelation of the Real. Here, the "case" of Schreber will provide us with another way to comprehend

Joyce's notion: we will move between the Bible and Schreber's writing. The epiphany then, to sum up, is a sudden emergence, the appearance of something lived that can only be part of existence in the form of the letter (which of course does not necessarily entail the domain of writing).

In addition, if the epiphany implies the emergence of the Real, this will not occur without a "touch" of the uncanny, one of the basic Freudian definitions of which is the encounter between the strange and the familiar. What Joyce recounts—something so elementary, insignificant, and vulgar, as he indicates himself—does not fail to produce a certain disturbance, in the way it bites across the unexpected into the uncanny. This resembles what Lacan conceives of as the "unhappy" encounter: no planned rendezvous, the encounter between the couple talking and the passing listener is contingent, out of place. In this sense, the attempt to turn it into letters is an effort to tame the experience, to make it "treatable." Whereas, on the contrary, in actuality it is the experience that possesses the writer.

The epiphanies were extremely significant in Joyce's decision to become a writer: he had a strong sense of what is ordinarily called a vocation. *Vocare* entails hearing a voice calling out—something that is certainly written into the epiphany. It is perfectly possible to isolate this dimension in the speaking-being; it is situated, of course, beyond any particular aptitudes or interests. It is a question of the occurrence, without it being sought, of a certain experience that leads to the unique point of inventing one's own *sinthome*. Thus, an *élan* or buzz is generated, which becomes indispensable and which works in a way quite unlike the symptom. The suffering entailed by the symptom is certainly not at work in the same way in the *sinthome*, linked as it is to the epiphanic quality of inventing something.

3

Epiphanies, Σ, Trefoil

Our study has two essential themes: on one side, the work of Joyce; on the other, the way Lacan introduces topological questions around the quadruple Borromean knot. It is thus doubly necessary for us to take up the topic of the Joycean epiphany and elaborate on it further than Lacan does in Seminar 23. As we have seen, arguably Lacan did not give that notion all the importance that it has in Joyce's work, even if, indirectly, the movement of his teaching on the subject of repairing the knot—which culminates, in the final session, with a knot ascribed to Joyce himself—indicates paradoxically that in practice he was able to posit the foundation of what the writer named "epiphany."[1] Let us return to this topic, then, starting with some notes that will help us understand it.

---

1. According to Umberto Eco, Joyce took the concept of epiphany from the work of Walter Pater, who in turn had adopted the term from D'Annunzio's *Il Fuoco*; cf. U. Eco, *The Middle Ages of James Joyce: The Aesthetics of Chaosmos*. London: Hutchison, 1989, p. 23.

First, we will call upon a literary critic interested in Joyce's writing, Sydney Bolt, whose work on *Dubliners* opens an important pathway toward the epiphany.[2] The stories in Joyce's first published work are distinguished by their abrupt endings—something ostensibly not at all innovative, given that it is one of the characteristics of the short story. But these endings are not merely sudden; they entail a breakdown of narrative coherence, a kind of bolt out of the blue that can completely cut the imaginary thread of the reader's expectations. It is not a matter of some obscurity, something not understood in the facts of the story; indeed, it is the facts that leave the reader in a veritable state of stupefaction. Let us put this in psychoanalytic terms: at these defining moments, the stories emerge as emptied of meaning. This implies that the endings cannot even be understood in the context that "prepared" them. Faced with such awkward perplexity, in the absence of a context to create an integrated whole, the spontaneous reaction is one of flight. Ironically, we thus arrive at a kind of "totalism," the attempt to immerse the enigma into a context that can illuminate it, make it a comprehensible whole. Yet at the endings of the stories in *Dubliners*, we have something that appears to be emptied of signification—the latter, in Lacanian terms, being always phallic, we recall. Let us clarify this point.

Signification is phallic because, in referring to nothing with concrete embodiment, to no empirical organ, the Phallus belongs to the domain of the signifier. It is precisely the fact that one is never able to locate it that leads to its continual slippage, the constant search to grasp directly something

---

2. S. Bolt, *A Preface to James Joyce.* Harlow: Longman, 1992, pp. 55–58.

impossible to seize. If it endlessly extends into the distance, this is because signification—the possibility of understanding, of producing a "brilliant" effect of meaning—is linked to a sense of oneness. Each time that we conclude, "at last I've understood," we affirm our corresponding immersion in the context, for we have reached an unified, unifying condition; otherwise, such a conclusion would be out of the question. Or else, as we shall see, following Lacan we can show that it belongs to the register of the Real, remains split off, unknotted. To knot it would imply giving to it the phallic dimension that it lacks. Whereas the procedure Joyce terms epiphany consists in leaving language unknotted. The result is a space of phenomena defined in advance as banal, everyday, and we could link this to Freud's explorations of everyday life, which found in banality the core of our being. By examining the slip or bungled action, for instance, Freud took up the residue that had been cast aside by all psychologists, before they came into contact with his genius; he revealed that such errors could embody thoughts away from the "higher"' mental processes. Joyce, for his part and in his own way, will rummage for the core of our being in the epiphanies that he collects, and on the basis of which he decides to begin his literature.

The *extasis* that comes over being at the moment of the epiphany does not generate meaning. This would also imply—as we have observed in Joyce's work—a failure of metaphorical production, given that according to Lacan metaphor is what creates meaning, in a poetic "sparkle." Of course, in our view a literary creation is potentially just as metaphorical as a symptom. In the latter, a particular phrase is made metaphor in the body and "presented" in the flesh, rendered incarnate. Why do we claim that Joyce's writing would correspond to the failure of metaphor? Because had there been a

successful effect of metaphor, the endings of the stories in
Dubliners would be laden with meaning. To work properly,
metaphor has to provoke in the reader an effect well known
in the traditions of philosophy and of art theory: aesthetic
enjoyment [*jouissance*]. The first condition of this is that the
metaphor must be understood, otherwise it is useless. In this
sense, it must be said that what Joyce does is in no way metaphorical; one could speak, rather, of metonymic residues, the
remnants of an ecstatic experience, dislocated fragments that
are displaced into writing and that, as broken pieces, make
us feel penetrated by a nothingness. We do not know where
we are going with Joyce, what he meant by that; we fail to
understand. And the endings that Bolt draws attention to are
not only banal, but also stereotypical—situations, in brief, that
always appear to be exactly as they are. Concerning this, and
to our astonishment, we find ourselves before a project that
Joyce himself formulated: to purify the language without com-
promise, by obliquely denouncing stereotypes by means of
satirical exaggerations that would show them to be laughable.
What a challenge! To accomplish such a task—and here, as
analysts, we must follow him, Joyce had to seek out habits of
signification, the hiding place of being. Martin Heidegger, in
his concept of truth (which was adopted, with certain reservations by the early Lacan), insists that Being is *unveiled*, its
truth exposed by the lifting of a veil. This was what the Greeks
called *alethia*: truth as unveiling and not, in its academic definition, adequation. Joyce sets out, by means of his epiphanies, to lift the veil, an act that, as a literary undertaking, can
only expose a "split," if it fails to give rise to a metaphor. In
the corresponding perspective of literary criticism, the Joycean
wager on "portmanteau" words (which were named as such by
Lewis Carroll, to account for the condensation allowing a single

verbal invention to "contain" several distinct signifieds[3]) dem-
onstrates, according to Derek Attridge, that

> Anything that appears to be a metaphor is capable of re-
> versal, the tenor becoming the vehicle, and vice versa. . . .
> All metaphor, we are made to realize by [*Finnegans Wake*],
> is potentially unstable, kept in position by the hierarchies
> we bring to bear upon it, not by its inner division into lit-
> eral and figurative domains.[4]

Now, to talk of the "failure"of metaphor is not to make a
judgment about the aesthetic value of Joyce's work, but to refer to what makes a Freudian slip emerge as a "failed" act; to
describe it as such goes along with the view that successful
communication has not been affected. Yet at the heart of this
failure there is a success: a true discourse wells forth, making
the Freudian slip into a successful act. This is why our judgment is not in any way derogatory: Joyce's "failure" forces us
to question ourselves, ultimately putting us in the subjective
position of the analyst. Isn't this what happens whenever we
raise questions about the signification of what remains beyond
interpretation in the analysand? Lacan constantly warns us
about the risks of overrapid clinical comprehension. If the analyst is in a hurry, he gives nothing to the discourse he hears
but familiar signification, riddled with prejudice, and thus
obscures any possibility of isolating the singularity Lacan repeatedly stresses. The Joycean epiphanies seem deliberately

3. Cf. J.-J. Lecercle, *Philosophy of Nonsense: The Intuitions of Victo-
rian Nonsense Literature.* New York: Routledge, 1994, pp. 59–68.

4. D. Attridge, "Unpacking the Portmanteau, or Who's Afraid of
Finnegans Wake?," in *On Puns: The Foundation of Letters*, ed. J. Culler. Oxford: Blackwell, 1988, pp. 153–154.

conceived to ward off rapid understanding: they generate constant enigmas, never being tied down to any one exact meaning. But in that case . . . when will this enigma ever be resolved? We do not know—as Lacan comments in the seminar, when Joyce sets out to make the scholars work, it is not only to procure commentaries but also commentaries on commentaries, thus launching criticism on an infinite task. One of those perspicacious critics is Sydney Bolt, and we will follow his remarks further in order to grasp more firmly the Joycean epiphany.

As already mentioned, if there is a point at which the Joycean epiphany finds something comparable in the work of Freud—certainly as both are conceived of by Lacan—it is that of the interrupted message, of the phrase seemingly broken off by suspension points. We take Schreber to be a prominent *craftsman* in such interruption; and we can immediately perceive one of the aims of this paranoiac of genius (as Lacan called him): to attain a *Grundsprache*, a basic language, a sort of fundamental proto-language. Joyce would initiate something not dissimilar: he aspires to create a primordial language that is radically *Other*, and in so doing to liquidate—in a phonetic sense—English. *Finnegans Wake* reaches the point of presenting us with the question of how to formulate what is unspeakable, the foundation of how we distinguish between written and spoken language. At one point, the text does this by calling on incomprehensible words of a hundred letters (one of which we used as an epigraph). How can these words be read or pronounced? Without introducing scansions, it is impossible to make sense of them.[5] These extended words

---

5. However, since it is not a question of a maniacal illegibility but of an enigma that can potentially be unveiled, the polysyllabic words in question

have of course nothing to do with terms belonging to familiar language; one can perceive in them a plan, a missionary
endeavor directed toward finding a kind of philosopher's
stone: an undertaking, in other words, with every appearance of being foundational.

The evacuation of phallic signification from what surges
up in the epiphany, touching on mysticism and devoid of all
meaning, means that it can be categorized—according to the
terms set out in Seminar 7, *The Ethics of Psychoanalysis*—as
being in contact with the Thing: that is, a Thing not included
in the world, not an object in reality, and also an instance
impossible to grasp. In Lacan's later work, this Thing will
link up, via the formalization of the knot, with the register
of the Real. Its predominance corresponds to the liquidation
of meaning: the Real is profoundly alien to meaning, being
ab-sens, punning on *absence* to negate meaning (*sens*).

Let us turn to some examples from *Dubliners* to account
for the perplexity we have mentioned. Following the approach
proposed by Bolt, we can point to two of the stories' endings.
First, the closing lines of "Araby":

> Gazing up into the darkness I saw myself as a creature
> driven and derided by vanity; and my eyes burned with
> anguish and anger.[6]

This is how the short tale ends; it does not suffer from
being taken out of its context, as we are dealing with an ut-

---

are open to the logic of multilingual games, which does not prevent their
evoking other associations. On this point one could point to the polysyl-
lables relating to thunder, including our epigraph. Cf. M. Teruggi, *"Finnegans
Wake" por dentro*. Buenos Aires: Tres haches, 1995.

6. J. Joyce, *Dubliners*, p. 40.

terance that is abrupt, categorical. There is apparently an indication of emotion here ("my eyes burned . . ."), although we do not know its cause, the context it relates to.

Likewise, in "Clay," the final fragments of the story refer to an ordinary situation:

> At last the children grew tired and sleepy and Joe asked Maria would she not sing some little song before she went, one of the old songs. Mrs. Donnelly said *"Do, please, Maria!"* and so Maria had to get up and stand beside the piano. Mrs Donnelly bade the children be quiet and listen to Maria's song. Then she played the prelude and said *"Now, Maria!"* and Maria, blushing very much, began to sing in a tiny quavering voice. She sang *I Dreamt that I Dwelt*, and when she came to the second verse she sang again: [The text includes a childish song]. But no one tried to show her her mistake; and when she had ended her song Joe was very much moved. He said that there was no time like the long ago and no music for him like poor old Balfe, whatever other people might say; and his eyes filled up so much with tears that he could not find what he was looking for and in the end he had to ask his wife to tell him where the corkscrew was.[7]

Do we laugh or are we baffled? The ending of the story is completely disconcerting: we can see how Maria finds herself in a fixed position when she is called upon to sing; but once she has finally got through the old ballad, the response of Joe, her "mistake," and why the last line centers on such a total irrelevancy as the location of the corkscrew are so many details that add up to something nonsensical.

---

7. Ibid., p. 88.

Let us take our last example from *A Portrait*. It is the moment referred to by Jacques Aubert when Lacan shows his surprise at the term "epiphany," and also connects back to the definition of epiphany in *Stephen Hero* with its "vulgarity of speech or gesture." Here, it is no longer a question of an ordinary situation, but of one that is openly vulgar, strikingly stereotypical in its characterization, even though the task of the epiphany is to unveil the essence of being, according to Joyce's "Thomist" definition:

> He was sitting on the backless chair in his aunt's kitchen. A lamp with a reflector hung on the japanned wall of the fireplace and by its light his aunt was reading the evening paper that lay on her knees. She looked a long time at a smiling picture that was set in it and said musingly:
>
> "The beautiful Mabel Hunter!" A ringletted girl stood on tiptoe to peer at the picture and said softly: "What is she in, mud?"
>
> "In a pantomime, love." The child leaned her ring-letted head against her mother's sleeve, gazing on the picture, and murmured as if fascinated:
>
> "The beautiful Mabel Hunter!" As if fascinated, her eyes rested long upon those demurely taunting eyes and she murmured devotedly: "Isn't she an exquisite creature?"[8]

Here, from the girl's first comment to her last, a certain progress toward ecstasy appears. It does not emerge all at once from the beginning: at first, the child reproduces exactly what she heard; she is then "authorized" to enter into the code she has been offered. At any rate, in this process she has passed

---

8. J. Joyce, *A Portrait of the Artist as a Young Man*, p. 67.

into an experience of *exstasis*; such a banal occurrence is prototypical of the Joycean epiphany. This is what made Joyce's
compatriot, the poet W. B. Yeats, declare rather tartly that he
couldn't understand how anyone could expect to do so much
with so little. The spitefulness of Yeats' comment perhaps does
not completely mask a certain involuntary tribute, with its
implicit acknowledgment of Joyce's unaccountable literary
powers.

As we have already indicated, Lacan's principle interest
in Seminar 23 is to explore, by means of the quadruple knot,
how Joyce's art is produced, how the process of its invention
can be made intelligible. We will propose the dimension of
artistry, of craftsmanship, that allows us to link this preoccupation of Lacan's to the question we raised at the end of the
last chapter: that of differentiating between the irruption of
the symptom and the force that accompanies the *sinthome*. The
impulse to write, for instance, is clearly of a different order
from an obsessional compulsion, not merely due to a difference in the respective positions of the subject, but beyond this,
due to metapsychological criteria. Let us take a familiar example: someone who washes his hands a hundred times a day.
There is no doubt that this occurs according to the pattern of
metaphor; as clinical work shows—if we are to be allowed this
kind of cliché, the action is to be read as a defense against
masturbation. However, the aim to keep one's hands clean,
to evoke the semblance of the absence of masturbation, ends
up becoming a way of touching part of one's own body with
one's hand: thus the return of the "repressed" masturbation,
now taking effect by means of the signifier, metaphorically.
It may not result in a poetic creation, but what it produces is
clearly a metaphor—one which strenuously demands, moreover, to be deciphered by the Other. In this sense, one ob-

serves an "obvious" message; at the same time—as Lacan maintains in his seminar *R.S.I.*—the neurotic *believes in* his symptom, considers it to be meaningful. And he thinks that if this "meaning" is unveiled, his suffering will cease.

This neurotic kind of belief differs in certain ways from that at stake in psychosis, of which Lacan remarks that what the subject believes in there is his hallucination. The psychotic feels the absolute certainty of concrete, empirical perception regarding what he is hallucinating or dreaming-up, whereas the neurotic only *believes in* the symptom, addressing it to the Other with a demand for it to be interpreted. But what happens in Joyce's case? What is the singularity of his subjective position—at what point, even, does it lead us to questions about Freud's theory of art? The answer is given by the famous anecdote about Joyce writing *Finnegans Wake*: as he wrote, he allegedly laughed continually, showed unbridled jouissance. This contradicts the Freudian aesthetic theory according to which the artist succeeds in expressing a universal fantasy, dares to give voice to what we would all like to do but cannot ever attain. In this theory it is *we*, the receivers of the artwork, who experience enjoyment, due to the fact that we see ourselves represented there, "hooked" onto it by a certain fantasmatic detail. This is not so with Joyce; on the contrary, his work is so full of riddles, so completely emptied of (phallic) signification, that it was to "keep the professors busy for centuries arguing over what [he] meant," as he put it.[9] It is impossible—Real—to feel oneself represented in the inscrutable *Finnegans Wake*, which does not of

---

9. Richard Ellmann, *James Joyce* (1959). Oxford: Oxford University Press, 1982, p. 521.

course prevent it from being a magnificent, highly stimulating work of art.

The splendor of the *Wake* has to do, not with metaphor, but with jouissance. This is the fundamental point about Joyce: he managed to work on his own jouissance, all the while convinced that what he was producing was something exceptional, and deserving of being recognized as such by the whole world. This amounts to a complete reversal of the Freudian view of art. Joyce never puts himself in the place of the reader; he demands, rather, that the other occupy his place. At stake here is a categorical difference, which cannot be understood merely by invoking a change of roles in the fantasy. Joyce's work is located one step beyond fantasy: that is, in a place where collective fantasies or desires cannot be grasped, framed, or represented, in such a way that they can be recognized by others. Indeed, it is extremely hard to "identify" with certain effects of the Joycean text: no one can feel himself represented by a hundred-lettered word. Yet this is precisely where the possibility of experiencing jouissance through our engagement with the text emerges, once we have accepted its radical *ab-sens*. This is certainly true of the epiphanies, which is why Joyce's writing is dominated—although Lacan doesn't put it in exactly these terms, we do not think this unfaithful to his thought—by *metonymy*. To grasp the defining Joycean characteristic, in short, one should not focus on the process of substitution—one word for another, because such a process for him hampers that of enchaining words, linking them together simultaneously, without repression.[10] Verbal explo-

---

10. Cf. J. Lacan, "The Agency of the letter in the unconscious, or reason since Freud," *E:S*, pp. 156–157.

sions and implosions, words that are decomposed and transmuted: this is the Joyce of *Finnegans Wake*.

Artistry, singularity: both are categorically opposed to any preestablished series or chain. On this topic, it is interesting to look up the dictionary definitions of these semantically related terms. The *Real Academia Española Dictionary* defines *artisan* as "one who makes by himself objects for domestic use, giving them a personal signature, unlike the factory worker." Singularity is thus emphasized as the decisive element. The word *artifice* derives both from *ars*, "art," and *facere*, "to make"; in this context, let us recall *Homo faber*. Further dictionary definitions of *artisan*: "A practitioner of the fine arts; an author, someone at the origin of a thing; a person skilled at obtaining what he desires." All of these definitions are relevant, for they emphasize a crucial factor—knowing oneself to be the cause or origin of a thing. There is no doubt that this is one of the fundamental supports of Lacanian clinical work.

Knowing oneself to be responsible entails occupying a position diametrically opposed to that of "blaming" the unconscious and thus distancing oneself from any participation in the origin at stake. Responsibility amounts to this: one cannot avoid being implicated in whatever is described as "unconscious." This is the complete opposite of the familiar pious and medical gaze that sets something to one side as it describes various subjective aspects of it—illness, unconscious, and so forth, thus making it completely unlike "what everyone knows it is." Let us formulate things after the manner of the *desideratum* Lacan stated concerning his *Écrits*: the unconscious, as something to be assumed by the subject, should allow no way out other than the way in. It is a dimension that has to be captured so as not to allow room for any

defense that would turn away from it. An author is thus someone who causes something, but at the same time someone
skilled at obtaining what he desires. This implies a certain
acceptance of one's own desire, such that the subject becomes
("well and truly," as Lacan puts it) a heretic, one who chooses
and thus succeeds in attaining his real logically.

Another term frequently used by Lacan is *artefact* ("a
thing made by human workmanship," according to *Chambers
20th Century Dictionary*). In French, too, there is the verb
artificier, "to contrive," "to do something with artifice"; and
also, of course, the adjective *artificié*, "artificed." These terms
denote the skilled treatment of an object such that it can be
singled out, separated from serial production. Here it must
be stressed, however, that if heresy entails a choice, that choice
must nevertheless be confirmed. If this latter point is not
sufficiently accounted for, one risks endorsing an "elective"
legitimacy of madness. We should not embark on a naive,
romantic return to the misguided views of antipsychiatry.

Artifice, a decisive word for Lacanian teaching, is defined
in the dictionary as "the predominance of skillful ingenuity
over nature." In other words, we are in the realm of the opposition art/nature, conceived as if they were separate domains. Here we could recall why Lacan began his seminar by
referring to Eve and the question of naming—precisely in
order to overturn a naive idea of nature. God, the author of
so-called divine Creation, is nothing but a signifier, an order
with no connection to what is "natural." To put it briefly, all
we ever encounter are the results of artifice. Let us note the
pejorative sense we usually associate with what is artificial;
as though, lacking natural daylight, we resign ourselves to
making do with artificial light, but we think the latter infe-
rior. Yet this natural light is really only a product of urban

civilization, of the signifier: light would not be "natural" if it were not cut out by the signifier, made part of a construction whereby certain holes can give rise to the semblance of "nature." There is no nature outside of "nature": thus, one cannot conceive of a nature that one can oppose to art, nor can art constitute a reaction against nature. The classical dichotomy nature/culture always implies that the latter is set up at the expense of the former; but we can never imagine nature as virginal, only nature founded by the signifier, in a paradox or concealed joke, as "virginal."

Let us continue to explore etymologies by turning to that of "symptom." According to its Greek origin, it means "that which falls together." This is not the case with the *sinthome*, which neither falls not comes together. In fact, the contextual or metaphorical condition that is a central constituent of the symptom is diametrically opposed to the level of the *sinthome*, which Lacan will situate as "extraterritorial."

Here we must pause over the topological writing brought in to account for this new psychical constellation. For this, Lacan reintroduces the schema of the tetrahedron, which he draws as follows (Figure 13):

Figure 13

The figure is a horizontal section with a line drawn from top to bottom, and Lacan adds to it the terms he uses in his four discourses: S_1, S_2, a, and $\mathcal{S}$.[11] Over the course of time, these letters acquire different functions and so our reading has to be adjusted to the distinct periods of Lacan's teaching. In Seminar 23, Lacan declares that S_2 denotes a "duplicity" between the symbol and the *sinthome*. This shows that in his conception of the fourth order, Lacan immediately situates it in the domain of the symbol. The latter term is unexpected, given Lacan's usual theoretical preference for the Symbolic. In Freud, on the other hand, we often come across the word "symbol": for instance, in his discussion of the "dream symbolism" that is invoked in the context of an analysand failing to offer associations in the face of a dream. In such a case, says Freud, the analyst interprets "by way of the symbol"— in other words, according to preestablished associations rather than the singularity we have emphasized. We will examine below the reasons for Lacan's return in this seminar to ideas that he had previously powerfully criticized.

If the symbol thus now comes to indicate the Symbolic order, it seems that the *sinthome* is very closely bound up with it. Together in the S_2, these two instances constitute another form of the Symbolic; if this takes place, what falls is not a symptom but the object a. Effectively, as is shown by the tetrad above, S_2 is oriented toward a.

We can thus affirm the following: S_1 represents the subject $\mathcal{S}$ for another signifier (S_2). If the former is not divided, it makes room for the object a. And this a is artifice: that which

---

11. Translator's note: For the four discourses, cf. J. Lacan, *Le Seminaire, Livre XVII: L'envers de la psychanalyse*, 1969–1970, ed. J.-A. Miller. Paris: Seuil, 1991; and B. Fink, *The Lacanian Subject*. Princeton, NJ: Princeton University Press, 1995, pp. 129–137.

is produced out of the coming-together of the two components of S_2. But this coming-together also results—and here Lacan brings in a new topological reference—in a false hole, produced by the overlapping folds of two circles, which can be presented as follows (Figure 14):

Figure 14

As previously, it is the crossing-points that interest us: the dotted line, when read along the upper/lower axis, passes under the unbroken line, then over it, before it again goes over, and finishes its course by going under the other line. We can thus see that the figure is not governed by an alternate over/under sequence, and this is what constitutes its "slip" [*lapsus*]. This arrangement, it seems clear, is absolutely unrelated to the Hopf chain. Moreover, there is no central hole here: the hole is "false" because the two elements can be isolated without the requirement of a cut. Yet we cannot avoid the fact that they are separate, as there is nothing passing through the middle. Therefore, if we include a third element, a line passing through the center—where the false hole can be situated—allows the two to be linked together, and in turn linked to the new line. The addition of an infinite straight line—the equivalent of a circle—to the false hole brings an end to the separation; in its place, now, a triple Borromean knot takes shape, "is written" (Figure 15):

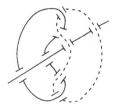

Figure 15

This "writing" thus presents the same structure as Figure 1 (p. 8).

Elsewhere, Lacan stresses that when the symbol and the *sinthome* are separated, this is an effect of the discourse of the master. But what is a true hole? The effect of a circle, in other words a closed line in space. The discourse of the master is precisely that which says: form a circle. What then happens when the initial false hole is no longer sustainable? If the structure is maintained—thanks to the inclusion of the third order—the hole will no longer be "false." But if this does not take place, if the symbol and the *sinthome* come apart, instead of artifice there will emerge a dominant discourse that is incompatible with artifice, given its command: "form a circle, in the name of the law." The latter refers to something universal, obligatory "for all," so that no one can plead ignorance in order to claim innocence of any transgression. In the end, an obligatory circle.

It is thus no surprise that Lacan isolates from this invention of artifice the properly human aspect in the *sinthome*. What is specifically human is the act of artifice: this constitutes a new advance, a new conception of what had been hitherto proposed, in other words that the distinctive human characteristic lay in language. Lacan now refers this to *invention*, in terms that certainly necessarily imply language—as shown by the order of the symbol—but also another order that we will attempt to conceptualize. Let us stress that, for the moment, we are dealing with another dimension than that of the Symbolic. This already indicates how subversive the fourth order must be.

In order to grasp the full importance of what emerges in Seminar 23 for this question, one should focus on Lacan's remarks there about his trip to America. It is one of those moments where he seems to reflect in a rather digressive, anecdotal way on his intellectual itinerary, setting aside the academic agenda of the seminar. By way of a general remark, he notes that he perceived a certain "lassitude" among American analysts, a kind of lack of interest in or weariness of psychoanalytic questions, something scandalous despite being "extensively addressed." Lacan's comments point to one of the debates where he is straightforwardly Freudian and where he once again expresses his doubts about the very possibility of psychoanalysis in the United States. He wonders about the rise there of an Erich Fromm, in whose work Freud (despite his having uniquely grasped the truth of the *parlêtre*) was above all "a bourgeois riddled with prejudice."

Leaving aside his concern with the figure of Fromm, Lacan has an encounter in America with Avram Noam Chomsky, one of the most important linguists of the 20th century. The encounter is frustrating for Lacan: he is disappointed by Chomsky's conception of language as a tool—a point where this brilliant intellectual is situated uncritically in one of the most steadfast American traditions of thought. Concerning this, Chomsky does not distance himself by even an inch from the utilitarian notion of language proper to Anglo-Saxon pragmatism: a tool adapted to its task and with the capacity to apprehend itself. Here, language is something that is useful, which is understood functionally. An erroneous message has no value for Chomsky: only the processes of successful communication are worthy of his attention. This is the exact opposite of what takes place in psychoanalysis, which is in no sense an applied linguistics. Linguistics can certainly furnish us with "useful tools," but only providing its concepts are reworked and recycled—not in order to falsify it, but to outline productive epistemological connections. Lacan gave an example of exactly this when he proposed a *linguisterie*. This *linguisterie* draws on Freudian teaching to show, for instance, that obsessional neurosis corresponds to a "dialect" of hysteria, the latter constituting the prototypical neurotic "discourse." This Lacanian sense of *linguisterie* is completely at odds with Chomsky's linguistics—thus the inevitable disagreement.

America was a series of disappointments: the lassitude of analysts, the presence of Fromm, Chomsky with his ideas of language as a tool. In the course of these remarks, Lacan allows us to glimpse another important point, providing we read closely enough. He does not only criticize the way Chomsky conceptualizes his field, but also the ignorance shown by the linguist of the subject of language that makes a hole in the Real. Lacan thus points to another function of language, its perforation of the Real—which opens a new way for us to understand it. Effectively, language is not to be grasped solely in terms of structure (as one finds dogmatically repeated); according to this perspective, Lacan's fundamental thesis is that the unconscious is structured like a language. And this idea is then transformed, according to a reading based on periodization, into a new one: that is, that the Symbolic makes holes by causing furrows in the Real.

Lacan thus breaks with the Kleinian notion of the symbol, which is sometimes wrongly attributed to him. According to Klein, when the object disappears, the subject recreates it by means of a symbol; it has been claimed that the same is true for the function of the signifier. Whereas the idea that language makes holes in the Real means that if something is lacking, this is precisely due to the effect of the signifier: language cannot make up for a lack which is its very consequence. A lack is installed: that of jouissance as plenitude. This lack and its effects lead Lacan to claim that everyone, including those who describe themselves as atheists, believes in God. Why should this be so? Because we are dealing with a belief that goes beyond all rational proof. In the end, such proof leads to nothing productive, due to the lack of universally convincing arguments. The overall function of language necessarily, inexorably precipitates belief in God. One can often hear "spontaneous" remarks such as: "I'm not religious, but there must certainly be something more. . . ." In other words, language makes speech possible and thus always provokes a certain excavation or extraction of jouissance, which pushes us into conceiving of the latter as something absolute, from which we have been unfairly and temporarily separated. We do not accept this, believing—this is also due to language—that somewhere that extraction has not taken place, that there must be a totality and an Other, full, absolute jouissance to which we can ultimately have access. This is why our most pressing concerns are directed to the hypothetical recovery of lost jouissance, through which we imagine that we can reconstruct the dreamt-of totality.

We have moved from language as an ordered set of structural rules, from that which is "structured like a language," to the Symbolic as the conveyance of holes. This idea is already present in *R.S.I.*, the seminar before *Le sinthome*, and in the latter seminar its elaboration is continued. For its part, the Imaginary is what gives things consistency, while the Real is that which—here we must refer to the work of Heidegger—ex-sists (or "is outside of"). We can sketch out these orders with the diagram of a circle: its consistent perimeter is imaginary, the hole it outlines is symbolic, while what remains outside the circle with no law or connection is real. R.S.I. once more, each with its specific characteristics.

But let us return to the question of God. It is here that Lacan makes another famous declaration, stating that the three orders were acknowledged by the only authentic religion, that of the holy catholic, apostolic, and roman church. Here, our reading of Lacan should note a certain rhetorical flair, understanding the claims he makes as a way of illustrating his point through learned allusion. Why is Catholicism the only true religion? Because it is the one that proposed the Trinity of the Father, the Son, and the Holy Spirit, thus illustrating—intuitively, of course—the triadic order of the Real, the Symbolic, and the Imaginary. In this sense, precisely, by grasping the resemblance of the Trinity to the triad R.S.I., Lacan indicates how Catholicism "understood" the knot. And here we should refer once again to Joyce.

In *A Portrait of the Artist as a Young Man*, Stephen Dedalus reflects on the Trinity in the following terms:

> He offered up each of his three daily chaplets that his soul might grow Strong in each of the three theological virtues, in faith in the Father Who Had created him, in hope in the Son Who had redeemed him, and in love of the Holy Ghost Who had sanctified him; and this thrice triple prayer he offered to the Three Persons [note the appearance here of a fourth element in this knot] through Mary in the name of her joyful and sorrowful and glorious mysteries. [p. 148]

In sum, the terms Stephen takes into account are three plus one. Let us continue with our reading:

> The imagery through which the nature and kinship of the Three Persons of the Trinity were darkly shadowed forth in the books of devotion which he read—the Father contemplating from all eternity as in a mirror His Divine Perfections and thereby begetting eternally the Eternal Son and the Holy Spirit proceeding out of Father and Son from all eternity. . . . [p. 149]

Here it is a question of the doctrine of *filioque* that gives entity to the third person of the Trinity insofar as it derives from the other two. On this topic, if we turn to a classic study of the history of religion—*Orpheus* by Salomon Reinach, a book almost a century old—we find a description of how opposing conceptions of Eastern Christian orthodoxy are at the origin of the Schism of the Christian churches. Effectively, it is different understandings of the third person that give rise to the proliferation of the various heresies, despite the fact that "the term 'trinity' does not appear in the Evangelists."[12] Reinach writes:

> The doctrine of the Trinity was fixed by the symbol wrongly ascribed to Atanasus, the author of which might have been the African bishop Vigilus (around 490): "We worship one God in the Trinity and the Trinity in Unity, without confusion of persons or division of substance. . . . Yet they are not three Eternities but One alone; not three All-Powerfuls but One alone. Thus, the Father is God, the Son is God, and the Holy Spirit is God; but they are not three Gods but One'.[13]

12. D. R. Dufour, *Les mystères de la trinité*. Paris: Gallimard, 1990, p. 199.

13. S. Reinach, *Orpheus* [*Orpheus: A History of Religion*. New York: Livecraft, 1932.]

We might see this as a powerful source for Lacan's claim that each of his registers is at once hole, consistency, and existence. If we consider the triple bo-knot, it is certainly possible to maintain the same thing about the Symbolic, the Imaginary, and the Real, given that the same knot, once it is tied, is clearly unitary—and that is what constitutes its real. Almost identical to what is claimed in the doctrine of the Trinity.

Let us continue with our reading of Reinach:

> The Father is not born, nor created, nor begotten. The Son derives only from the Father; he is neither shaped not created but begotten. The Holy Spirit derives from the Father and the Son; neither created, nor begotten, nor shaped but proceeding.[14]

These are exactly the same terms taken up by Joyce in *A Portrait* concerning the derivations and ways of knotting the Father, the Son, and the Holy Ghost. Lacan specifically addresses this topic in the course of one of his American lectures that coincides with Seminar 23. On December 2, 1975, at the Massachussets Institute of Technology, he states that "the alleged mysteries of the Holy Trinity reflect what is in each one of us, and what that best illustrates is paranoiac knowledge."[15] Now, one of the features of paranoiac knowledge is the ability to recognize in the other what is misrecognized in oneself. We can thus state that the figure through which we "recognized"—as well as misrecognized—the subjective knot by way of paranoiac knowledge, was the doctrine of the Trinity. This misrecognition

14. S. Reinach, ibid.

15. J. Lacan, *Conférences et entretiens . . .* , op. cit., p. 58.

is shattered by Lacan when he discerns the structure of the triple Borromean knot in this procedure. This powerful arc of thinking will be constantly developed throughout Seminars 22 and 23.

During the same lecture at M.I.T., Lacan adds that his remarks "might make it look like I'm making fun of the Holy Trinity. . . . It is precisely to avoid this," he goes on, "that there must be a fourth term." He thus aims to push his heresy beyond R.S.I., making it depend upon the inclusion of the fourth element. With the three registers, we remain in an order of equivalence: all three analogous, somehow equal or equivalent. We propose giving this configuration a name that we will return to: the paranoiac clinic of the Trinity. This is why the fourth term opens a new field that we can call the clinic of suppletion, referring to an inherent aspect of the *sinthome*. In *A Portrait*, Joyce ratifies and radicalizes the question of the Trinity, without at the same time breaking with the doctrine. Yet such a break comes to be figured when Mary appears as that which the "three persons" refer to (we recall that the design of the quadruple knot consists of three plus one: three alike and one different). In *Finnegans Wake*, finally, the quadruple knot will be fully attained.

In a typically analytic mode, Lacan's unveiling impetus leads him to another reference to paranoia, via the following knot (Figures 16, 17):

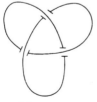

Equivalent
by continuous
deformation to:

Figure 16   Figure 17

As we mentioned at the outset of our study, Lacan had already worked with this kind of trefoil knot in Seminar 9, *Identification*.[16] The knot has only one feature, a single line defining a single element, which indicates the continuity of the three Lacanian registers. Nothing allows us to separate them clearly from each other. This fact makes Lacan write in the knot what is the simplest, the most logical kind of madness: paranoia. This kind of psychosis is situated, then, in the continuity of the three registers. But that continuity is equally that of a speech-act passing from one subject to another without interruption, or one that weighs up the pros and cons of a situation with the same level of realism, coherence, and energy, without paying attention to any possible contradictions or paradoxes that might inhibit it. Now, if one examines Figure 19 carefully, one can see how this trefoil knot underlies the triple Borromean knot. It is beneath it, or better: the trefoil is a knot, whereas the triple knot is in fact a Borromean chain linking up lines closed in space (thus making them "trivial" knots) (Figures 18, 19):

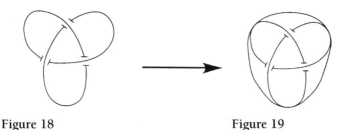

Figure 18   Figure 19

We could sketch this out differently. Let us draw a triple Borromean on top and, as was done inversely above, let us

16. J. Lacan, *Identification*, seminars of May 2 and May 16, 1962, unpublished.

again outline a trefoil knot (with a dotted line), in which we can clearly discern the four zones defined in the first chapter: JΦ, JA, *a*, and meaning (Figure 20):

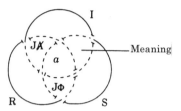

Figure 20

Thus, R.S.I. can be read both clockwise and anti-clockwise. We can read the diagram R.S.I., then, by moving on to the next element, S.I.R., and lastly I.R.S. Beneath this series Lacan draws a line and writes *SINTHOME*, so that it is present—simultaneously three and one—whatever one's reading of the chain:

R.S.I.

S.I.R.

I.R.S.

SINTHOME

But if the trajectory can equally take place the other way around, it is just as valid to link the terms up as follows: R.I.S., I.S.R., S.R.I.; these are modalities whose result is the *sinthome*. In sum, our reading can equally be clockwise and anti-clockwise (Figure 21):

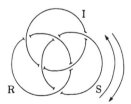

Figure 21

Thus the *sinthome* is written as a result, as if it has been produced by a sum in mathematics. Lacan will henceforth assign it the Greek letter sigma (Σ); this will serve as the *sinthome*'s graphic trace, its *grama*—written, as if to mark its singularity, with a "hellenization."

We have now reached another interesting point in Lacan's seminar, which can be isolated in the third session (December 16, 1975). He confesses to attempting something complicated: instead of enchaining circles, he has tried to link together four trefoil knots.[17] Lacan clearly wishes to be able to "construct" four trefoils in a Borromean chain; the resulting schema, as one can easily imagine, is extremely complex. He confirms this complexity, adding that he spent months trying to do it until he finally saw a solution thanks to help from two topologists who participated in his teaching, Michel Thomé and Pierre Soury. The latter mathematician, in particular, was to be greatly involved in the subsequent seminars (as he was already in Seminar 22), providing Lacan with numerous schemas, and even instructing him.

Concerning his encounter with this strange topological object, Lacan declares that when they brought it to show him, he felt nothing but enthusiasm; not that blend of awkwardness and powerlessness sometimes caused by another's success, but enthusiasm. We could pause there, with an imaginary reading; or we could take it a step further. In fact, "pure and simple enthusiasm" indicates a good way to thwart the

---

17. Concerning this, some versions of the seminar (including Chollet's) have "triple" where in our view it should say "trefoil." The error is very probably due to the similarity of the terms; but if one retains "triple," the text becomes practically impossible to understand, whereas "trefoil" makes perfect sense.

position of the divided subject: "enthusiasm" is etymologically linked to inspiration, which hardly entails an effect of teaching. Enthusiasm is actually what the working of the *sinthome* produces: a site of unification, but not an imaginary one. Recognition thus occurs at the site of "pure and simple enthusiasm" and not in the divided subject.

It is curious that one of these mathematicians is called Thomé, a signifier that links him to sin*thome*. The family name of this man who cracked the problem of the quadruple trefoil Borromean chain is very similar to that of another French mathematician, an important theorist who became friends with Lacan around 1971: René Thom. Thom triggered off a veritable crisis in scientific theories—especially in physics—with his theory of catastrophes. This work, along with the theory of dissipative structures formulated by Nobel Prize-winner Ilya Prigogine, the general theories of chaos and the theory of fractals produced by B. Mandelbrot—this whole set of morphogenetic theories, in our view, are extremely relevant to Lacan's fourth order. Thom is the author of a now classic text, *Stabilté structurelle et morphogenèse* (1972), as well as *Esquisse d'une sémiophysique*, among other works that include some vulgarizing and less important books. In an issue of the journal *Ornicar?*, Thom joins Lacan and other thinkers (mainly linguists) in a joint study of language.[18] A little surprisingly, perhaps, the mathematician reveals there a conception of language that differs from Lacan's. However, for our part, we think—on the basis of certain of his remarks in the last seminars—that if Lacan had lived longer he would have leaned to-

---

18. R. Thom, "Entretien sur les catastrophes, le langage et la métaphysique extrêmes," *Ornicar?* 16. Paris: Lyse, 1978, pp. 73–111.

ward Thom's morphogenetic perspective. For instance, Lacan makes a valuable comment concerning the hole of the Symbolic, indicating that what he is thus seeking to denote is the vortex. It is this vortex that comes to replace the old notion of dialectic that, as he notes, he had made so much of and used so often. These remarks come in 1975.[19]

The vortex was one of the central reference points in morphogenetic theories. How could its emergence be predicted? How could its cycles be analyzed? How could the irregular circuits of its ostensibly chaotic movements be outlined? These are extremely complex questions. It was no longer a question of a simple circle, with hard or malleable edges, which in any case came down to topology as the study of continuous deformations. The vortex is something radically different. Moreover, the ability to decipher it implies a profound reformulation of the concept of science, above all the one corresponding to the classical model of the 19th century (which is so praised by Mario Bunge, among others[20]). The latter model is predictive, whereas the model implied by morphogenesis is explicative. Here we reach a point of intellectual affinity with psychoanalysis. Indeed, our discipline does not aim to predict but to explain, according to an *a posteriori* epistemology. It therefore does not "expect" something to happen because of some general law.

Concerning what happened when Thomé and Soury came to him with the model he was seeking, Lacan adds something very revealing. The event was not "trivial," as he

19. J. Lacan, "Séance de clôture. Journées d'étude des cartels de l'Ecole Freudienne," *Lettres de l'E.F.P.* 18, 1975, pp. 263–271.

20. Cf. R. Harari, "Del psicoanalisis/del Norte," *Psicoanalisis in-mundo*. Buenos Aires: Kargieman, 1994, pp. 177–185.

puts it (perhaps again evoking the Joycean epiphany), but neither was it an uncanny one. Why should we expect it to be
uncanny? Because this would imply that something unexpected had suddenly arisen, which was not the case, given the
amount of time he had already spent on his research. But
Lacan's remark here is worth pursuing. He states that the event
was not part of the order of experience outlined by "a remarkable article." This article, "Vautour rouge" ["Red Vulture"], by
Sarah Kofman, had recently appeared in a collection entitled
Mimesis. Désarticulations. Oddly, Lacan states with a cabalistic
touch that he has only read Chapters 1, 3, and 5 of this book
(his original title for Seminar 23, of course, was *4, 5, 6* . . .).

We will focus on only one point in Kofman's article,
which we can relate to the internal logic of Seminar 23 and to
our own trajectory. "The Elixirs of the Devil," the story by
E.T.A. Hoffmann that is discussed in the article, is made up
of two distinct narrative parts; Kofman comments:

> Heterogeneity: is it not the essential characteristic of
> every text? Does the first part, for all its masterly construc-
> tion, escape a certain gap which makes it differ from
> itself, which makes it a text? Is it not particularly unavoid-
> able that a work where everything concerning the double
> [Hoffmann's classical subject. RH] is in play, in all its forms
> and variations, should be more than any other marked by
> a double seal? At the very least.[21]

"The Elixirs of the Devil" is double because "its entanglement is neither contingent nor secondary; it would have oc-

---

21. S. Kofman, "Vautour rouge," in *Mimesis. Désarticulations.* Paris:
Aubier, 1975, p. 98 [our translation].

curred anyway, even without the particular circumstances of this process." Here we reach an especially interesting passage in Kofman's article, both for how it deals with the Trinity and for the style of the writing: "The ability to knot and unknot the text implies at least two hands. Effectively, the duality of parties is joined by the fiction of a double manuscript edited by a third person, the author." This very Borgesian account continues: "The latter figure only repeats, with slight modifications, texts already written by others. Because it is double, the text is triple—or even quadruple, for one of the manuscripts turns out to have been finished by the hand of Father Spiridion relating the last moments of the monk Medard."[22] From the moment we encounter such a sequence, we find ourselves very close to Lacan's ideas.

Now, the book containing this article also contains several authors in Jacques Derrida's circle, and indeed, a piece signed by Derrida himself. As is well known, the philosopher has kept his distance from Lacan, despite the efforts of some scholars to find more common points than differences in their respective work. A relatively recent book, *Lacan avec Derrida*, by René Major, tries to go beyond the differences between these two great theoreticians in order to sketch out a productive way of combining them. In Seminar 23, however, Lacan confesses to not having read the article written by his enemy (the book's fourth chapter), thus implicitly maintaining the polemical tone of their relation.

To conclude this chapter, we turn to another heterogeneous text that will return us once more to the divided subject and the continuity of the trefoil knot. Lacan states in the

---

22. Ibid.

seminar that for a long time he has been asked for permission to republish his doctoral thesis, *De la psychose paranoiaque dans ses rapports avec la personnalité*. The reason that he has resisted this for so long, he says, is that he now sees a fundamental conceptual error in that work: he now considers that, rather than there being a *relation* between paranoid psychosis and the personality, they are in fact one and the same thing. Personality, to take one of the classical definitions (that of Allport), is "the dynamic organization in the individual of psychophysical systems which determine its specific adjustment to its environment." It is global, all-encompassing, like paranoia. Both are given "comprehensive" definitions, which are situated in a register of absolute continuity, according to what is presented by the trefoil knot. This link implies a severe criticism of psychology, not just that of personality but of the discipline as a whole—for the psychology of personality entails a central notion of all psychology. Let us not forget that Freud had already expressed this, by referring to the "decomposition (*Zerlegung*) of psychical personality." He thus sets up an important point in his teaching: we take up the personality in order to decompose it, to analyze the instances that make it up; and not in order to see there an allegedly harmonious integration, with nothing left over or not connected. It is on this basis—which is made into a classic of his work—that Lacan offers the opposing notion of the subject and allows himself a play on words. With the swift force of an epiphany, he states that the subject is always supposed. The audience is stupefied, as is the reader. What can this mean? Is this put forward to allow the subject some undefined quality, or as a radical critique, to rule it out? Certainly neither of these: if the notion of the subject—unlike the classical paranoiac personality—is useful for psychoanalysis, this is because it comes from the Latin *subjectus*, "cast down," "sub-posed," subjected. In this sense, to indicate that the subject is supposed is nothing new, but is rather somewhat tautologous. It is supposed by its very definition: it is posed (hierarchically) beneath a structure that determines it. It is diametrically opposed to the personality, as the latter boasts that it is its own master, it is self-born. It is the notion of the subject that accounts for the condition of being supposed, determined by the field of the Other.

4

Jouissances, Responsibility, Riddles: Doing with Know-How

The previous three chapters have given an overall presentation of the themes dealt with in Seminar 23. As we progress, we will see how this presentation becomes more precise and reaches deeper levels. It is far from easy to grasp the final, decidedly Joycean, period of Lacan's work. The proximity between these two monumental figures is very clear, above all at the point where Lacan's practice becomes notorious for giving rise to riddles, in its frequent capacity to formulate aphoristic phrases that go completely over our heads. In our "dialogue" with Lacan's formulations, it becomes as impossible not to "demand" explanations from him as to forgo our own sense-making constructions. In other words—adopting the tone of Lacan's teaching on Joyce—why does he not insert more of the Imaginary? Why are there not more coherent, more unifying connections in his work? One response to this will emerge from what we will explore below, which will provide an initial outline of cohesiveness. How will this be done? Through isolating certain signifiers and drawing up an itinerary, partly on the basis of our own imaginary, aiming to produce an effect of meaning.

It is worth retracing the subject dealt with in this seminar (as well as the one before it and those after), as it is the central goal of our research. Here, the level of complexity involved does not prevent us from perceiving that these are new questions for Lacan, that a third period of his work is opening at this point, where he progresses with his own signifiers. We must accompany him on this journey, if we wish to follow his work to its conclusion and not remain stuck halfway along it like so many of the "adepts" who don't get beyond the early seminars where Lacan discusses Freud. This early work is of course illuminating, but can in no way be understood in isolation from the later developments. What needs to be stressed about this third period of Lacan's work is that it is a time of invention, of *in-venire* (a theme that we will find explored in the seminar). Lacan no longer reads Freud here—with his undoubted mastery, his methods of interrelating texts and lucidly reformulating the problematics they generate—but he produces new signifiers. The return to *reading* Freud is undoubtedly an achievement of Lacan's, but it is not his only one. In sum, we must locate an epistemological break in his last seminars.

In the preceding chapter, many apparently disparate themes were presented. We must recognize, however, the coherence of these themes in Lacan's repeated return to the question of number, and specifically that of the disjunction between three and four. Concerning the number three, we noted the trefoil knot drawn with a single line, consisting of only one element, which allowed Lacan to write paranoia, also dubbed personality. The new perspective on Lacan's doctoral thesis shows the study of the personality to be nothing but the examination of the paranoiac element in everyone. The trefoil, as we have noted, is the knot which underlies the triple Borromean chain, which is drawn as follows (Figure 22):

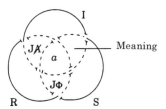

Figure 22

Why does Lacan return to the trefoil knot, beyond using it to account for the identity of paranoia and personality? It introduces a new precision, allowing him to isolate zones of intersection in the Borromean chain. As we have already observed, these can be drawn in a two-dimensional topological writing that can take different forms on the sole condition that the over- and undercrossings are maintained exactly. Lacan will add, at any rate, that this is not only a question of intersections; he will in fact redefine them as zones of suture. We thus come back to metaphors of string, in a definition that is, to say the least, surprising: "Analysis is a matter of sewing [*suture*] and splicing [*épissure*]." What is he seeking to indicate here? That our project, as analysts, our ethic, is to accompany the analysand until he is able to find his own knot and stitch something new into it by putting artifice to work. A new theory of the end of analysis: to succeed in enabling the subject to suture, stitch, unstitch—that is, to tie or untie something, to retie things otherwise. According to our aphorism, there is no unknotting without reknotting, and vice versa. In this sense, the metaphors of suture and splicing allude to effects of sewing things together.

The number of zones in the trefoil diagram is not accidental: there are four, of course (another Joycean "quaternity," according to Lacan). The fourth zone is located in the center of the drawing, and Lacan writes the object *a* there. Since Seminar 16, Lacan had associated this with surplus enjoyment [*plus-de-jouir*]. This is how he introduces it as such, comparing it with capitalist surplus value. Let us briefly reconsider this idea. Freud had identified the existence of a symptomatic benefit or gain of pleasure; the *Lustgewinn* implied a single addition to what came before. Now Lacan develops an implicit re-reading of this on the basis of the *sinthome*. Thus, the symptom constitutes a site well suited to the jouissance of the neurotic; or else we could say that the jouissance of the neurotic symptom accounts for the subject's resistance to being separated from it. Analysis proposes not enjoyment through the symptom, but enjoyment with the *sinthome*.

Lacan installs his surplus enjoyment in a retranslation of Freud's *Lustgewinn*. In his view, it is here that his own *in-venire* is to be situated, on the *a*: it is this, above everything else, that gives his theory its particularity and logic (at least until Seminar 23). This *a*, as surplus enjoyment, has the singularity, once found, of offering a little more jouissance. The latter term is a translation into French of a notion Lacan takes from Hegel (it can be found in the *Phenomenology of Spirit*).[1] This word also appears in Freud: it is *Genuss*, and the creator of psychoanalysis uses it in the context of his ideas about the end of analysis.

It is commonly claimed that according to Freud the goal of all analysis is to love and to work. Yet both verbs

---

1. Cf. R. Harari, "Del goce de Hegel al goce del fantasma," in *Fantasma: fin del analisis?* Buenos Aires: Nueva Vision, 1990, pp. 217–231.

are incorrectly translated here. Freud wrote *Genuss und Leistungsfähigkeit*, terms that we can link in particular to Lacan's teaching.[2] *Genuss* in fact means jouissance, while *Leistungsfähigkeit* means effective or productive capability. These two terms will thus be the first two parameters of this chapter.

In Freud, *Genuss* is different from *Lust*, "pleasure." Jouissance and pleasure are two separate instances, and it has certainly been one of Lacan's accomplishments to have outlined a distinct place for jouissance. The concept does not appear in his very early work; it gradually emerges until it comes to occupy a central place there, and is given a definitive, regulatory status. On this topic, we should reconsider our statement in the previous chapter that Joyce experienced jouissance in writing. What did this refer to, in generic terms? Not to a reduction in tension; not being a hedonist, Joyce did not aim to reduce tension to its lowest possible level. Here, the pleasure principle is linked to the Nirvana principle: a psychical tendency toward zero. On the other hand, jouissance does not tend to reduce toward zero; on the contrary, it consists of a push toward raising the level of tension. Indeed, the strange business of speaking beings seems to us very far removed from Epicurean ideas. It is not a matter of the least possible jouissance—the ideal condition for the ethical and philosophical model of Epicurus, but of enjoying more and more, right up to the limit of death as the only unavoidable finality. Such a scenario is portrayed in Abel Ferrara's film *Bad Lieutenant*, in which the protagonist's search—neither delib-

---

2. S. Freud, "Vorlesungen zur Einführung in die Psychoanalyse," *Studienausgabe*; *Introductory lectures on Psycho-analysis* (1917), *Standard Edition* 15–16.

erately nor consciously—goes progressively toward a limit that is none other than death.

Nevertheless, we must not simply confuse jouissance with the pursuit of death or masochism (a serious error made by some neo-Lacanians). The increase of tension does not necessarily imply suffering, just as its diminution does not always lead to a feeling of well-being. These concepts require a necessary differentiation, especially given their important clinical consequences. For Lacan, there is also room for a sublimatory jouissance, a spiritual jouissance, a jouissance of being, of life, of the production of knowledge, among other kinds. It is a question, in sum, of a dimension of the speaking being that should not be conceived of in hydraulic terms, the rise and fall of tension. Centering his work on jouissance, Lacan is forced to posit an opposition between *Genuss* and *Lust*, making one the limit of the other, or even its "bridle." But one should reject any idea of jouissance as an ailment that harasses the subject and that must—as they put it—be "tempered"; if not, one risks failing to understand it completely.[3]

In the trefoil knot, Lacan finds a topological writing appropriate for figuring *Genuss*, jouissance. Surplus enjoyment, like surplus value, is the excess "able" to provide the speaking-being what is not bestowed by JΦ (phallic jouissance). In this seminar, Lacan calls phallic jouissance "parasitic," because it is impossible to get rid of it. As it nourishes itself, this parasite does away with any possibility for us to enjoy the hypothetical absolute jouissance. The parasite is unavoidable, since

---

3. On this topic, the point made by F. Perrier is valuable: he recalls the etymology of jouissance, from the Latin *gaudium*, meaning "to have full power over" and/or "to enter into possession of." Cf. *Le Mont St. Michel.* Paris: Arcanes, 1994, p. 64.

it is located in the Phallus; and, paradoxically, it also causes the Phallus to be an instrument of jouissance. At the same time as making it possible, however, it blocks the way to this hypothetical absolute jouissance. Consequently the latter is rendered partial, circumscribed and defined by the phallic agency. As we have mentioned, Lacan terms this dimension of absolute jouissance the "jouissance of the Other"; the genitive being of course ambiguous, given the usual neurotic modality of being enjoyed by the Other.

Now, the jouissance of the Other is characterized in the sixth session of Seminar 19, *ou pire*, in the following terms: "One enjoys it, it must be said, in the Other [*de l'Autre*], one enjoys it mentally." The jouissance of the Other is thus given the status of mental jouissance. It is important to take account of the disconcerting theoretical strategy adopted by the final Lacan: he makes progress using terms from traditional psychology like feeling, mentality, mind . . . and then we run into symbol, sign, thought, that which is individual. These terms could come from an essay on general psychology. We might, if we felt malicious, attribute this to some sort of decline into senility on the part of the author. He in fact calls upon the categories of paranoiac or personality psychology in order to reintroduce an even worse category: that of man. Since his most important work has consisted of an intricate effort to dismantle that category, and propose that of the divided subject as an alternative, this idea seems extraordinary. Yet we find in the very title of Seminar 23, *Le sinthome*, a pun on *homme*, "man." We will have to return in more depth to this rich theoretical fracture.

Let us return to the trefoil knot. We have isolated surplus jouissance there, as well as phallic jouissance and the jouissance of the Other; but Lacan will later concentrate on the intersection where "meaning" is written. In a first moment, he writes "meaning" in the sense of practical linguistics—that is, which relates to signification. This site, as we can understand, is a stitch between the Symbolic and the Imaginary. However, in the text of *Television* (almost exactly contemporary with Seminar 23), we see how Lacan plays on and breaks up the term jouissance, making it into *jouis-sens* [enjoy-meaning].[4] This pun, repeated in Seminar 23, might almost be taken as an imperative: *jouis sens*, "enjoy meaning"! We can understand this as follows: having outlined a "three" of jouissance (surplus, phallic, Other), Lacan now introduces a fourth kind, a "meaning-jouissance." This indicates that we are dealing not with a piece of linguistics, nor an attempt at psychological understanding, but with the observation that when meaning arises, there is jouissance. This can be situated at the edge of various kinds of psychotherapy, since we know that Lacan's statements are more than harmless wordplay; indeed, we can gauge the importance of the point only if we succeed in grasping its clinical relevance. What, then, does this consist in? Many kinds of psychotherapy work toward naming things, fixing in place words with a calming effect; that is, they function according to the pleasure principle. Giving names to feelings should reduce or "temper" anxiety; thus, referring to an inclusive and empathic meaning keeps us on the edges of the psychotherapeutic field. Now, if we go to work with jouissens, the chain tends to come undone: instead of calming down, like an Epicurean subject reducing tension through mortifying practices, the analysand would on the contrary relaunch the chain of associations. This entails the enrichment

---

4. J. Lacan, *Télévision*. Paris: Seuil, 1975, p. 22.

of jouissance, the extension of its versatility, rather than its stopping short before the fixed sense of a word and saying "Aha! So that's what is happening to me," as happens in many so-called moments of "insight," in accordance with the typical jargon of Anglo-Saxon psychoanalysis. This "insight" (Is it a matter of vision?) leads only to stagnation, to an impasse of signification. Conversely, to think of jouis-sens provokes, stimulates, leading to what Lacan terms an analytic task. In this manner, analysis comes to be recycled due to the condition of jouissance, and does not remain stuck fast to meanings. This permanent adherence to meaning, Lacan will state, is a characteristic of "mental debility." This is certainly not a reference to the features of mental debility as understood in psychopathology, but to something in which we are all implicated: making the least possible effort. The laziness of the average speaking being consists in rapidly seizing a meaning, smoothing it out into a self-identical "thing," and concluding that "that's exactly what's happening to me" in order to take hypnotic comfort in this refuge from the omnipresent discourse of everyday life.

The opening implied by jouis-sens also entails another, closely related sense: *j'ouïs sens* ["I hear meaning"]. With this, a fundamental element comes into play: that of the voice. Concerning Joyce, Lacan will work on the singular question of what he terms *imposed words*. These are *paroles*, spoken words, and not *mots*: not isolated words, but phonic structures that are articulated (even if particular types of articulation may be enigmatic, latent). The effect of these spoken words is sharply more visible in psychotics. This is how *j'ouïs sens* is to be understood: "They"—the voices—speak to me, interpellate me in different ways. This can be experienced as a hallucination, or—as in the case of Joyce—it may be worked on with letters, making this "hearsay" [*ouïe*] into *sinthome*. The point of *j'ouïs sens*, moreover, is to indicate a dimension beyond the textual realm: meaning is not read, it is heard. What does this imply? That we are dealing with an intrinsically psychoanalytic category, an interlocutive one. There is no "bibliotherapy," no self-supervision with the particular dissolved into the general. No, for the meaning in question is bound up with a wholly singular act of listening. Many analysands bear witness to this in terms of their own neurotic structure when they say something like "I don't know how, but I heard your voice booming like thunder, like something you shouted at me terribly loudly." It is clear that "in reality" the analyst spoke in his normal tone of voice, with its usual ups and downs. But here a factor ex-sisting the interlocutive chain has taken effect, making the voice into an object *a*. The latter, isolated, produces the *j'ouïs*.

If we let ourselves play with these various puns a little, sliding from jouissance to *jouis-sens* and *j'ouïs sens*, we can formulate what we have just outlined: meaning, as written in the trefoil knot, becomes jouis-sens, so that all four intersections on the knot diagram are written as kinds of jouissance. Here, we must refer to a unifying point that comes at the end of two sessions in the seminar (the third and fourth sessions), concerning the theme of the different kinds of jouissance that we have outlined. This will be one of the fundamental aims of this chapter.

Our next question can be described by means of two terms considered to be "not very Lacanian": *responsibility* and *riddle*. These familiar words are apparently alien to our theoretical field; yet Lacan will nonetheless give them a singular inflection. In the fourth session of the seminar, Lacan declares: "One is only responsible to the extent of one's *savoir-faire*."

The latter notion refers not only to the capacity to make something (acquired over the course of time), but to something else as well: dexterity, deftness. Whoever has *savoir-faire*—a composite expression that can of course be split apart, but that amounts to a single unit of sense—is one who knows how to do something with a certain singular dexterity or cleverness. Now why would this make the subject responsible? This last notion, which we briefly alluded to in the previous chapter, is a relatively new one, being no older than the American and French revolutions. It derives from a political context: effectively, one tends to judge whether or not a government is responsible for something, in other words whether it takes upon itself the role of causal agent concerning a determinate event. Very frequently, a small step further takes us onto the terrain of legal imputation. Taking all this into account, we see Lacan addressing our *savoir-faire*, in other words that of anyone at all. Being responsible implies having to give a response. The etymology of the term is often forgotten: responsibility comes from responding. When I am interpellated, then, I can respond to the extent of my *savoir-faire*.

The notion of responsibility is crucial, given that Lacan has made the interlocutive center of his theory of neurosis a response to demand (another juridical term, even if here it is not a question of the legal concept). The neurotic, as we proposed in the opening chapter, is someone who confuses his desire with the demand of the Other; hence the discontinuities, the disjunctions, due to why and for whom he does or stops doing such-and-such a thing. It is at moments like these that he cuts out the shape of an unknown knowledge [*savoir*]: "I don't know why I do that." The neurotic sets out on this premise; we could also describe him as occupying the place of the object, which leads to the following paradigm: "I'm forced to do it, there's no alternative. I'm asked to do it and I accept, I *respond* immediately." We should note the importance of this dimension of the response: responsibility is thus articulated around the question of demand, of "what is to be done" when faced with it. Of course, the minimum criterion for the end of a neurotic's analysis consists in the modification of his relation to the demand of the Other. The obsessional, for instance, "knows" very well how to do nothing without counting in advance on the permission of the Other. By "childlike submission"? He tells us, rather: "Okay, I'll ask permission, but so long as it is understood that I'm doing this for you"—returning responsibility in this way to the Other and thus strategically escaping castration, in the imaginary. On this level, he does not take responsibility. The question is not confined to asking him why he submits, or why he seeks out a slave's position, instead of being himself. This kind of questioning, wittingly or not, looks very like the unlikely advice offered in many "alternative therapies," encapsulated in a superegoic "Be yourself!" or similar fierce, obscene imperatives. Such propositions cannot avoid falling into the naive instigation of a "counterphobic" dimension that can only end up producing "alternative" frustrations. Things are not so simple: one cannot hope, by making the ego swell up, to "pull it out of" *that* [ça, "the id"].

Savoir-faire, then, emerges, for the final Lacan, as a new concept with consequences for a different understanding of the end of analysis. He links it to artifice by stating that we are responsible for and through our savoir-faire, because of it. In this claim we can see a metaphorical reference to art; it is a question, effectively, of *savoir-faire* with art—in other words the capacity to bring off certain tricks [*trucs*]. In a Spanish translation of this seminar, this has been well captured by translating *truc* as "ruse," "knack," or "trick." We understand by this the art of working out a way of obtaining what one wants. Of course, this means confronting—and here we see the nonneurotic side—a certain risk that is involved. This is precisely what the neurotic avoids by asking permission, by submitting to the demand. We should emphasize that we are not faced with a binary opposition between authority and submission, since we look to the relation between castration and the ways in which it is either avoided or confronted. This takes place according to what was put in place by the fantasmatic imagery of castration, corresponding to the imaginary dangers "mastered" by that situation.

The question of responsibility is, as we have said, a relatively new one in the history of the representations and ideas produced by each social formation in order to explain its functions. Lacan was already working on the topic very early in his career, in the text "A Theoretical Introduction to the Functions of Psychoanalysis in Criminology" of 1950; there, he writes of responsibility as a "punishment." By contrast, in 1965 he writes (in "Science and Truth"): "We are always responsible for our position as subject." This means that it's no good saying, "It's a symptom (that I don't wish to have)" or "It's because of the way my father was," and so forth. Such alibis are given support and justified by many analysts: "What can you expect, with parents like that?"—or "What happened to her, it's not her fault." For Lacan, it's no good arguing in this virulently rationalist way: the unavoidable question remains that of assuming responsibility, in other words, responding for and by oneself. Without this, the analysand will never be able to take charge of her life, falling back on her illness as a protective "comfort."

"We are always responsible for our position as subject" does not imply that responsibility is immediately associated with punishment, as long as one's conception of ethics is not a crude one. Eleven years after "Science and Truth," Lacan makes the statement we have referred to (in Seminar 23): we are responsible to the extent of our *savoir-faire*. What therefore emerges here is a way of *responding* that will need to be situated in relation to certain of our categories.

In the subsequent seminar, the title of which Lacan makes into a long translinguistic pun (we'll call it simply *"L'insu"*),[5] he pursues his preoccupation with this problematic. In the session of January 11, 1977, he takes up the topic of *savoir-faire* somewhat obliquely, without informing his audience that he is returning to a theme from the previous year's seminar. We also find one of his sharpest critiques of Freud there:

> Freud thus had only a weak grasp of what actually constituted the unconscious. But it is my impression, on reading him, that we can deduce that he thought this to be the effects of the signifier. Man—we must indeed give this name to a certain generality, from which no-one can be said to escape. Freud's work is in no way transcendent: he was an ordinary doctor—heavens, doing what he could to reach a so-called cure, which doesn't amount to very much. . . .

And the argument continues:

---

5. Translator's note: Lacan's title for Seminar 24 (1976–1977) is *L'insu que sait de l'une bévue s'aile à mourre*, which can be read as "The failure (*l'insuccès*, but also *l'insu que sait*, "the unknown that knows") of the unconscious (*de l'Unbewusst*, quoting Freud's German, but also *de l'une bévue*, "of the oversight") is love (*c'est l'amour*, with a nonsensical pun)." Harari refers to his discussion of this seminar in *Discurrir el psicoanálisis*. Buenos Aires: Nueva Vision, 1986, pp. 123–125.

> Man, then, since I've spoken of man, can hardly free him-
> self from this business of Knowledge [*Savoir*]. It is imposed
> upon him by what I term effects of the signifier, which
> means that things aren't easy for him: he does not know
> what to "do with" [*"faire-avec"*] Knowledge [*Savoir*].

Lacan thus reintroduces the earlier theme: Man does not
have any "know-how" with knowledge. This lack corresponds
precisely to what, as we saw above, Lacan terms mental debility: the lack of *savoir-faire* with *Savoir*. Before we go on,
we must underline that this knowledge is not what can be
obtained from books, the sciences and arts, and so forth; it is
a question of unconscious Knowledge—concerning which we
have no *savoir faire*. Thus, when Lacan refers to the speaking
being's mental debility, he states that he "does not know what
to 'do with' this material." In other words, we do not know,
have no influence upon, are not in control of its processes.
Seminar 24 stresses this "doing with" in a new way. Doing
with what, though? With precisely what produced the symptom, in other words with factors relating to the domain of
causality. This is not of course linked to the exercise of any
task that one can learn, or to the mastery of any preset code
or recipe. We repeat that it takes place in the same domain
and in the same elements that produce the symptom.

The *sinthome* will be invented, little by little, out of bits
of this knowledge, by means of this "material" determining
the symptom, but in a purified form. Here, it is not a question of the traversal of fantasy, but of another path, a third
mode of ending analysis which Lacan terms the *identification
with the sinthome*. Concerning this, we have proposed the transition, as it were, across "three Lacans": the first tending toward the interpretation of symptoms; the second focusing on

the traversal of fantasy; and the last arguing for identification with the *sinthome*.[6] Lacan thus distances himself from fantasy, which (as we have explained in an earlier work[7]), being situated in the *Wirchlichkeit* of life, tends to take on the form of punishment, as figured symbolically by the many varieties of "being beaten." The position of the neurotic in fantasy is that of a being who is beaten in an endless variety of different ways. Now, taking a distance from that position does not entail reconciling oneself to it, as a certain pessimistic resignation would imply, nor changing to a more active position, the subject becoming the agent of punishment. All this would mean would be simply to change places within the fantasy. It is certainly possible to point to a certain irreducible quality in fantasy, but it is a question of the position one adopts toward it. Thus, subjecting oneself to it leads, with an inevitable, unperceived bluntness in the Real, to a destiny compulsion— in other words, to the serial recurrence of situations of punishment or failure.[8] This neurotic pattern should not be conceived as a "syndrome" but as a romantic principle that captures the subject insofar as, paradoxically, he enjoys it. What Lacan will propose, once again, will consist in highlighting another form of jouissance that is not neurotic suffering but identification with the *sinthome*. It is thus a certain "knowing what to do with": this is our responsibility.

---

6. R. Harari, "Del sujeto dividido finalmente puesto en cuestion," *Las disipaciones de la inconsciente*. Buenos Aires: Amorrortu, 1997, pp. 89–100; given as a paper at the Latin American Psychoanalytic Congress at Porto Alegre.

7. R. Harari, *Fantasma: fin del analisis?* op. cit.

8. R. Harari, *La repeticion del fracaso*. Buenos Aires: Nueva Vision, 1988.

Lacan teaches us, in sum, another knowledge: a knowledge linked to facts, to Freudian *Wirchlichkeit*. Previously, he had differentiated textual from referential knowledge (for instance, in the "Proposition of October 9, 1967"). Knowledge as "familiarity" [*connaissance*] is a *savoir* or knowledge of the referent, to the extent that it "alludes to" a denotable entity. We can have this kind of knowledge, for example, of physical or chemical objects. By contrast, textual knowledge [*savoir*]—that of the unconscious—is unknown. But from now on a third category comes into play, which is neither referential nor textual: that of *know-how-with*.

Introduced between Seminars 23 and 24, this category is sketched out at various points in the latter seminar. A certain modification to the sense of "know-how" takes place between the two seminars: if in Seminar 22 Lacan refers to *savoir-faire*, the following year he makes this into *savoir-y-faire*. What is the difference between these two phrases? *Savoir-y-faire* means something like "dealing with it," with connotations of "getting rid of it," "untying oneself from it"; it does not involve learning a skill, but sorting something out, getting rid of a burden or irritation. It thus implies an unknotting or *dénouement*. Concerning this, Lacan says something remarkable: "But this *y-faire* ["sorting out"] indicates that we cannot really take this phrase to be a concept." We have no knowledge, in fact, of how each analysand will put together his own way of *dealing with it*. Here we confront an essential point: there is no possibility of predicting things. As Freud already states, in psychoanalysis there is no predictability (despite what will be claimed by the devotees of a crude medicalization of its discourse). As for Lacan, he will guard against a "preventionist pharisaism," because psychoanalysis must be situated in an epistemology of actual effects and not one of some future presumption. This situation introduces a certain element of chance, as a real to be supported by clinical analysis.

In the seminar of April 19, 1977, Lacan modifies a central aspect of his theory. If we naively suppose that psychoanalysis is an (almost) ethical pursuit of the truth—as do many who refer to Lacan, we will see that this seminar will challenge that notion. Lacan is to claim there, in fact, that the *sinthome* is an obstacle to truth. This is a surprising transformation: this notion of *dealing with it* comes to change the theory of the end of analysis so that the latter is no longer associated with a search for truth. Lacan tropes the term "truth" [*vérité*] into a half-pun "variety" [*variété*]: there are varieties of truth, to be expressed through condensation as "varity" [*varité*]. This singularization of truth can be linked to the "all, but not that" we looked at in Chapter 1; it goes beyond the aphorism about truth being always half-said, and thus not-all. This declaration is no longer enough, given that the truth in question cannot emerge since the *sinthome* blocks it. The latter will make room for a crucial category: that of the necessary. This is Lacan's new definition of the *sinthome*, as "not ceasing to write itself" [*ne cessant pas de s'écrire*], which it is clear can only correspond to what he terms "the necessary." A moment later he states that the "varity of the *sinthome*" is what "the analysand says awaiting verification." This *varity* is thus posited at the expense of *the* truth—and as an inflection of the necessary. "That which does not cease to write itself" alludes to a theoretical constellation that returns inexorably, incessantly. In the last instance, the necessary is that which must not be gotten rid of; if it comes away, it must be tied back in—it's necessary, one cannot hide it. In colloquial terms, we could say "I can't live without it," or "it's part of

my life, it's irreplaceable." Here, of course, we are not referring to any intersubjective relations; it is a question of "Without that—entailed by my way of dealing with it—I cannot live.
It is necessary for me." A nodal category, in sum, illuminated
by Seminar 24.

But let us return to the question of responsibility, now
that we have slipped into the domain of know-how [*savoir-
faire*]. In his seminar, Lacan implies—according to our reading—that this responsibility can be separated into two vec-
tors. According to one of these, we are always responsible
"obliquely," for a response linked to sex: our sexual response
is produced in one way or another. This kind of responsibility entails the position of the unconscious in terms of the
absence of the sexual relation. "There's no such thing," given
that nothing pushes toward or endorses a perfect encounter
of the sexual couple. We must nevertheless also consider
another kind of responsibility, which goes "well beyond" this:
that of artifice. Let us draw the following schema:

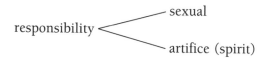

One aspect of responsibility finds its origin in sex, which
gives rise to lots of misunderstanding; the other lies in know-
how, which is ostensibly strange because it highlights a non-
sexual reference. Or is it simply nonphallic? What does Lacan
mean by this? Let us quote him: "Know-how [with artifice]
goes well beyond . . . the artifice that we quite gratuitously
ascribe to God." Such a gratuitous act no doubt points to
another instance or paranoiac (mis)recognition: it is God the
creator, not the speaker. Lacan indicates, finally, that raising

such a question "exceeds by far the enjoyment [*jouissance*] which we can have of it. That absolutely slender jouissance is what we call the spirit." Yet another disconcerting term: spirit. For Lacan to claim that a jouissance implies the spirit, whereas he had always maintained that there was only jouissance of the body—what on earth can this mean? Firstly, this jouissance seems to "fall" outside the limits of the body: it ex-sists the body. At the same time, he extols its "slender" quality, an effect of the fact that we are not able to acknowledge its importance due to its evanescence. Since it concerns, in the end, a jouissance largely in excess of the register of our experience, it constitutes a category that cannot be located in consciousness. We are in fact barely conscious of the agency of this jouissance. Let us call on ideas from Lacan's earlier seminars in order to situate this problematic.

Let us pause, for instance, at one of the passages where Lacan reexamines that troublesome scab scratched at in and by psychoanalysis: the notion of sublimation. On this topic, he recalls a point that is impossible to trace back to its origin: that in sublimation there is no inhibition of the drive, due to the absence of repression. Where does this lead us? To the following scandalous statement: the act of sexual intercourse provides exactly the same level of enjoyment that I am currently experiencing as I write this book. This is without any doubt *heretical*, given that in terms of psychological introspection it amounts to perfect idiocy. Is it another textual error, or is it an effect of some alteration of Lacan's mental capacity? It must be acknowledged, however, that sublimation is nothing but a drive-destination, insofar as that is defined as an absence of repression, of drive inhibition. As for spiritual jouissance, which seems slender because we only partly perceive its consequences and its way of engaging us as men (we underline the latter category)—this jouissance, then, is what is often attributed to God, as supposed artificer, so-called maker of artifice. This happens because, instead of doing what we can ourselves, we always first put our faith in a constructed universe, created by God. Such a universe is a totality, as it is governed by a vision of the world that "guarantees" the existence of the Other. Hence the question of divinity, to be posed to any theologian: Did God experience enjoyment in what He did? The question—certainly a paranoiac-projective one—signals the absence of the hypothetical universe: for if God had enjoyment, He did not make the universe; while if He had no enjoyment, He did not create.

Now, throughout his teaching Lacan maintained the castrating Freudian idea of the nonexistent universe. The Viennese master always claimed that the task of philosophy was to seek to patch up the holes in the world by producing a totalizing vision of it. This, for Freud, was the very *quid* of philosophy: a conception of the world, of man, that we could term "totalist," corresponding to the notion of the universe. By contrast, Lacan posits—in another strange aphorism, from Seminar 19—that "There is One," in isolation, but no universe. For this one is no longer an index of itself: it is not the mark of totality, of the unification inherent in "personality." It does not even refer to a trait allowing partial identification in the Other. Better still— we are no longer dealing with the one that can be counted, situated in a problematic of repetition. This is why "There is One" can be said to invoke the *One of the sinthome*, thus indicating a marginal instance, since it can be neither totalized nor added up. Situated elsewhere, on another edge, it operates as the support of the speaker. We could define it as an uncoupled One, outside any sequence; it answers to no integration, no context, no history, no full or anticipated meaning. It therefore persists in an awkward, troubling manner. And it is from this One, not the universe, that there arises the possibility of invention, if we are aware that this invention *has no meaning*. Let us return, then, to this latter notion and to the question of ascribing "to God what falls to the artist."

Concerning the problematic of sexual responsibility, Lacan makes a very lucid comment about the act in question. If we pay attention to etymology, in fact, we see that the term "act" already entails a certain misunderstanding, given that it inevitably suggests at the same time the other pole (i.e., passivity). The act designates an activity, comments Lacan, illustrating one of the traps we are led into by our way of representing ourselves. A matching error is to believe that when one knows, one is active. Man wishes to obtain a so-called knowledge of something, and considers himself to be "active" in this. What is mistaken about such a notion? In Lacan's view, it is the object (of knowledge) that marks us and commands us, beyond our grasp of this process. Already, in Seminar 11, he quotes Picasso's famous words, "I do not seek, I find"; for if I am seeking, what I find is not what I wanted ("love was there in front of me, but I couldn't see it," as they say). This is why, according to Lacan's teaching, love is contingent: it is not there, until one day it is, all of a sudden. In terms of Lacan's modalities: it has ceased not to write itself. Again, here we are not dealing with any prediction, any required willingness to "form a couple" or something of that kind. We do not seek, we find. We depend far more on the object than we believe. The illusions of thought invert this situation, naively referring to how knowledge is "handled."

Lacan returns to the topic of the sexual act, now opposing his own declaration that "there is no sexual relation." As we have argued, there is no way to attain some perfect union, with everyone finding his or her ideal partner, and so on. There is no inscription of such a sexual relation in the unconscious; what there is, rather, as Lacan puts it, is a "sexual opacity." The belief in the sexual act is as mistaken as a belief in the role of the "active pole" in the act of knowledge: these are the imaginary snares of thought. All these questions touch on the notion of responsibility: we must say how we respond indirectly to them.

This manner of para-responding may also entail another detour: supposing that when we create something, whatever that may be, we do so in order to totalize it. Lacan will stress, on the contrary, that we do this in order to continue to support the hole. To make this point, he takes the potter as the model for the artist (a Heideggerian reference that we can trace back to Seminar 7), and he comments that his task consists in constructing a pot around a void, in order to preserve this *lack*. Let us turn to our guest James Joyce, to find out what he has to say on this subject.

In *Ulysses*, the author reflects on what is certain and what is uncertain in this world; in other words, on where we can suppose a void, and where something solid. What is it that guarantees an absolute certainty for us? Let us see:

> Fatherhood, in the sense of conscious begetting, is unknown to man. It is a mystical estate, an apostolic succession, from only begetter to only begotten. On that mystery and not on the madonna which the cunning Italian intellect flung to the mob of Europe the church is founded and founded irremovably because founded, like the world, macro and microcosm, upon the void. [*Ulysses*, p. 170]

That is the point: founded upon the void. Stephen's theory that this foundation is linked not to the maternal

Madonna but to paternity evokes—beyond ecclesiastical matters—creation. The text continues: "Upon incertitude, upon unlikelihood. *Amor matris*, subjective and objective genitive, may be the only true thing in life." Lacan referred on several occasions to this peculiarity of the double genitive. The Latin phrase means "the love of the mother," but does this refer to an emotion felt *by* the mother or felt *for* her? A similarly ambiguous genitive occurs with "desire of the Other"—is it a desire felt by me toward the Other or vice versa?

Concerning the mother, Freud quotes another Latin tag (which moreover is in accord with the findings of contemporary genetic research): *Mater certissima, pater semper incertus est* ("The mother is absolutely certain, the father always uncertain"). The certainty lies in the fact that the body of the mother guarantees our origin: there can be no doubt about it. This is the starting-point of certainties: we are certain in the fullest sense there. The mother represents plenitude, with all the risks that that entails. The function of the father is different, and here Joyce shows a strong conceptual kinship with Freud and Lacan. At the next line, we read, "Paternity may be a legal fiction." This is very close to declaring that it is ultimately no more than a symbolic given, detached from the *ment* (cf. Chapter 2 above). And then: "Who is the father of any son that any son should love him or he any son?" The subsequent paragraphs amount to a good basis for supporting Lacan's conjectures about the relation between Joyce and his father. A few lines later, Joyce has Stephen joke that when Shakespeare

> [in the comedy of errors wrote Hamlet] he was not the father of his own son merely but, being no more a son,

> he was and felt himself the father of all his race, the father
> of his own grandfather, the father of his unborn grand-
> son who, by the same token, never was born, for nature,
> as Mr. Magee understands her, abhors perfection. [p. 171]

We are reminded of the famous "uncreated conscience
of my race" in *A Portrait*: he must engender all fathers, become the father of his unborn grandson and his own great-
grandfather. This is exactly what Lacan had to teach about
Joyce: that he had to invent himself by making a name for
himself, in order to make up for the paternal absence. The
father is *radically* lacking, and also absent in the Real. It is
not a question of a symbolic lack, which is precisely limited.
This is why Lacan considers that what Joyce has his character say designates the author's own problematic, which he thus
seeks to reveal. Effectively, Joyce both is "burdened" by, and
at the same time suffers from an absolute lack of, the father.
He is sick of, has too much of, a father—but of a lacking father—for which he tries to make up with his entire work. He
denies, and remains rooted in, the father.

At this point we must outline a relation between the two
types of responsibility, as also between responsibility and
artifice. Let us focus on the latter relation. It is here that Lacan
opens up some "psychological" ideas in a literal, insistent
manner. Concerning thought—which, we recall, always requires words, there being no thought outside language—
Lacan remarks that words can set up false "facts." That is, all
facts are the effect of words; and here he adds something decisive: there are thus only facts through artifice. A fact exists
insofar as the speaking-being says it is so; and through this
speech, artifice comes about. Thus, if there were no artifice,
there would be no facts; but if there is, those facts may be false.

There is a striking shift of emphasis here, truth no longer being confined to the simple analysis of discourse. Of course, we are capable of sliding surreptitiously toward some other mistaken notion to explain what the facts may "truly" be. Lacan remarks that this is quite within our mentality—deliberately using the term to pun on *mentir*, "to lie" (we recall the discussion of *ce qu'on dit ment* from Chapter 2). Our *mentality*, then, lies to us, is subjected to the Imaginary. Why is this? Because it is adoration of the body, self-love, senti-mentality. It is hardly necessary to add that Lacan is seeking to lead us along a different, nonmental path. Consequently, once this mentality has been made visible, he makes a simple connection for didactic purposes: the famous "trivial" knot. Its simplicity makes it no less a knot,[9] one which one obtains by joining together the two ends of a string, in other words by knotting it together. The string circle then becomes a point of departure for opposing the imaginary *mentality* (Figure 23):

Figure 23

We all know what "trivial" means. Yet there is more to say about this, as we will show. We will focus on something from Joyce that is explored by Richard Ellmann, the author not only of a biography of our author that has become a classic, but of other works including an extremely enjoyable book entitled *Four Dubliners*. The book has a chapter on Joyce, alongside those on Wilde, Yeats, and Beckett. We will pick out just

---

9. However, due to its simplicity, Adams prefers to term the "trivial" knot an "unknot"; cf. G.C. Adams, *The Knot Book*, op. cit., p. 2.

one point from the wealth of information provided by Ellmann: concerning Joyce's singular, surprising manner of responding to his critics. This is yet another thing Joyce has in common with Lacan; the responses of both were ironic, paradoxical, disconcerting, humorous. For example, when, during the events of May 1968, Lacan was asked by the "revolutionaries" to explain the existing difference between capitalism and socialism, he replied, "Capitalism, according to Marx, is the exploitation of man by man; socialism is the other way around." This mirror-image response was a way for Lacan to attack a certain illusion of "progress." Likewise, when asked, "What can psychoanalysis do for the revolution?" Lacan answered, "Tell me instead what the revolution can do for psychoanalysis?" When Joyce was criticized, writes Ellmann, by those who alleged that the verbal games in *Ulysses* and *Finnegans Wake* were "trivial" (the same term used for the simplest knot, we recall), he replied, "Yes, sometimes my methods are trivial, and sometimes quadrivial."[10] Again, we have three and four, here in terms of a classical reference. In Antiquity, education was based on the two terms Joyce alludes to, the *Trivium* and the *Quadrivium*.[11] The *Trivium* refers to the three Liberal Arts relating to eloquence: Grammar, Rhetoric, and Dialectic.[12] Clearly, these lie

---

10. R. Ellmann, *Four Dubliners*. London: Penguin, 1982, pp. 53–78.

11. In *A Skeleton Key to Finnegans Wake*, J. Campbell and H.M. Robinson propose an interpretative table for Joyce's last work (cf. Chapter 8). When they get to Book II, the "Book of Children," they give its second chapter the same heading, "The Trivium and the Quadrivium." This chapter certainly contains the text's longest treatment of mathematical questions; we can even discern there ideas from geometry and algebra.

12. These have been intensely studied by Roland Barthes in his works on rhetoric. Cf. R. Barthes, *Elements of Semiology*, tr. A. Lavers and C. Smith, London: Jonathan Cape, 1967.

within the domain of the signifier, and thus of *mentality*. As for the *Quadrivium*, it comprises what were once called the four mathematical arts: Arithmetic, Geometry, Music, and Astronomy. In other words—although Lacan makes no mention of the *Quadrivium*, we can assume this, disciplines that are linked to writing as a way, precisely, of avoiding *mentality*. From the *Trivium* to the *Quadrivium*, then, we pass from the signifier to the letter, from that which has been heard to that which has been written. It is this movement that makes Joyce a being located within the episteme of the *Quadrivium*, given that writing is indispensable to him, amounting to a decisive, irreplaceable support. Here it is a question of the same writing that allows Joyce to seize fragments of the Real: through it, one can gain access fleetingly to that register.

Hence Lacan's recourse to mathematics, and topology in particular, as well as his interest in writing, understood as always implying the knot or chain. And it is here, indeed, that we come back to Joyce. For if he often works with the *Trivium* and shows eloquence, he makes it irrefutably clear that the letter is his master. Joyce's art is fed not by the resources of eloquence, but by those of writing, which for Lacan is to say mathematics: this point is crucial. And on this subject, we might ask what it is that the final Lacan is defining here. He is undertaking a thorough reconsideration of the linguistic foundation of psychoanalysis—seeking not to deny it, but to rethink it in terms of writing. It is no longer a question of an interlocutive dimension, but of the traces that a subject, on the basis of its *savoir-faire*, leaves in the world. This question has a bearing on every single speaking-being (without, of course, anyone needing to make the ludicrous claim of being a "new Joyce"). We will reiterate, in order to avoid misunderstandings: we are not simply dealing here with a theory of art, nor with a so-called "profile" of creative genius, but with a new theory of the end of analysis where the function of writing—not of the writer—plays a major role.

Having clarified these points, we now return to the "trivial" knot to see how Lacan will move, along with Joyce, to the quadrivial knot. If the trivial knot is a circle, we might also use "trivial" as an allegorical description of the triple Borromean knot; this is because each of its registers includes all three categories, so that each circle of the knot is simultaneously made up of ex-sistence, hole, and consistency. Thus the absolute risk that each link in this chain will come to resemble the others; this indicates its proximity to the trefoil knot, and thus to paranoia. This is why the Lacanian *Quadrivium* introduces a very important distinction.

This is where we should bring in another notion, mentioned at the beginning of this chapter: that of the enigma. Lacan writes this in a singular manner, as Ee. How should this be read? As signaling an enunciation in search of its enunciated. Lacan's concept of enunciation, his characterization of its subject, is that it contains hidden words, a certain non-sense; and of course the same is true of the enigma—we don't understand it. Moreover, there is something to be read between the lines, which is no clearer as its meaning is withheld. Likewise, in Lacan's eyes, every enunciation is in pursuit of an enunciated it will never find. Here, we can refer to a riddle in Joyce, and to the commentaries of two French critics, to give a good illustration of what is at stake in the enigma. When, in the "Nestor" episode of *Ulysses*, Stephen is giving his class, he suddenly presents the pupils with a riddle (which Lacan will pick up on in his seminar). At first sight, it looks fairly odd:

> *The cock crew,*
> *The sky was blue:*
> *The bells in heaven*
> *Were striking eleven.*
> *'Tis time for this poor soul*
> *To go to heaven.* [*Ulysses*, p. 22]

Of course, a pupil asks what this means; another says, "Again sir. We didn't hear." At last they give up, and Stephen, "his throat itching, answered: 'The fox burying his grandmother under a hollybush.'"

Analysts Jean-Guy Godin and Annie Tardits, contributors to the volume *Joyce Avec Lacan*, take account of something missed by Lacan himself: another riddle that occurs shortly before the one quoted, which Joyce leaves unfinished, and which might offer us a key for reading the second riddle. The text reads:

> *Riddle me, riddle me, randy ro.*
> *My father gave me seeds to sow.*

Joyce breaks off there, but Godin and Tardits complete the riddle:

> *The seed was black and the ground was white.*
> *Riddle me that and I'll give you a pipe* [or *"pint"*]

The solution of the riddle is: *Writing a letter*.[13] Here we find a perfect version of the gift of the father: seeds, letters,

13. A. Tardits, "L'appensée, le renard et l'hérésie"; J-G. Godin, "Du symptôme à son épure: le sinthome," in *Joyce Avec Lacan*, ed. J. Aubert, op. cit. Paris: Navarin, 1987, pp. 117, 187.

white paper. It is now a question of writing the letter. Lacan insists on this point: it was through his *savoir faire* that Joyce was able to invent his art, but also through knowing himself be to employing—paradoxically—the paternal gift (which as we will see is already a matter of debate).

A little after the strange riddle of the fox, Joyce returns to this question. This extract from *Ulysses* is very interesting if one reads between the lines:

> Across the page the symbols moved in grave morrice, in the mummery of their letters, wearing quaint caps of squares and cubes. Give hands, traverse, bow to partner: so: imps of fancy of the Moors. Gone too from the world. . . . [*Ulysses*, p. 23]

We have here the same type of idea as that which allows us to consider the One as something outside the world, exiled. Likewise, *Exiles*, Joyce's play, seeks to confront the sexual nonrelation, setting out a fantasy that a sexual relation exists. *Exiles* is also a work known to be "autobiographical," where a recurrent fantasy of Joyce's can be found: the act of imagining—and why not: desiring—that his wife Nora is betraying him. It's as if he wishes to have a kind of absent, but simultaneously knowing, witness. We could even say that Joyce sought to set up a scene so that the betrayal would occur in a way familiar to him, which is no less enigmatic. Lacan will claim that Joyce's desire to decipher his own enigmas does not take him very far. This is because he believes in his sinthome; and due to this belief, he is not greatly interested in resolving the enigmas. This would distinguish him from the neurotic, as we have already pointed out. In neurosis, we suppose a knowledge in the symptom that makes the subject suffer because he doesn't possess that knowledge; and thus, the neurotic searches courageously to decipher the enigma of the symptom.

We might declare that this is why Joyce omitted the part of the riddle concerning the paternal inheritance. That is, he has no interest in unveiling his enigmas because the paternal inheritance that would oblige him to do so has not been accepted. At any rate, he tries to pass on his enigma to others: to us, his readers. And at this point we come back to the opening of this chapter. What should we do with these theoretical developments? Lacan gives us his definition of the task of the analyst: we have to give—note the subtle trajectory of the phrase—responses. We are responsible insofar as we have *savoir-faire*: we have to give responses. What responses are these? Responses that look very like the solutions of a riddle. Lacan even gives a description of our work that is quite conventional: ". . . it is the answer to a riddle, and one, it must be said, that is quite especially stupid." Thus, the dimensions of responsibility and of the enigma—which after these clarifications appear in a new light—are to be given emphasis. The adjective "stupid" [*conne*], far from being derogatory, alludes to the character of this response—dumb, absurd, displaced—which no dialectic of general/particular can account for. Thus, the analyst has to make possible a jouissance—"enjoyment"—that is equally a *jouis-sens*—"enjoy-meaning"—and a *j'ouïs-sens*—"I hear meaning." Of course, the act of finding a meaning, as Lacan teaches, "implies knowing what the knot is and sewing it up properly with artifice."

5

Between the Père-sonnores *and the Folded Glove*

In this chapter we will refer to two strands from Seminar 23. The first, where Lacan again asks himself why he is interested in Joyce, will be our major preoccupation. In question is something that had been a principle concern of his for a long time, going back, in fact, to 1931, more than forty years before he delivers *Le sinthome*. In that year, Lacan published a text, in collaboration with two colleagues, entitled *Écrits "Inspirés": Schizographie*. Lacan was only 30, he hadn't finished his doctoral thesis (he had another year to go), but he was already interested in writing and madness. The writings in question were "inspired" according to the usual sense of the term, that is, to do with creativity, but they were also— and above all—inspired in the sense of "breathed," making the term into a metaphor for a kind of respiration. This is very much bound up with the "imposed speech" we have already mentioned, a problematic that Lacan addresses in 1976 on the basis of an interview with a patient at Saint Anne Hospital (which we will consider in detail).

Lacan never in fact employed the classic model of a psychiatric case presentation. He used a presentation as an opportunity to ask some questions, in an effort to elucidate a central problematic, as well as perhaps giving a therapeutic prognosis for a patient not in analysis. Lacan "exploited" the psychotic's lack of privacy, the fact that, unlike the neurotic, he is interested in the public. For a psychotic, the presence of others—in the ordinary sense of the term—is indispensable; in particular, we would refer to those mad people who require an audience to be interested in a story, often one not without a certain power to command attention. By contrast, the neurotic is ashamed if what is happening comes to light; he therefore seeks to pass over in silence at all costs—and struggles not to acknowledge—his central sexual fantasy. The neurotic places enormous value on privacy, in stark contrast to the psychotic's *penchant* for the public. Those who have been in the hospital or who have worked with psychotics will confirm this as a feature of everyday experience. When faced by psychosis, in sum, Lacan directly asks us not to turn away—which is to say, to seek to go as far as one can, to do everything possible for the psychotic. In other words: putting psychoanalysis to work with psychosis, without of course attempting to direct the treatment as one would with a neurotic.

Écrits "Inspirés": Schizographie appeared together with Lacan's thesis in an edition from Seuil in 1975.[1] This is the text we will focus on here.

---

1. Strangely, this work is not included in the Spanish edition. We might understand this—without accepting it—as due to the notorious difficulties of translation produced by the verbal games there. In this sense, we might associate it with the problems of translation presented by *Finnegans Wake*. (Victor Pozanco has recently produced a first edition of the *Wake* in

We will begin in a roundabout way by returning again to the question of hearing [*ouïr*], of the *j'ouïs* ("I hear" punning on "I enjoy"). Let us stress that this is not a matter of a shared, interlocutive hearing, but of hearing imposed voices. Here, in terms that we will have to reconsider in detail later, we could say that the imposed voice, where the subject does not recognize itself as emitter, requires a response: it is imperative speech. The response is not required in an exchange, but as a kind of commentary. In the *Écrits* "*Inspirés*," we find the case of a woman patient, which we will try partly to explain and simultaneously to overcome the difficulty caused by the multiple *jeux de mots* involved. What can we isolate, a posteriori, as an implicit concern of Lacan's here? Certainly, the question of the voice as autonomous object, implying not merely the act of speech, but the voice as something detached from the subject itself. Voices that insult, that demand, that coerce: as we mentioned in Chapter 1, this presence of the "invocatory" object offers a differential diagnostic criterion with a bearing on Lacan's conception of psychosis.

As for Joyce, Lacan's view is that he needed little by little to break up language, to take it to the very edge, in order to show how he could throw off the traditional habits of language—those habits and tendencies in which almost everyone partakes. Joyce rebelled against them, accepting the task— or rather, according to Lacan, the "calling," in the sense of being called by God—of becoming the champion of such a mission. We recall from *A Portrait of the Artist as a Young Man* how Joyce searches to become this "genius," the "uncreated conscience" of his race.

Spanish—Barcelona: Lumen, 1993—but it is only a résumé, comprising less than half of the work. Is it then still *Finnegans Wake*?)

Let us therefore pause over this question of hearing, referring back to some of the topics from the previous chapter. Hearing is thus linked to meaning, as Lacan indicates with his *j'ouïs-sens*; from the imposition of meaning, he formulates a sort of goal for analysis, describing it as "a matter of sewing and splicing." The metaphor, of course, relates to the knot or the chain: untying and retying. As Lacan says, we must know about the knot of each individual and sew it together using artifice. To do this, we have to locate a meaning, something produced by stitching, unstitching, deploying suture. It is worth reiterating: Lacan claims that Joyce succeeds due to the singular manner with which he connects up his "chain-knot" by means of the *sinthome*. This implies believing in the latter: thus Lacan's emphasis that Joyce was nonanalyzable. In a joke that is of course also meant seriously, Lacan says that he regrets not having been able to analyze Joyce, and thus having no other recourse than turning to his writings. Again, we need to read this metaphorically: Is it really a matter of Lacan regretting Joyce's failure to ask him for analysis? Or is this rather a way of saying that what interests him here is not listening but writing—vividly expressed when he talks of "grasping" the letters?

Joyce poses his riddles through writing; what we discover is an enunciation searching fruitlessly for its enunciated. What, then, for Joyce, was the enunciation in question? Above all, it concerned the fact of having received a mandate from the father, which we could discern in the answer to the riddle: *Writing a letter*. This very word takes us to the first of Lacan's quotations from Joyce, in the "Seminar on *The Purloined Letter*" (1955); it occurs again in *Lituraterre* (1971): *A letter, a litter*.[2] In both

---

2. J. Lacan, "Le Séminaire sur 'La lettre volée,'" *Écrits*, op. cit., p. 25.

English and French, "letter" has the sense of both postal item and graphic sign. A letter, a litter: Would this be a letter to be gotten rid of, thrown in the dustbin [*poubelle*]? In this sense, is writing to consist of throwing a letter in the dustbin? Not merely due to abjection, something to be simply thrown out, but because the means of getting rid of it is writing. Lacan stresses the notion of imposition, for it is a question here of something necessary: something that does not cease writing itself [*ne cesse de s'écrire*], functioning as excreta that must be urgently eliminated. A letter, a litter: What does Lacan say when his *Écrits* are published in 1966? That it is a matter of *poubellication* ("publication" punning on *poubelle*-ication, "dustbin-ification"). It is not wrong to detect a certain Joycean influence here; it is also, of course, part of a series of playful ideas meant seriously. This is not an attempt by Lacan at simple humor, but a question about whether his text will end up in the dustbin, as is the case—and rightly so—for the major part of analytic writing. Here, we must take the "joke" literally: it asks whether his book is litter, waste paper, for instance in the sense of being useless or tautologous. If the book did not exist, would anything be different? Lacan's ambition— very Joycean, to be sure—was that his *Écrits* would not share the common fate, that they would be able to overturn the history of psychoanalysis, not partaking in the sheer point- lessness of the mountains of analytic "papers." In fact, Lacan's *poubellication* has been so successful that it indicates how well he was able to use the signifier to bite into bits of the Real. Let us return to Joyce. Through the character of Stephen Dedalus, he listens and "searches for" a solution to his riddle. By means of his writing, he sought to make up for the shortcomings of his father. The father who renounces his place belongs to Joyce as "individual," and not as the one we can trace, Daedalus-like, in his writings. We will refer to a Joycean critic in order to explore this in more depth, for in what follows we will ascribe great importance to Joyce's father and to his wife. These are two major figures in Joyce's life, and Lacan constantly returns to them. We will organize our investigation around these two axes, proposing a singular new term of our own to clarify Joycean *père-version*—that is, both a version of and a turning toward the father.

Let us pause to look at a book about Joyce by John Gross.[3] This is a valuable text insofar as it predates Lacan's intervention, offering the perspective of a judicious and intelligent observer. Gross outlines categories that will later be engaged by Lacan (we do not know if he had read the book in question, but there are clear correspondences between it and his own work on Joyce). Gross writes:

> Of all Joyce's emotions, as they figure in his work, the strongest were undoubtedly those centring on his father. In the earlier books they tend to be predominantly negative, not without good reason. From most points of view, John Joyce was a highly unsatisfactory parent: selfish, irresponsible, a heavy drinker, "a praiser of his own past."[4]

Lacan reaches similar conclusions, remarking that this father failed in almost every respect. These are without doubt solidly based remarks. The father in Joyce's early work, adds Gross, "is coarse, menacing, liable to crush the son to death"

---

3. J. Gross, *Joyce*. London: Fontana, 1971.
4. Ibid., pp. 18–19.

(p. 19). We find the father in Joyce's work accused, at one point, of simony, of the buying and selling of ecclesiastical benefices; in other words, he is accused of taking part in the corruption and decadence of the Church.

Nevertheless, we should pay attention to Gross's next remark: "It would of course be an oversimplification to say that as an artist Joyce was his father's son. Whatever he inherited, he added to and immeasurably transformed" (p. 20). But why this thematic of artistic inheritance? Gross provides us with the answer: "Along with his faults, John Joyce was a man of considerable accomplishments: a gifted singer [Let us note that for a singer the voice as object *a* has a structural dominance] . . . a mimic, a raconteur, a seasoned Dublin character with an explosive turn of phrase and an outstanding talent for vituperation" (p. 20). This last characteristic is certainly present with marked persistence in Joyce's letters to his wife Nora. Gross continues: "Most of these attributes, notably his humor and his love of music, were transmitted direct to his favorite son . . . *Ulysses* and *Finnegans Wake* both represent a turning back toward his father's world" (pp. 20–21). A little further on, in the last of our quotations, Gross notes something that we have already addressed in Chapter 1, no doubt with his book in mind: "Father and fatherland count for so much in Joyce's work that at first one can easily underestimate the strength of his attachment to his mother" (p. 22). It must be observed that, for all the attempt by Gross here to give a more balanced picture, the father and patrimony remain the fundamental coordinates of Joyce's world.

We discussed *père-version* in Chapter 2. We saw that this new concept was able to account for questions that were not encompassed by the notion of the Name-of-the-Father, and that the latter, even before *père-version*, had lost its unique status, become the plural "names of the father." Now if we flee toward reality, as we analysts like to say, and begin to outline a more or less "faithful" account of John Joyce—what he was and wasn't like—to bring together different opinions and views, and so on, we cannot get beyond the imaginary domain, marked by its standard inversions and fascinations. For all that, Lacan makes his wager forcefully: he remarks that Joyce's point of departure was extremely difficult, suffering from the failings of that man which led to a *de facto Verwerfung* or foreclosure. How could foreclosure be *de facto*? Precisely by not being *de jure*, a matter of general law. Would it thus be empirical? Lacan sheds no light on this, but carries on along his path. On this topic we must be careful, given that if, when we come across the word "*foreclosure*," we seek to understand it too quickly, we can go seriously wrong. The term Lacan borrows from Freud and which he translates *forclusion* must no doubt be situated as a properly psychotic mechanism; this is how it is accepted. But, precisely on this question, Lacan specifies the *Verwerfung* of the Name-of-the-Father, the fore-closure of a particular signifier—not foreclosure *tout court*. But what takes place in 1975? When Lacan proposes other kinds of determination, *Verwerfung* becomes the mechanism of an unavoidable dimension of the psyche, that of the con-stitution of the subject. We have already touched on this question, that of the role of a constitutive hole. Something is lacking in an inevitable, irreparable way: this is why we are such gossips, why we never stop talking and believing that by doing so we can make up for this irreducible lack. Lacan writes this as a matheme: S Ⱥ, in other words there is a signi-fier of the Other as lacking; this indicates that what we find at the place of the signifier is what is absent by definition. We can thus say that the signifier is foreclosed. Here, we are dealing with a "normal" foreclosure, so to speak, a foreclosure that is constitutive, irreducible, bearing on the very condition of being a speaker.

Thus, referring to a *Verwerfung* does not necessarily imply a mechanism proper to psychosis. A "*de facto Verwerfung*" does not, then, put Joyce in the position of a psychotic. Let us propose something different. Doesn't the final Lacan envision the incidence or effect of an irreducible "psychotic" kernel in every individual, by means of which we are identified with our *sinthome*, the ever-present modality of our jouissance? And that it is on this basis that we come to be constituted as speaking subjects? Lacan gives us an account of "finding" this constellation. This, of course, is our own reading, but we do not consider it ill-founded, given Lacan's refusal to speak at any point of Joyce's madness. He often asks rhetorical questions on this topic in the seminar—"Was Joyce mad?"—but he never makes any claims about it, even when talking of Joyce's *de facto Verwerfung* (to which we will return).

Lacan observes that Joyce, instead of honoring or rendering homage to his father, makes into his life's goal the effort to honor his proper name. Honoring his father would amount to a way of linking up with symbolic debt. John Gross says something relevant here, if we read him carefully: What does James owe to John? Apparently, he thinks, much more than is allowed by Lacan. But we are still on an imaginary level. Beyond these opinions, so to speak, why does he not attempt to write *père-version*? We propose at this point to do this by means of a "true" word-game: Joycean *père-version* is written as *Père-sonnores*:

Honneur ["honor"]

Personne ["person"]

Raison ["reason"]

Père-sonnores

Père   son   ores

son ["sound" or "his"]

résonner ["resound"]

Several terms are condensed in this table, in order to
conjugate *père-version*, by homophony or paranomasia. *Père-
sonnores*: the father, certainly, but which one? If we play on
the word *personne*, we get *son père*, "his father," strictly speaking that one: just his father, in no sense a universal father.
Thus, there is no reference to biology here, but to what is taken
to represent a symbolic order that, determining it, goes beyond it. At the same time, there is something that *sounds*
[*sonne*], taking us back to the question of *j'ouïs*, of hearing
and the voice. Something sounds, returns, seeks to compensate, precisely, in the fact of being heard. We should not forget, of course, the double meaning present in *personne* ["person" and "nobody"]. As for *ores*, this has a sense similar to
"now." We next get to the question of honor, of rendering
honor or paying homage—but in a special sense, that of "prid-
ing oneself" on something. It is not only a matter of honoring
someone, but of "boasting" or "flaunting" them. The expression contains another term: *to resonate* [*résonner*], referring to
an effect of the voice, its sound resounding with the persistence
caused by an acoustic box. At any rate, one ceases to hear it
insofar as it can be written; and that is the point—the emer-

gence of this (ultimately) epiphanic moment. But the associations do not stop there: with *re* and *son* we can produce
the homophonic "reason" [*raison*].

Where does this complex, overdetermined structure
lead? Our aim was to set out a writing to indicate how we
can go to work and make a "choice" without lapsing into a
simple alternative produced by conventional language. The
linguistic structure necessarily calls for explanation. Thus,
the condensation it embodies accounts for a parasitic signifier, one that tends to lead to Joycean jouissance. We would
propose the following reading of this insistent signifier: "His
father, nobody, re-sounds now masks reason [*son père, personne,
ré-sonne ores masque raison*]." "Mask," of course, takes us to
the Latin etymology of "person." So, his father, nobody, re-
sounds now—as effective transformation—masks reason. And
the latter is what Joyce takes pride in, a boastful reason—for
he believes in his *sinthome*. This belief, which makes reason a
source of such pride, means that his father, nobody, becomes
in a compensatory manner, after the search, that which works
(*Wirchlichkeit*) to allow him to make a name for himself (a
question we will come back to). Lacan asks whether or not
Joyce was mad; then, in an apparently sudden leap, indicates
that this takes us into the problematic of the true and the Real.
The introduction of these categories is resituated by the following observation: the true is in pursuit of pleasure; and the
Real, of jouissance. Why does Lacan think that these two categories can shed light on the question of whether or not Joyce
was mad? Here, we should recall the distinction between *vérité*
and *varité* [see above, p. 122], between general truth and its
singular "variety." But this definition defers the role "of" the
true until later. There is no doubt that the thinking of the final
Lacan gravitates around the Real, a register to which he gives

increasing emphasis, so that its place becomes decisive. Hence he introduces the question of the Real to his consideration of the relation between John and James Joyce, and asks (ironically mocking analysis in general) whether this relation can be considered sadomasochistic. John Gross considers things in practically the same terms, falling into the trap of imagining a sadistic father and his poor masochist son. Throughout his teaching, Lacan shows that the couple involved in the so-called sadomasochistic relation are not two sides of the same coin, in some sense complementary. There is no question here of a couple in search of one another, the sadist seeking the masochist and vice versa. Lacan refutes such assumptions, referring to the following schema to illustrate the point (Figure 24):

Figure 24

This is a torus, defined as such by the disk being pierced by a straight or "infinite" line. In other words, the line—whatever its imaginary dimensions—reaches its topological objective by making a hole in the "flat" sphere, and thus making it a torus. The latter would correspond to masochistic receptivity, while the line would stand for the sadistic element passing through that disposition. As the line is infinite, we know that its ends join together, making it equivalent to the circle. Lacan does not write out the conclusion here, which is self-evident: the figure presents, with the torus and the line, a chain of two or Hopf chain. Was this chain what linked the two Joyces, father and son? Lacan answers in the negative, emphasizing another aspect of this singular Joycean *père-version*. He asks his assistant on matters Joycean, Jacques Aubert, if he sees any trace in the writer of a "redemptive" madness: Did he think of himself as a redeemer? Can we trace such an idea in his writing? Did Joyce believe he could redeem somebody? Presumably, to think in these terms one would have to have gotten rid of the belief in only one Redeemer, Jesus Christ. But was there another for Joyce, precisely himself? Lacan comments, again with irony, that in fact Joyce did not think that he was the redeemer, but God himself. This was of course God the creator, as artist. But why then raise the question of redemption? The answer is that, for Lacan, Joyce somehow supposed himself to have saved his father. In effect, he states, the "loony idea" of redemption flourishes to the extent that there is a "relation of the son to the father." The point to consider, then, would be what Joyce has to do in order to save his father, to rescue him from the precarious, contested position we outlined above. Here, Lacan moves between Joyce and the Christian *père-version* of redemption, as something opposed to psychoanalysis. He thus explains that Freud responds to the naive idea of sadomasochism—the idea of the son submitting to the father in order to save his creation by means of redemption—with the problematic of castration. This presents a very different situation than that of a sadistic father assaulting a masochistic son.

This argument is very interesting from a clinical perspective. Lacan refers to the notion that, due to castration, the father renounces the Phallus even before the son receives it, in other words before he obtains the right to possess it. This is important, as it postulates an intermediary moment when the father, making use of his paternity, abandons possession of the Phallus. He renounces being the absolute Phallus, the Omniphallos, a Priapus with an eternally erect phallus. In doing this, he makes possible symbolic transmission—an act that in various senses resembles that of the analyst. To put it more bluntly, if the analyst did not lay mines along his own path in order to make himself destitute, his analyses would never finish. And this is paradoxical: the analyst is the "victim" of his own act, which a too rapid reading would surely label as a sign of masochism. On the contrary, if one gains an understanding of this problematic, one sees that here it is a question of an act of transmission. Perhaps the supposition of "masochism" is based on the belief that any self-destitution would be a sign of this; in other words, the guarantee of a nonmasochistic analyst would be an interminable analysis. For, reading between the lines, we see that Lacan is not only alluding to Joyce and his father, but also to the relation between analyst and analysand. In what way is there a symbolic transmission in this relation? Not that this would imply any kind of salvation: there is no redemption, only castration.

In his work on the two categories we have discussed, Lacan formulates a new aphorism that is highly significant: "The Real is located in the entanglements of the true." This remark takes us very close to the analyst's interest in babble, as opposed to structured language. We have already noted this in our discussion of Chomsky: unlike him, we do not focus on language that is supposedly well constructed or "full," but on language with structural faults. In the same line of thinking, the following question is interesting for analysts: How is the true articulated? The answer is that it is *found*—not sought—and in the form of an entanglement. There is nothing "clear and distinct" here, not even partially; but rather, bits of the Real: limit points, marks of the end of analysis. These are not, however, insurmountable obstacles that must be accepted with resignation, but rather bear witness to the singular identification with the *sinthome* where an irreducible jouissance takes shelter. Here, then, it is not a question of a search for the true, but of "finding" this bit of the Real and the jouissance it can offer. To be sure, when he asks what is the greatest jouissance that can be procured by the Real, Lacan responds that it is masochism. But this does not, as we have said, mean we should confuse jouissance, marked by its uncaring imprecision, with masochism; simply that the latter entails the greatest scope for the drive it is possible to obtain from the Real.

Let us return to the relation we have already mentioned between hearing [*l'ouïr*] and sound, the re-sounding we heard in *père-sonnores*, by examining the text we cited at the beginning of the chapter, the *Schizographie* co-written by Lacan with his colleagues J. Lévi-Valensi and P. Migault.[5] The text begins with the question of schizo-aphasia, a term related to aphasia that designates frenetic division and verbalization. The article does not, however, deal only with this specific pathology, as the authors aim to discover (let us recall the date: 1931) whether this illness might illustrate something general about the developing stages of thought or its inner mechanisms. It turns out that in certain cases such "deep problems" can only be detected in the domain of written language. There is thus an intriguing return on the part of Lacan, forty-five years later, to an early preoccupation.

---

5. J. Lévi-Valensi, P. Migault, J. Lacan, "Écrits 'Inspirés': Schizographies," *Annales médico-psychologiques*, 1931 II, pp. 508–522.

The text presents the case of Marcelle C., a 34-year-old who suffers from a multiple delirium, fundamentally characterized by vengefulness and hatred, and also periodic episodes of aggression, loss of control. Here, we should read *à la lettre*: "In listing the basic phenomena that are 'imposed' or said to be caused by an external act." We note that the word given emphasis is the same that Lacan uses in 1976, when he talks of "imposed words." It is important to observe that here the voice is given a decisive role as an axis of the patient's suffering; in fact, she hears voices. The authors of *Schizographie* note frequent and intense "feelings of being influenced" on the basis of the lines written by Marcelle C.: "psychical affinities," "intuitions," "spiritual revelations," and above all, feelings of "being directed." We could term all this "inspiration"; hence the title, referring to "Inspired" Writings. These inspirations, of course, give rise to the writing—and here we come to our chief interest: the authors center their analysis, to a massive extent, on these writings. Their research leads them to a sort of classification of disorders based on their work with the patient's language. They refer to Head, to his studies of aphasia and similar conditions. We will give some examples to make clear the resemblance (at least in formal terms) of this method and the later confrontation with Joyce's work.

The descriptive analysis produced by the three psychiatrists in 1931 first indicates some of the features of Marcelle C.'s attitude to her writings, above all her earliest ones. To start, they stress how she was "absolutely convinced of their value." This certainty appears to be based on a state of "sthenia"—the opposite of "asthenia"—in other words, on what Lacan refers to at the beginning of Seminar 23: mania. It is a swelling-up, an elation caused by her having to obey orders from on high, coming from the truths proper to that glorious order. The authors next state that they were perplexed in the face of the "meaning contained in her writings." She did not understand what they were about, there was an enigma in her inspired words. But what was the aim of Marcelle C.? Nothing other than what she states: "I am making language evolve. Its old forms must be shaken up." Is this not, for all the alleged distance between irreconcilable individual "heresies," a profoundly Joycean project?

In accordance with the work of Head, Lacan and his collaborators argue toward an implicitly phenomenological goal. Lacan had in fact not yet entirely accepted psychoanalysis. This text is thus situated at a point where—as Philippe Julien puts it ironically[6]—Lacan was still a Lacanian; he subsequently becomes a Freudian. That is, he is still carrying out his research in a fragmentary, disordered manner, and would have been unable to say, as he does in Caracas in 1980, "I am a Freudian. If you so desire, it is for you to be Lacanians." In other words, Lacan is saying: I am constituted on the basis of the place of the Other. In this sense, it could be said that Marx was not a Marxist, only his followers were. Did Freud not claim that psychoanalysis had been born with Breuer? If we read Freud attentively, we will find frequent references to his masters (although we may well ask how this can be so, given that their practice was not psychoanalytic). It is a question of maintaining, through an effective method of teaching, that one is on a path opened by the Other—otherwise, one risks suffering from a delirium of self-engendering.

---

6. P. Julien, *Le retour à Freud de J. Lacan. L'application au miroir.* Toulouse: Erès, 1986, pp. 11–23.

According to Julien, we can find in this early "Lacanian" period of Lacan's work a trace of phenomenology that will orient the ensuing classification of disorders. These are categories relating to the semiology of psychiatry; we should therefore not overlook the fact that we require another set of criteria to interpret this material. According to the writings of Head, the functions of language are based on "the organic intersection of four functions that relate to four orders of problems that are effectively treated separately in clinical work." These problems are:

1. Formal or verbal
2. Concerning meaning or names
3. Grammatical or concerning syntax
4. Semantic or concerning the overall organization of a phrase's meaning

The authors pick out, with rigorous accuracy, examples of each of these problems from the writings of Marcelle C. We will examine a few, to show what we have already anticipated: the remarkable resemblance of these writings to Joyce's method. At any rate, to avoid accusations of reductionism (sheltering behind a false analogy), let us refer to a point Lacan makes, mentioned in our first chapter:

> . . . once [the choice] has been made, there is nothing to stop anybody from subjecting it to confirmation, in other words, from being heretical in the true sense—that is, once the nature of the *sinthome* has been recognized, not denying oneself the logical use of it, which is to say, pushing it until it attains its real.

This was not the case for Marcelle C. "Attaining its real" implies succeeding in grasping what invention circles around,

by biting into the lack of the Other. Lacan thus opens the way
to the logic that belongs to the *sinthome*—something that does
not of course amount to any fixed phenomenological entity,
insofar as it entails a singular manner of working with a choice.
In sum, the *sinthome* has a logic, in other words it emerges as
an articulated register grounded, necessarily, in the Real. By
contrast, Marcelle C. is not "heretical in the true sense": her
choice is fulfilled by a furious vengefulness directed against
those whom she feels have wronged her. On the other hand,
it is true that Joyce was extremely sensitive to criticism and
was never the least bit friendly toward those who offered it.
He persistently thought that any criticism was due to a failure to recognize his talents. Nonetheless, we should reiterate
that unlike Marcelle C., Joyce knew how to make logical use
of the *sinthome* and attain its real.

Concerning the first in the list of disorders, formal or
verbal problems, we will shortly see the striking similarity
mentioned above. The three authors write: "The imposed
quality of certain phenomena is clearly shown by the fact that
their image is so completely acoustic that the patient transcribes them in several different ways." Let us consider this
point: that of "hearing" words and transliterating them, putting them in writing, making various different choices. We
see the patient doing this in a manner very close to the technique of *Finnegans Wake*:

> *là mais l'as* ["there but you have it"]
> *la mélasse* ["treacle"]
> *l'âme est lasse* ["the soul is weary"]

The first phrase has no discernible meaning, but all three
phrases sound almost exactly the same. The autonomous dimension of the voice gives rise to incongruous transliterations,

which cannot be brought together in a single meaning to be communicated. In the case of the patient, it is a question of "poubelling" (making public/chucking in the dustbin) what is acoustically imposed, getting rid of it with an "inspired" writing. To do this, she has to appeal to the piece of paper, which here has the function of containing such a "production." At last, she manages to get rid of it.

This is one of the examples given by Lacan and his colleagues of what they term verbal disorders; they subsequently give illustrations of trouble with naming and grammar. If we look more closely at the domain labeled semantic disorders, we will see how the pre-Freudian Lacan orients his reading on the basis of affects. As we know—as Lacan subsequently demonstrated, the latter refer back to the signifiers to which they are connected. But in this early classification, Lacan commits an error that is very common among analysts: that of using a magic word that says everything and nothing—the word in question being "ambivalence." What is ambivalence? It is not clear. On the whole, as Lacan will observe later, one talks of ambivalence in order to avoid talking of aggression. If one did not aim to connote a certain violence, nobody would call on this famous "ambivalence" to explain what relates to the speaking-being. In other words, the term says practically nothing.

Having set out these reservations, then, let us begin with ambivalence. "I have suffered," says Marcelle C., "the yoke of defense"—or to quote her exactly, write the authors, "the yoke of oppression." We have here a perfect example of how these authors understand ambivalence. What is this "defense" doing there? The anticipation of meaning is broken, in the same way as often occurs in jokes: we expect a word to appear that is coherent with the thread of the discourse, but something else entirely suddenly crops up. This one example of many, which mostly illustrate "displacement," in terms of "image projection"' and "condensation" as the "buildup" of these images (according to the classical Freudian categories). We find an extremely interesting point here, as well, which is often mentioned by Lacan: "Her writings also manifest a profusion of proper names (several linked together, joined up with a = sign, for instance, to indicate the same individual), nicknames, the diversity and the fantasy of her own signatures." This point might be linked up with the massive valorization of the proper name in Joyce: more than one proper name, it is true, and moreover for Joyce a name "can only take place as a nickname," states Lacan, referring to the name "Dedalus." That is, the goal of exceeding the S_1 requires the S_2, the nickname. Moreover, with the nickname we see the proper name returned "to the domain of the ordinary noun." To sum this up, when Lacan comes to the end of a session he says something like this, according to the transcription: *Jaclaque han!*

That's him: Jacques Lacan. The pun on his name also alludes to *la claque*, a "slap": the irony is that the audience will be obliged to applaud him, even though they might *en a eu leur claque*, be "fed up to the back teeth" with him. And Lacan adds to this ambiguous tribute to his audience the interjection *Han!*, almost an onomatopoeia, implying the effort needed by the audience as well as the speaker. To make clear his reasoning, Lacan notes that the proper name must be "reduced"—de-idealized?—"to the most ordinary noun," as he now puts it more emphatically. Such a reduction, he adds, causes him "relief." Is he thus referring to the analyst's relief when he manages to dislodge himself, in the analysand's eyes, from the place of "more than S_1," and thus produces a good

scenario for the end of analysis? Concerning this, there is a
suggestive echo in the work of M.-D. Vors on *Ulysses*, where
we read: "One observes that the proper name aiming to become a common noun can in fact be a common name that is
taken on."[7] And M. Moulon claims, in more draconian vein,
"Every proper name was originally a common noun."[8]

But why does the name have so much significance here?
According to what Lacan states in Seminar 9, the proper name
is not, as Bertrand Russell had claimed, "a word for something particular." Lacan is equally opposed to the common
assumption that the common noun means something, while
the proper name does not. As everyone knows, this is utter
rubbish; clinical experience completely refutes such ideas.
Lacan teaches that, on the contrary, we have to be especially
attentive to the analysand's name and forename, as these are
usually bound up with his or her plans, likes, choices, moods,
opinions, and so on.[9] The proper name is just as important
as the common noun, owing to the effects of a powerfully
imperative semantics. It is unnecessary to recall how many
there are whose activity conforms to their name, to the extent that the S_2-articulation contributes to this a posteriori. It
is not an accident, for instance, when someone called Carpenter seeks a job as an artisan. Here, a personal experience
can be mentioned. A friend and colleague of mine, who has
been living in Israel for some years, sent me the gift of a tre-

7. M.-D. Vors, "Les noms propres dans *Ulysse*," in *L'Herne: 50-James
Joyce*. Paris: Editions de l'Herne, 1985, p. 291.

8. M. Moulon, "Curiosités lexicales," in *Nom, prénom—La règle et
le jeu*. Paris: Autrement, 1994, p. 37.

9. J. Lacan, *Séminaire IX: "L'Identification*," session of December 20,
1961, unpublished.

foil knot carved in wood, which he commissioned from a local carpenter, whose name turned out to be highly appropriate to his trade—Dubois [literally "Of wood"].

What, then, does Lacan contend concerning the proper name? He claims that we will understand its function when we have grasped why we are so upset by any alteration of the name. In Seminar 12, he situates the essential characteristic of the name in the fact that it is irreplaceable; it is effectively located in the place of a lack, which it at once suggests and conceals. If it cannot be replaced, this is because there is no equivalent term in discourse. The person interpellated automatically becomes angry when someone accidentally gets it wrong, as I myself can testify when—as happens fairly often—people omit the "H" of Harari. One thus touches on, or exposes, something irreducibly lacking, a lack that cannot be alleviated or substituted. The speaking-being is stitched to its name, dependent on it: we are suspended from it. The name can travel, can move around, can even be made plural ("the Smiths"). At the same time, it can even be given to a microorganism—as in the Koch bacillus.[10] But above all Lacan emphasizes one crucial problem: the fact that names cannot be translated (as he puts it, "I am called Lacan in every language"[11]). Whenever one tries to translate a name, this is due to a desire—whether or not one is aware of it—to insult the person being named.

As an illustration of this, we should refer to an anecdote concerning the great author Jorge Luis Borges. When he gave his second lecture to the Mayeutica-Institucion Psicoanalitica

---

10. J. Lacan, *Séminaire XII: "Problèmes cruciiaux pour la psychanalyse,"* session of December 6, 1965, unpublished.

11. J. Lacan, *Séminaire IX: "L'Identification,"* session of January 10, 1962, unpublished.

in 1981, our conversation on the way to the venue turned to celebrity in general, and his own fame in particular. Borges' comments were at once acute and markedly modest, and he added distractedly: "These days, everyone is famous. Take that man, what's his name? Who is so well-known, the television presenter . . . you know—Newton." He had translated the name, *Neustadt* [German for "new town"] becoming *Newton*. Without saying anything explicitly about the theory of names, Borges was showing rigorously that names do not translate, that there is no way of doing it without a subtle implication of hostility.

On this topic, some time ago an article by the music critic Napoleon Cabrera appeared in the journal *Clarin*, which criticized what had happened in the Spanish-speaking market to the name of a piece by Mozart: the one entitled *Doncel* ("lad," the masculine of "doncella"). For the composer had dedicated it to someone called *Jeunehomme* ["young man"] and they had dared to translate it as "doncel," even though it was a name. It would be like asking somebody if he were fond of the jazz musician Louis Brasfort, in place of the incomparable Louis Armstrong; or, likewise, a French reader translating the title of Stephen Hero as *Stephane le héros* ["Stephen the hero"].

We are therefore outlining a place for the proper name that is ex-sistent, extraterritorial. It is thus extremely relevant for Lacan to point out the link between *joy—enjoy yourself*, as the Americans say, in other words the product of jouissance, and the first syllable of Joyce. Could we also see a relation between that word which figures in Beethoven's 9th Symphony, *Freude* or "joy," and the name Freud? Would this be a way of articulating Joyce and Freud? Possibly, but we cannot be sure. Lacan shows, however, with further convincing examples, what passes through the proper name as an irreplaceable site, the channel of tasks to be accomplished.

By contrast, Marcelle C. plays with her own signature, making it into an object of fantasy by altering it. We can see here how fragile is the core constituent of her self-identity. In what she does we see—as we saw earlier in our reading of *Ulysses*—signs caught up in a kind of Morris dance. Usually, faced with such a phenomenon, one thinks of depersonalization; while in the case of a literary producer (above all a narrator?) we can see how a singular world is organized through proper names, personal nicknames. There, a metaphorical dimension is at work, a dimension of suppletion and wordplay, as in *Jaclaque Han!* The latter example entails, as we argued, the destination of the analyst's name, its reentry into the category of the most common noun as an indication of a "cease-fire" in the transference.

At the same time, what is emphasized very judiciously in the 1931 text is the writing mechanism of rhythm. This is a point developed with great lucidity by Julia Kristeva in her 1974 text *Revolution in Poetic Language*. There, she isolates the incidence of a presymbolic, presemantic level she terms the "semiotic," which is present in rhythms, scansions, in phonetic traits and emphases, and which is closely related to what we think of as a writer's "style." These rhythms are bound up, above all, with breathing, with phrasing and pauses, with the manner of linking together written expressions. Writers reveal this level with great clarity, by showing how the (Kristevan) symbolic is secondary to the rhythmic semiotic. In other words, it is not so much what is said that matters, as the "music" of the way one says it. Kristeva is especially interested in harmonies, in the way speech can become rhythmic.

So—having considered rhythm and melody, the psychiatric text of 1931 ends on a rather striking note, where we can again see the daring way that Lacan circles back to his own work after almost half a century. We read the following conclusion: "There is, in short, nothing less inspired, in the spiritual sense, than this writing which is felt to be inspired [by the patient]. It is when thought is meagre and scant that the automatic phenomenon supplements it." The phenomenon is "automatic," evidently, due to its uncontrollable occurrence, but in addition it has the role of a suppletion, which is in our view the key point. The text continues: "It is experienced as something exterior because it makes up for [*suppléant*] a deficit in thinking." Briefly, thinking is replaced by a supposed creativity. Having said that, this notion of suppletion is the same as what is isolated by Lacan in Joyce. In order to clarify this, we must trace Lacan's new emphasis on knots by looking at the famous trefoil (Figure 25):

Figure 25

In this knot, there are three crossing-points that follow an alternating pattern. If one makes a mistake at some point, not keeping to the right pattern of over- and undercrossing, when the string is pulled one gets, not a trefoil, but a circle—in other words, a prototypically "trivial" knot. In Chapter 7, we will explore the different consequences that can be identified when each of the three crossing-points is incorrect, when a line passes over instead of under or vice versa. But what interests Lacan in particular is the case where the error in the knot is located at the following crossing-point (Figure 26):

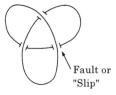

Fault or
"Slip"

Figure 26

Now, when a crossing-point is wrong, a suppletion must be called in to avoid the knot "lapsing" back into a circle. This idea, which is already present in the *Écrits* "*Inspirés*," returns in Seminar 23 at exactly this point (let us remember that the emblem of Ireland, its national symbol, is none other than the trefoil-like shamrock). In the earlier work, there is an explanation of how, although the patient experiences thought that is brief and fragmentary, she can believe herself to be "inspired," and thus make up for [*suppléant*] the shortcomings of thought. By contrast, with Joyce the suppletion is already inscribed in an incorrectly tied knot, at the place indicated. What is this place? It is the site where the paternal lack is made up for [*supléée*]: the radical absence of the father leads to the error in the knot, giving rise to what Lacan terms a "knotted compensation." This takes effect by means of a new register or supplementary element that comes to repair the knot. According to this first approach to the question by Lacan, it is here that we can locate Joyce's *sinthome*: it is the artificial cord, the act of adding it to the knot, which prevents unknotting (Figure 27):

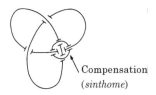

Compensation
(*sinthome*)

Figure 27

We will have to come back to this point. To conclude this chapter, we will now turn briefly to Joyce's relations with Woman [*La femme*]. We deliberately write it thus; on this point, the final Lacan stressed two points that he expressed aphoristically. It is well known that one of these is written as [barred] *La femme*.

This formula, with *La* written barred, means that woman does not exist as a single, unified prototype that can be given universal representation. To the extent that this is so, Lacan writes that "there is no sexual relation." This is not to deny copulation—quite the contrary! If there are sexual relations—this is because there is no sexual relation—there is nothing predetermined or prescribed, there is not an instinctive plan here, or anything of the kind. The existence of a sexual relation is, at any rate, a naive, biologistic, pre-Freudian way of thinking about sexuality. What did people think before the appearance of Freud's *Three Essays*—that sexuality suddenly emerged at puberty, that it was restricted to heterosexual intercourse, and that its aim was reproduction? But Freud showed that the opposite is true: since there is no predetermined definition of sex for speaking beings, there is no sexual relation.

Lacan makes another claim, however, concerning Joyce and his wife Nora Barnacle (her maiden name, which she kept for a long time as they only married in 1931 after a relationship of 27 years, bearing witness to a desire not to legitimate the union before others). Joyce and Nora did have a sexual relation, says Lacan—she fitted him like a glove turned inside out. What does this mean? Take a glove, turn it inside out and put the other hand inside it: it adjusts marvelously well, fitting exactly. This is how well Nora "fitted" Joyce, for Lacan; thus she was the only woman of his life: *The* woman, as he constantly tells her in his letters (which are recommended reading).[12] In his preface to the Argentine edition of these letters, Luis Thonis refers to Lionel Trilling's book *Beyond Culture*, where it is claimed that Yeats, Pound, and Joyce "are the survivors of a tradition that worshiped The Woman." In this, Trilling very much echoes Lacan's theorization of Joyce.

Clinical work teaches us, however, that in the case of those analysands with such a "Joycean" problematic, a sort of inversion takes effect. Freud worked on something similar when he dealt with the split between virgin and whore. Much has been written on this dichotomy, and many attempts to analyze it have failed because they have taken it, in an essentialist manner, to be a "natural" given of masculine sexuality. Yet such subjects, like Joyce, actually *find* at the place where virgin and whore divide, *The* unique Woman, an Eve on whom they massively and neurotically depend. At the same time, there is the "Pygmalion"' fantasy that entails imagining The Woman as something designed, sculpted. We find in Joyce's letters the desire to choose clothing for Nora and organize her diet, so that she will end up with the form he requires. As their relationship progresses, the letters take on a scandalous, obscene note; we can read there accounts of and demands for some fairly bizarre sexual practices, which are hard to distinguish from perversion. Here is one, without all the accompanying verbiage: to lie down under her anus in order to see how she defecates and to savor her farts and excrement; all that written with an indescribable jouissance. Or this: "I wish you would smack me or flog me

---

12. Translator's note: Harari recommends an Argentine edition of Joyce's letters, with a preface by Luis Thonis: J. Joyce, *Cartas de amor a Nora Barnacle*. Buenos Aires: Leviatan, 1992.

even. Not in play, dear, in earnest and on my naked flesh. . . .
I would love to be whipped by you, Nora dear!"[13] Furthermore,
he often addresses her as "my sweet little whorish Nora" or
something of that kind; and then of course claims never to have
known anyone as pure and holy as she.

It is no doubt better to deal with _the_ than with The
Woman. Why is this? The consequences of being linked to
the latter are very like what Freud, at the end of _Narcissism:
An Introduction_, describes as the "cure by love." He refers to
those who suddenly "get better" during their analysis when
they encounter the love of their life, and no longer have any
reason to carry on with the treatment. Freud does not claim
that these people are wrong, but he points to a slight difficulty: the overwhelming dependence of these "cures" on being loved by the providential person. Effectively, there has
been no change of subjective position: the individual simply
gets stuck with a new other, with whom he or she repeats
worryingly stereotypical fantasies. As Freud tells us, therefore, this is nothing but one of the neurotic modes of loving.
In short, this situation does not really amount to a "cure by
love," as Freud calls it somewhat ironically. At any rate, the
difficulty is no less, being now focused on the success of what
we know to have been Joyce's aims. Thus, he writes to his one
and only: "O take me into your soul of souls and then I will
become indeed the poet of my race."[14]

In short, through Nora, Joyce discovered love and sex,
linked to what was low and to disdain for women, but with a

13. _Selected Letters of James Joyce_, ed. R. Ellmann. London: Faber,
1975, p. 188.
14. Ibid., p. 169.

parallel dependence on The Woman, to whom—as he explicitly states—he owes everything and by whom he constantly fears he will be betrayed due to excessive transgression. Joyce was extremely sensitive to anything that concerned his relationship with Nora, however insignificant it seemed. Moreover, he feared many times that their relationship was close to collapse. During a trip back to Dublin, he was told—without any proof—that at the beginning of her relationship with him, Nora was seeing another man every other night; Joyce believed this quite literally. Here, we may read his fantasmatic desire, despite his incessant protestations, his desire to possess Nora body and soul, to appropriate her completely.[15] The implied geometry of the inside-out glove is valuable here— although not, of course, topologically—to see what is at stake in this fantasmatic desire. We might associate this with entering the body, turning it "inside-out," coiling up inside it; as Joyce writes, "I want to be the master of your body and your spirit." If Nora's body is like an inside-out glove, he seeks, like an allegorical hand, to penetrate the glove, to see excrement falling from her, to savor "the very stink and sweat that rises from your arse," as he writes.[16]

Joyce's desire, then, is to get all the way inside Nora, right to her guts, and for her to do the same with him. Here, a too rapid reading would talk of a form of symbiosis—to which

---

15. On this point, Brenda Maddox's conclusion is highly relevant: "Nora is not important because she belonged to Joyce, because in reality she never belonged to him. She was the stronger of the two, an independent spirit who had far greater influence on Joyce than he had on her." Cf. B. Maddox, *Nora: A Biography of Nora Joyce*. London: Hamish Hamilton, 1988.

16. *Selected Letters of James Joyce*, op. cit., p. 181.

Lacan responds by recalling our separation from the botanical kingdom. For the relation between fungus and algae cannot be used as an analogy here, but rather serves to efface the difference: it is a question not of the formation of a distinct new organism such as lichen—the classic example of symbiosis—but of an imbrication that is *different* from the one perfectly illustrated by the inside-out glove. We would emphasize the letter of November 1, 1909, where Joyce, writing from Dublin, addresses Nora as "my dear little Butterfly" and goes on:

> I hope you got my little present of gloves safely. I sent them just as I sent you my first present five years ago. . . . The nicest pair is that one of reindeer skin: it is lined with its own skin, simply turned inside out and should be warm, nearly as warm as certain districts of your body, Butterfly.[17]

In my view, this letter may be the actual source of Lacan's notion of the "glove turned inside out," for all his allusions to Kant. Our inference fits well enough: in his letter, Joyce uses the gloves as a means of signification, and wishes his wife to take him in such a way.

At this point, we may ask what, ultimately, is the problem raised by this singular position ascribed to Nora? In principle, such a constellation serves to close off the couple defensively, so that any children are shut out. Each time a child comes along, it tries to burrow into the inside-out glove, but is not welcomed, not given a place there. At moments of Joyce's obsessive jealousy, when he is informed of the presence of an

---

17. Ibid., p. 176.

alleged third party at the beginning of the relationship, he even casts doubt on the paternity of his son Giorgio, questioning Nora about it.[18] Like his sister Lucia, who is to become schizophrenic, the son is given an Italian name. We are reminded of the passage quoted above, concerning *amor matris* as the only certain thing in life. As for Joyce's daughter, as we will see, he will seek to discredit psychoanalysis as a therapy by attributing a singular quality to her: Lucia is not schizophrenic, he will claim, but "telepathic." Concerning this, in the next chapter we will consider the case presented by Lacan, that of a patient suffering from "imposed speech," where telepathy also plays an important role.

We will begin by outlining Joyce's position regarding psychoanalysis in general. In the *Selected Letters*, there is one written by Joyce to his patroness Harriet Shaw Weaver from Paris on June 24, 1921, where we read:

> A batch of people in Zurich persuaded themselves that I was gradually going mad and actually endeavored to induce me to enter a sanatorium where a certain Dr. Jung (the Swiss Tweedledum who is not to be confused with the Viennese Tweedledee, Dr. Freud). . . .[19]

Joyce's characteristic irony becomes still more barbed when he adds that Jung "amuses himself at the expense (in every sense of the word) of ladies and gentlemen who are troubled with bees in their bonnets." Having a bee in your bonnet may be rather like suffering from imposed speech; the metaphors are similar. Let us recall the topic that we ad-

---

18. Ibid., p. 158.
19. Ibid., p. 282.

dressed, following John Gross, at the beginning of this chapter: the meaning of vituperation, of the ability to set people up in a position of denigration. This trait of John Joyce's is thus taken up by his son James vis-à-vis, among other people, analysts. Hence Joyce's position beyond analysis, his belief in his *sinthome*. There could never have been, on his part, a demand for analysis, or an acceptance of his daughter's treatment. Yet this is not to imply that Joyce was a "stabilized" psychotic. Lacan emphasized that in such a situation it is only in the third generation that psychosis breaks out; and Lucia Joyce belonged, precisely, to that generation.

Joyce's belief in his *sinthome* makes necessary a new form of credibility: henceforth, the question lies in grasping the singularity through which he succeeded in tying-up his "knot." Even if this singularity does not correspond to the division proper to the neurotic subject, it in no way implies psychosis. And this is the point of obscurity, which in our view points to the subjective position of the end of analysis, not that of psychosis. This is not to say that there is no question of division here, but concerning the *sinthome*, identification, becoming-one, predominates (insofar as division denotes, obviously, at least two). Joyce's position is therefore exemplary, above all, of an identification that allows him, according to the logic of the *sinthome*, to attain his real. This is distinct from other moments in Lacanian analysis, such as when the end of analysis is characterized not by an identification with the *sinthome*, but by subjective destitution.

6

Jeems Jokes, *Telepathy,*
and the Verbal Parasite

Bloomsday, says Joyce, the day of flowering. It is the day of his first sexual encounter with Nora, and he transcribes it into *Ulysses* by making the action of the book unfold on June 16, 1904. It was then that Joyce *encountered* Nora: the term allows us to bring in one of Lacan's aphorisms, which will then punningly engender another (a sort of aphorism "squared"). As mentioned in Chapter 4, Lacan liked to quote Picasso's remark "I do not seek, I find"; he sees it as relevant to his conception of love as bearing on the domain of the contingent: love is not written until it ceases not to write itself. Quite suddenly: that's how love works. What is at stake here is the relation between looking for something and finding it: such an aphorism leads us to talk of the encounter as chance, something accidental; it jeopardizes all teleological schemes, in art as well as in love. Furthermore, as we have emphasized, what is evoked is a dimension of the "failed" encounter [*malencontre*] rather than of a fixed rendezvous.

In Seminar 23, Lacan's position shifts explicitly. His advancing years, and his sense of the work he still has to do with what life remained, make him declare that he is in the midst of his research, which amounts to him "turning full circle." What does this mean? Firstly, it indicates a 360° turn, returning to the same point from which one set off: the famous "circle" of the discourse of the master. This is one reading, but not the only one: in Seminar 25, *The Moment to Conclude*, Lacan will state that the end of analysis consists in precisely that, turning full circle—but, he adds, doing so twice. This, then, is Lacan's meaning: a return to the same thing, but one that no longer entails, in his writing, a circle, but rather an "interior eight." The latter figure, as we know, embodies a singular topology of recurrence (Figure 28):

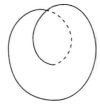

Figure 28

This form of writing provides us with a useful way of illustrating the points to come about the psychoanalytic work that remains to be done on the determining conditions of the symptom, and on the basis of those conditions, to reach the invention of the *sinthome*. Let us continue with our reading of Seminar 25. It is here that Lacan changes Picasso's aphorism into another, which is full of unexpected consequences for his teaching. Whereas beforehand he used to say "I do not seek, I find," he states, he has now inverted the order, to say

"I do not find, I seek."[1] He then moves on to something extremely revealing: other people, if they are willing, may accompany him on this path. It is striking to see the extent to which Lacan's colleagues begin to take the floor in these last seminars. It is Lacan who invites them to do this; they thus explore and resolve problems together, on an equal basis; or even end up giving Lacan himself instruction, as did the topologists we mentioned earlier, Soury and Thomé. We should also mention Michel Vappereau, who gave a presentation in Lacan's penultimate seminar, *Topology and Time*. These teaching developments show how in this last period Lacan found himself urgently seeking a program of research oriented by his increasing attachment to topological terms. This is undoubtedly a question inherently bound up with issues of the knot and the chain, in other words with the "scriptive" operations and transformations linked to them.

As we observed in Chapter 4, after the initial "shock" we return in one way or another to the questions that have been posed, left open—and thus we go along with Lacan's own method. We might say that our trajectory does not consist in returning to our point of departure having made a 360° turn, but in turning full circle—at least twice—in an interior eight. Due to this, we will have to return to a crucial question we touched on in the previous chapter: that of the proper name. Here, it is a question of what travels or circulates and cannot be translated—at least not, as we have mentioned, without a parodic, mocking, or degrading effect. As we saw, with *Jaclaque*

---

1. J. Lacan, *Séminaire XXV "Le Moment de conclure*," Session of March 14, 1978, unpublished.

Han! the speaker transformed his name into a common noun. This amounted to a kind of "relief," dislodging the name to which we may be attached or which may encumber us.

Let us return to Joyce. We recall how *joy* echoed "joie" and "jeu'" [play]; and we noted that the name can often entail a project, a motivation, signpost, or obligation, among other symbolic effects in the Real. It was Joyce himself who played with humorous transformations of his name, as we shall see. This chapter will explore some of the material in the *Selected Letters*, an exemplary text for studying a whole series of important points, beyond those proposed by Lacan in his seminar, even if in the same spirit. In a letter of November 15, 1926, to his frequent correspondent, Harriet Shaw Weaver, sent together with the beginning of *Finnegans Wake*, Joyce writes:

> Dear Madam: Above please find prosepiece ordered in sample form. Also key to same. Hoping said sample meets with your approval
>
> yrs trly
> Jeems Jokes[2]

The signature exemplifies Joyce's method: a joke coming after a formal, stereotypical statement. Joyce's self-mockery playfully violates some very serious protocols—those of phonic identity as well as genealogy. Ultimately, it amounts to yet again reducing the proper name to a common noun. Lacan was similarly "inspired" with his *Jaclaque Han!*; although the shift from James Joyce to Jeems Jokes is also, obviously, a reference to humor and cheekiness. In short, the pun sets up Jeems Jokes as nominative suppletion.

---

2. *Selected Letters of James Joyce*, op. cit., p. 316.

For Lacan, what constitutes us as proper name also covers "a meaning." We must, however, point to one instance that nothing can reflect, as meaning itself is located there: the Borromean knot. In this chain—to give its correct designation—meaning is an effect of structure, which logically precedes it, once again reminding us that topology *is* structure. Thus, meaning is located in the intersection of the Imaginary and the Symbolic.

In the next chapter, we will investigate those points where the trefoil knot comes undone. When such a failure of the knot to cohere occurs, Lacan—perhaps half-jokingly—dubs it a "lapsus," as in Freudian "slip." We must, however, emphasize a crucial difference here. A "slip" in the knot is a *conceptual* mistake that occurs in the domain of knowledge (as in the simple geographical error of someone declaring, "We are in Buenos Aires, the capital of Rio de Janeiro"—easy to correct and easily accepted by the speaker); whereas with a Freudian slip, the subject is ashamed and disturbed by the error. When a speaker makes this kind of slip, he is caught by, shown to depend upon, his condition as subject of enunciation, which makes him seek to conceal the error. This explains what we have noted concerning Lacan's joke here, which is probably aimed to show that we are always partially "mixed up in" the chain-knot. It is important to bear this in mind if we are to grasp how Lacan's project is a *Work in Progress*, in other words a constant search, no longer defined by "I do not seek, I find" but by its inverse.

What, then, is Lacan searching for in this instance? To isolate the knot or the chain that is appropriate to Joyce. To do this, it is first necessary to locate the points where the triple Borromean knot "slips." We will trace Lacan's commentary here, beginning with the two minimal elements for drawing the chain: the circle on the right-hand side (S) is here placed below the other circle (R) (Figure 29):

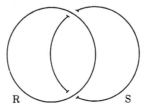

Figure 29

The third circle (I) that knots together the two others must pass, each time it crosses S, underneath the latter (Figure 30):

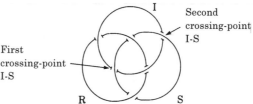

Figure 30

What happens if, on the contrary, I passes above S? The circle remains detached, the Symbolic is unknotted. Here, Lacan makes his first proposition in the attempt to understand Joyce's knot: there is no doubt that this knot is not a triple Borromean chain, as such a chain has not been able to form. This leads to the next claim made by Lacan on his Joycean trajectory: in order to make up for this failure of the chain to form, a fourth order has to be included. This will bind together the chain, and thus grant it Borromean status: it becomes the quadruple Borromean knot, now dubbed *sinthome*. As emphasized in Chapter 2, it is impossible for the quadruple chain to form unless, initially, the first three orders have come apart.

Does this entail a lapsus, or is it a structural condition? Or to put it another way: Is the *sinthome* a kind of repair, or does it bind together the structure in a way that is indispensable? For in fact—and this is something Lacan sheds no light on—if these slips in the knot take place, not only does S become detached but so do R and I too. This, as we have shown, is a necessary condition of the quadruple Borromean layout. Here, we can perhaps see that using the knot as a theoretical support is not wholly congruent with Lacan's argument; only through an arbitrary reduction can one say that the S alone comes free in such a disintegrating knot. This is how it is written (Figure 31):

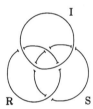

Figure 31

By the final session of Seminar 23, Lacan will no longer support this conception. Instead, he argues for something different: the circle that comes away is now I, the Imaginary, and it is there that the reknotting to tie it back in takes place. Thus, it will be necessary for something to be attached to the Imaginary if it is to be prevented from drifting away; and this is linked to what we have already indicated: R and S enchained, and no longer superimposed. (We will come back to this point below.)

We now turn once again to the question of *imposed speech* that we have already touched on at various points. It is important to stress that our activity of sewing (and we must account for both the metaphorical character of this, and its structural quality: "sewing" entails a vital activity to which one devotes one's life—hence its status as *sinthome*) cannot occur in an identical manner at any two places. What Joyce carries out with his art, which Lacan terms *sinthome*, is not a restoration of the knot that can take place simply at any point at all. And as if this were not enough, Lacan introduces another knot (composed of only one element) with five crossing-points that he baptizes, with humor rather than megalomania, "Lacan's knot." If we keep to the principle of under/over alternation, this knot might be written as follows (Figures 32, 33):

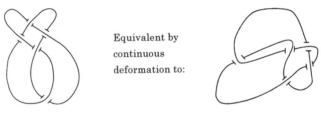

Equivalent by continuous deformation to:

Figure 32   Figure 33

Lacan would admit that, if he had been an entomologist, he would have liked to present the world with, say, "Lacan's tarantula." It is not a matter of vanity; such names are quite common in medicine (as in "Koch bacillus" or "Alzheimer's"). Just as we might therefore refer to "Lacan's knot," we can also talk of a "Lacanian psychosis," as we shall see. In both cases, Lacan does not specify what is at stake in applying a proper name to a knot or a psychosis, but he shows us this through what he does. Likewise, Lacan teaches that Joyce was able to make his name travel: he first made himself a name and then put it into circulation far beyond his own "neighborhood," by introducing a new signifier.

Nevertheless, Lacan appears not to ascribe the least importance to the knot made up of five elements, while he gives greater significance to the psychosis associated with it. We will now examine this psychosis, as, among other peculiarities, it entails a constellation that cannot be located within established diagnostic limits. It resembles a paranoiac delusion and was diagnosed as such; but Lacan claims that the classical categories cannot account for it, and thus gives it a new name.

The "Lacanian psychosis" is characterized as a case of imposed speech. In what way does this connect with Seminar 23? Due to the fact that the patient in question is spoken to by voices. "They speak to him": let us note this formula, which as we know constitutes a good diagnostic criterion for distinguishing between neurosis and psychosis. The patient does not know where these voices come from; he can only say that they are not his. There is clearly no sense of it being a "voice of consciousness," as the subject has no knowledge of—has foreclosed—his place in enunciation. But Lacan comments perceptively—like Freud in his ability to grasp essential questions—that this man is "canny" insofar as he sees that these words that are so disturbing and ungovernable derive from the Other. Of course, something must have taken place to allow him to formulate a structural condition in this way. If we recall Freud's text *Mourning and Melancholia*, we might note a similar kind of argument here. We can paraphrase the melancholiac's discourse as follows: "I am excrement, I am worthless, I upset everybody, I don't know how anyone could love me. I am an egotist and a miser, so I do not deserve to live." In short, the melancholic lays claim without modesty to having perpetrated the worst of the world's disasters. And with his usual brilliance Freud, when confronted with this, does not contradict the speaker but confirms his utterance. Is there not a truth being spoken here, one applicable to everybody? Freud's conclusion is that to attain such an overwhelming degree of honesty, the subject must have fallen ill. For we all think of ourselves as having good intentions, acting for the good of our neighbors and so on; and crimes are even committed in the name of love, religion, the wish to cleanse hygienically the filth of the world. This is always based, of course, on the noblest intentions and the defense of high ideals. This degree of hypocrisy, evidence of a cynical jouissance utterly lacking in honesty, seems to be natural in the speaking being caught up in *ce qu'on dit ment* ["what is said is a lie"]. In the Freudian tradition, Lacan concludes that this patient is speaking the truth when he claims that voices are speaking to him. We should note here Lacan's use of didactic examples and the irony he brings to bear. He is certainly not seeking to "promote" such a psychosis, but he shows how its logic gives it a certain appearance of truth. What interests Lacan about this man he questions in a clinical interview (in our view, an exemplary one) is his claim to be telepathic. He does not, however, claim to be a telepathic receiver, as one might expect, but an emitter: he can, he says, transmit his thoughts to another.

In the previous chapter we emphasized the psychotic's lack of privacy. The very act of submitting to a public clinical interview is a pathognomical equivalent of the man's affliction. Words pass into and out of the psychotic, as it were, without the slightest hindrance by any sense of privacy, something that is bound up with the structure of neurosis. Lacan thus begins his interview with the subject by focusing on his questions, in other words, with no interpretation. We can nevertheless observe, in the course of the interview, a guiding thread that indicates a hidden objective. In this case, Lacan shows how one should work if one understands how to direct the treatment, and if one has a certain experience: he makes use of a technique that in fact is far from obvious. Thus, he never announces "I will do such-and-such," but rather tacitly suggests to his audience what he is seeking in a singular manner. How does Lacan begin the presentation? By asking the patient about his name.[3] The theory of the proper name is thus brought into play. The patient had first of all stated that he felt "a little disjointed in regard to language," which entailed a "disjunction between the dream and the reality. . . . I am constantly making the imaginative flow." What he calls the imaginative is his own world, as opposed to "what is called reality." Now, the man replies to Lacan that his name is Gérard Primeau, which seems to leave the questioner in doubt as to the patient's "true" name. What follows is the patient's account of how he punningly transformed his name—precisely like a Joycean joke—into *Geai Rare Prime Au*. He thus imagined that he had "created" a name different from the one imposed upon him. As he puts it: "I had fragmented my name to create."[4]

Lacan tells Gérard that he has heard about his affliction, which the patient himself has termed *imposed* speech, and asks him about this. The man answers:

> [sentences] emerge as though I was perhaps manipulated . . . I am not manipulated, but I cannot explain myself. . . . It comes all at once [the voices tell him]: *You killed the*

3. "A Lacanian Psychosis: Interview by Jacques Lacan," in *Returning to Freud: Clinical Psychoanalysis in the School of Lacan*, ed. and trans. S. Schneiderman. New Haven, CT: Yale University Press, 1980, pp. 19–20.

4. Ibid., p. 20.

bluebird. It's an anarchic system. Sentences which have no rational meaning in banal language and which are imposed on my brain, on my intellect.

Another imposed sentence, he states, is "Mr. D. [a doctor] is nice," and here he has to add a "reflexive" sentence beginning with "but." That is, the imposed sentence occurs and subsequently has to be "counterbalanced" with another sentence of his own. Only this second kind of sentence, beginning with "but," is acknowledged by Primeau as his own.

Let us recall our discussion in Chapter 1 of the *sinthome*'s "formula" *tout, mais pas ça* ["everything, but not that"]. In psychosis, such a constellation becomes purely oppositional or negative; it should thus be considered in this structure as a refusal of the external world, a refusal to be captured through adaptation to collective fantasy. Hence, by extension, the fact that the place of the "but" in the formula of the *sinthome* indicates precisely the place of the subject, its initial inflection as emitter. This is why, conversely, Primeau suffers the imposed speech as receiver. Let us pursue the example quoted above. Beginning with "Mr. D. is nice," it continues "but I am insane." Here, it is not the content that interests us; we can easily see that it does not entail—in terms of the place of the subject—a self-eulogy or anything of the kind. This is why the statement following the "but" marks the recuperation of the subject's place, something that goes beyond any semantic signal of a narcissistic kind. What Primeau does is, in his own words, "compensate," "recover the imposed sentences," at the same time recognizing in himself "several kinds of voices" in order to deal with what he calls "emerging sentences." Consequently, we have imposed speech, emerging sentences, and later on, the arrival of the "reflexive."

Of course, as usually happens with this type of patient, Primeau knows perfectly well how he has been diagnosed, is familiar with his doctors and recalls what took place in his encounters with various psychiatrists. He can thus state that in 1974 he was diagnosed as suffering from a "paranoid delusion." Interestingly, as he says this, Lacan notices how the patient turns in his chair—he is in a room crowded with people—and suddenly gazes at someone. Lacan asks him what is going on, and Gérard responds: "I felt that he was mocking me." This comment makes Lacan justify the presence of others in whom he has "full confidence"; in an apparently naive, but effective, way, he tells the patient that these people are interested in hearing him. Primeau continues, explaining that his "imagination creates another world," and that he lives much of his life from and in this other world. He next states, "All speech has the force of law, all speech is signifying"' (the psychosis here is clearly a Lacanian one). Lacan's inevitable question is, "Where did you find this expression, 'all speech is signifying'?"; and Primeau's response, "It's a personal reflection," is evidently untrue—he had found the phrase in precisely the *Écrits* produced by his interviewer. The patient knew very well who was to question him; as he comments, "You are a rather well-known personality." This was why he was anxious in Lacan's presence. In short, Primeau's extremely sensitive willingness to learn from the voices, which were really nothing but letters, highlights another element that justifies us calling his case a "Lacanian" psychosis: the patient begins to talk in "Lacanese," with a fair amount of transitivist, specular "adequation," a kind of robotic engagement with his interviewer's discourse. Let us consider certain other features of this case, in order to link them to another case of overwhelming significance to our investigation—that of Lucia Joyce.

Primeau tells Lacan that he suffered a depression due to a disappointment in love. Immediately afterward, he brings in a point that confirms a crucial stage of Lacan's reflections on psychosis. He is led to reformulate Freud's ideas about the case of Schreber, which Freud had claimed showed the homosexual basis of paranoiac dementia. Lacan's clarification here is very shrewd: it is not a question, in such a psychosis, of homosexuality but of a transsexual dimension. This is clear. At a certain moment, what breaks out in Schreber, in the famous ecstatic fascination and fantasmatic appropriation, is not homosexual desire. He writes that "it would be marvelous to be a woman during the act of coitus"; and thus is oriented to a transformation of sex, not to homosexuality. Moreover, a notion as vaguely defined as homosexuality almost amounts to empty speech; as an explanation of the background of paranoia, such a notion is too general to produce any actual knowledge. Analysands themselves, indeed, take such an allusion to "underlying homosexuality" as a weapon for further "rounding off" the Imaginary; in the treatment of neurotics, such an explanation leads only to effects of narcissistic resistance. In Primeau's case, what occurs is what Lacan terms a "push-to-woman," resembling the Schreber case with its theme of becoming a woman. For a little boy with a "rather limp dick," as Lacan puts it, the weight of the phallic position becomes hard to bear; this situation ends up as a "push-to-woman." As with Schreber, the inability to be the Phallus lacked by the mother leaves only the solution of being the woman lacked by men.[5] Primeau confirms the "energetic'" force powering this push-to-woman. Speaking

5. J. Lacan, "On a Question Preliminary . . . ," *Écrits: A Selection*, p. 207.

of a particular woman, he says, "Claude did not wear make-up. This lady [pointing to a woman in the audience] has put on make-up." Lacan, once again showing how the incorporation of theory into his work allows him a relaxed, spontaneous method, asks: "Do you ever put on make-up yourself?"

> Mr. Primeau: Yes, it happens that I put on make-up. It has happened to me, yes (he smiles). It happened to me when I was nineteen, because I had the impression . . . I had a lot of sexual complexes . . . because nature endowed me with a very small phallus.
>
> Dr. Lacan: Tell me a little bit about that.
>
> Mr. Primeau: I had the impression that my sex was shrinking, and I had the impression that I was going to become a woman.
>
> Dr. Lacan: Yes.
>
> Mr. Primeau: I had the impression that I was going to become a transsexual.[6]

What is interesting here is that transsexualism responds to a medical demand; in one sense, it is produced by that demand. Who really sets this kind of story in motion? Normally, whoever wishes to change sex. But unless there were someone, empirically speaking, able to carry out the required operation, transsexualism could not exist. How, then, can Primeau speak of being able by himself to become a transsexual? He is no doubt referring to a "spontaneous" sex change with no recourse to surgery, to a "feeling" of shrinkage in what supports the place of the Phallus.

---

6. "A Lacanian Psychosis," op. cit., pp. 30–31.

Lacan continues to question the patient in order to discover if he has already felt himself to be a woman. Primeau responds, "No, I saw myself as a woman in a dream, but . . ." (note once again the occurrence of this "but"). There follows a fascinating exchange in which Lacan comes to state that if Primeau lives, as he believes, inside a "solitary circle," where imagination or the "imaginative" governs, he must be constrained inside the circle. A kind of debate then arises: Lacan seems to wish to corner the patient with implacable logic, indicating that he is confined to the inside of that zone, while Primeau insists that it is "my solitary circle where I live without boundaries." And he tells Lacan, somewhat surprisingly, "You think in geometrical terms."[7] Lacan of course immediately accepts this description, but replies by asking if Gérard too does not think geometrically.

We thus get to the fundamental issue: what has most perturbed Primeau is in fact the question of telepathy. It drove him to a suicide attempt, as he could no longer bear having no privacy, not having his own thoughts. Telepathy, precisely, is the hinge that will allow us to move from Primeau to Lucia Joyce. The telepathy of the Lacanian psychotic, we recall, is that of emission; as Primeau puts it, "It is the transmission of thought. I am a telepathic emitter." Lacan tries once again to contradict him, telling him that in general telepathy relates to "the domain of reception." The patient, however, is certain: he "is" the emitter, he is absolutely sure of it. Besides, it is easy to "verify": you only need to observe that others respond to any stimulation at all, and the subject attributes this fact to his being the center of emission. In one way or

---

7. Ibid., p. 34.

another, this confirms, in addition, that others know what happens to him.

The interview conducted by Lacan no doubt deserves closer attention; but the present work is not the right context for the task. Conversely, we should draw attention to the end of the interview, given what we have said concerning the proper name, Lacan's knot, a Lacanian psychosis, and so on. There, he states: "When we get into details, we see that the classical treatises do not exhaust the question." He once again gives emphasis to the particular, whereas the "classical treatises" generalize. And he continues:

> A few months ago I examined someone who had been labeled a Freudian psychosis. Today we have seen a "Lacanian" psychosis . . . very clearly marked. With these "imposed speeches," the imaginary, the symbolic and the real. It is because of that very fact that I am not very optimistic for this young man. He has the feeling that the imposed speech has been getting worse. The feeling that he calls "telepathy" is one more step. Besides, this feeling of being seen puts him in despair. I don't see how he is going to get out of it. There are suicide attempts which end up succeeding. Yes. This is a clinical picture which you will not find described, even by good clinicians like Chaslin. It is to be studied.[8]

No doubt, Lacan's prognostic remarks do not augur well. This Lacanian psychosis allows Lacan to return to what happened to Joyce's daughter Lucia, and the episode where her father defended her by claiming that she had powers of telepa-

---

8. Ibid., p. 41.

thy. For Lacan, Lucia was an "extension" of Joyce's *sinthome*. We would add that this went as far as blocking off Joyce's ability to grasp the disruptive effects of his symptoms. This was why he defended his daughter: he believed in her. Another way of putting this would be to describe Lucia as "syntonic" with her father. According to Joyce, she was more intelligent than everybody else, and she was able to inform him miraculously about the fate of certain individuals. In Lacan's view, the respective correspondences no doubt bear witness to this. As far as we are concerned, after a thorough examination of the letters we would say that this testimony is at the very least debatable, not being at all clear. On the other hand, what is clear is the discussion of these questions by Richard Ellmann, Joyce's biographer and major editor. We will quote him at some length, which will give rise to quite a few surprises concerning Joyce, Lucia, and the triple Borromean chain.

In his edition of Joyce's *Selected Letters*, Ellmann gives an account of an occurrence belonging to the domain of *Tuche*, of unexpected accident: the coincidence of the death of Joyce's father and the undeniable collapse of Lucia's mental health. As Ellmann explains in his biography of Joyce, Lucia had always suffered from psychical problems, although this had been treated by her parents merely as childish eccentricity. Here, Lacan is able to make a resonant clinical point: that what happens to Lucia is a direct index of Joyce's radical paternal deficit. The argument, as we deduce, is tri-generational; what determines Joyce's conception of his daughter's state is the radical lack around paternity, in relation to his own father, John Joyce. How does Joyce react to the obvious schizophrenic episodes afflicting Lucia? Ellmann reports that in 1932, Lucia's schizophrenia, "which had presumably begun during her girlhood," started to show full-blown symptoms; and Joyce's father had died at the end of 1931. This was the dangerous, or *tuchic*, coincidence. Ellmann goes on to narrate how Lucia's father made "a frantic and unhappily futile effort to cure her," trying "every means known to medicine as well as . . . simples of his own devising. He felt in some sense responsible for her condition, and refused to accept any diagnosis which did not promise hope. It seemed to him that her mind was like his own [this is certainly echoed by Lacan's claims], and he tried to find evidence in her writing and in her drawing of unrecognized talent."[9] Here, it is worth mentioning that Lucia even came to produce drawings and designs for her father's books. Ellmann continues:

> Lucia spent long and short periods in sanatoriums and mental hospitals, between which she would return to stay with her parents until some incident occurred which made it necessary she be sent away again. Joyce found doctors to give her glandular treatments, others to inject sea water, others to try psychotherapy; he sent her on visits to friends in Switzerland, England and even Ireland.[10]

As can be imagined, this was a profoundly distressing period, and it provides some "background" to the jokes aimed at Freud and Jung. To sum up, then, Joyce's refusal to accept what was happening to his daughter is read by Lacan as a sign of the radical paternal deficit that culminated in his own inability to assume the place of father.

There is no doubt that Lacan's formulation here has a wider significance, beyond the story of Joyce's family. In effect, the

---

9. *Selected Letters of James Joyce*, op. cit., p. 263.
10. Ibid.

place of the son—since it caught up in a compound, not merely a dual relation—is never simply a single place. This basic psychoanalytic teaching is ignored by many contemporary theories, including some proclaiming themselves to be psychoanalytic. For such conceptions, paternity and maternity are to be thought of in terms of what the child accepts or rejects, in a purely dual relation. Lucia was clearly greatly loved by Joyce, who made immense efforts to cure her of her "eccentricity." Yet he was never able to assume the place of her father. Here, we encounter a significant "detail," which returns us to a question we have already touched upon—that of whether or not Joyce was mad. Our response must be negative: his knot is not simply a trefoil, but a repaired trefoil. Conversely, his daughter was mad.

To explore this in more detail, we should focus on another of Joyce's letters, written to Harriet Shaw Weaver on May 1, 1935. Concerning

> . . . a proposal to bring Lucia to a medical gentleman who has studied psycho-analysis in the United States, I at once cabled calling that off. . . . After a good deal of talking I induced my wife to write to Lucia so that letters which now arrive are addressed to us both. This is a slight advance. But while I am glad in a way that Lucia is out of the dangers of Paris and especially of London every ring of the doorbell gives me an electric shock as I never know what the postman or telegraph boy is going to bring in. And if it is bad news all the blame will fall on me.[11]

It is truly astonishing here to see Joyce assume the typical parental position of heroic and sacrificial jouissance, and,

---

11. Ibid., p. 376.

absorbed by this image, scorn any assistance offered by the Other. He continues:

> . . . everybody else apparently thinks she is crazy. She behaves like a fool very often but her mind is as clear and as unsparing as the lightning [this is indeed the basis of Lacan's understanding of her "telepathy"]. She is a fantastic being speaking a curious abbreviated language of her own. I understand it or most of it.[12]

Hence Lacan's conclusion: Lucia is an extension of the Joycean *sinthome*. Only he can understand her, nobody else can: the code is shared by none but the two of them. As Joyce comments: "So long as she was within reach I always felt I could control her—and myself."[13] This position of complementarity—which does not constitute the place of a subject—of mutual control, to-and-fro: this position justifies Lacan's notion of the extension of the *sinthome* and the consequent mutual identification.

We will now attempt to outline certain points that are not tackled in Seminar 23, although they are in a sense implied by some questions raised there. We begin with another of Joyce's letters to Weaver, this one from June 1936:

> The reason I keep on trying by every means to find a solution for her case (which may come at any time as it did with my eyes) is that she may not think that she is left with a blank future as well.[14]

---

12. Ibid.
13. Ibid.
14. Ibid., pp. 380–381.

He goes on to refer to a "mysterious malady" afflicting his two children, and says that he is ready to endure economic misery if he can thus obtain the funds for Lucia's cure. But this pledge is made in a very curious manner: if we bear in mind Weaver's role as patroness—what is the debt that Joyce thinks he is owed?—we will be able to see the place occupied by this dysfunctional exchange of a phallic token, at once a hinge and an ecstatic, wretched jouissance. Joyce writes to Weaver: "If you have ruined yourself for me as seems highly probable why will you blame me if I ruin myself for my daughter?" A son has ruined one father; and more or less the same occurs in the next generation. Once this new aspect of the *père-sonnores* has been stated, Joyce adds: "Of what use will any sum or provision be to her if she is allowed, by the neglect of others calling itself prudence, to fall into the abyss of insanity?"[15] Note that it is only other people who will allow her to fall into insanity, while Joyce insistently pictures himself as the healer, defending Lucia against anything to do with psychoanalysis.

This rejection of psychoanalysis can also be seen elsewhere. We might turn to information provided by a close friend of Joyce's, Italo Svevo, the celebrated author of *Confessions of Zeno*. Svevo—or, to give him his real name, Ettore Schmitz—got to know Joyce in Trieste, and asked him for English lessons. Joyce repeatedly refused this request, holding up Svevo's work for a long time; only later did they come to assist one another in crucial ways. Although Svevo was older than Joyce, he looked on the Irishman as his master; his book *James Joyce* testifies to this, as well as making some interesting points. We

---

15. Ibid.

should start with an editorial note in this little book, referring to Svevo's notion that Joyce was completely unaware of the work of Freud: "This is a surprising claim for Svevo to make. Joyce was certainly familiar with Freud's work: as his brother recalls, he owned a copy of *The Psychopathology of Everyday Life* (1901) and was particularly interested in the essay *Leonardo Da Vinci and a Memory of His Childhood*. Moreover, Edoardo Weiss, who first introduced psychoanalysis to Italy in 1910, was a relative of Svevo's."[16] Why, then, this strange attempt to put distance between Joyce and Freud? Was it in order to attribute, regardless of facts, an absolute originality to Joyce's work? Svevo would have us believe that "Freud's thought did not appear soon enough to have aided Joyce in the creation of his work."[17] The point here is evidently to emphasize that Joyce had not been influenced in any way by the unfolding of psychoanalysis, and thus to uphold the creative originality of the master. But is to acknowledge the fact that Joyce knew Freud's work really to detract from his own? Not in our view; but Svevo, by contrast, continues his argument:

> This claim will astonish those readers who find in Stephen Dedalus so many elements that seem directly suggested by psychoanalytic doctrine. . . . Did Joyce not take from psychoanalysis the idea of transmitting the random thoughts of characters so that they appear without any constraint? Regarding the contribution of psychoanalysis here, we can

---

16. Editor's note: I. Svevo, *James Joyce*. Barcelona: Argonanta, 1990, p. 67.

17. It was, according to Jacques Aubert, Schmitz himself who introduced Joyce to reading Freud around 1910; cf. J. Aubert, Prologue to *Portrait de l'artiste en jeune homme, Letra freudiana: 13*, Retratura *de Joyce. Uma perspectiva lacaniana*. Rio de Janeiro, 1993, p. 47.

rule it out, given that Joyce himself indicated where he had found the technique: his comments were enough to bring fame to the elderly Edouard Dujardin, who thirty years before had invented that technique.[18]

Svevo is referring to the famous "stream of consciousness," and its variant the interior monologue; in other words, to the quasi-free association in the style and order of writing that we find, for instance, in the dense closing pages of "Penelope," the final episode of *Ulysses*. There Molly Bloom, with no recognition of grammatical breaks, gives free rein to the stream of her consciousness, the full expansion of her thoughts. According to Joyce, Dujardin was the master of this technique, as shown in his novel *Les lauriers sont coupés*. "As for the rest," concludes Svevo somewhat unconvincingly, "I can bear witness: in 1915, when Joyce left Trieste, he knew nothing about psychoanalysis." Svevo "bears witness" to their encounter in 1919, as follows: Joyce "was then in full rebellion against [psychoanalysis]: one of the scornful rebellions by which he warded off anything that might disrupt his thinking. He said to me: 'Psychoanalysis? Well, if we need it let us keep to confession.'"[19] This is a common misconception; in confession, however, one speaks of what is known and in terms of sin, whereas in psychoanalysis one speaks of what one does not know and in terms of a lack central to desire: castration. Here, we would point out how Svevo's fascination with Joyce precisely duplicates the shape of the latter's misrecognition of the father's traces: in an inversion, it is through Joyce that the "father" Dujardin will

---

18. I. Svevo, *James Joyce*, pp. 41–43.
19. Ibid.

become famous, according to Svevo. For Lacan, Joyce refuses to pay homage to the father; while for Svevo, this is only ultimately to win him collateral glory, putting him in (inverted) debt by "making" the name. In this sense, Svevo shares Joyce's denial of any trace of Freud, a denial that, as we will see, is a clinical as much as a literary matter.

We next turn to an astonishing letter by Lucia Joyce. It was written in one of her more lucid moments, on September 3, 1933, and addressed to Frank Budgen. What is so striking about this letter? We must recall here our opening chapters, in which we explored the question of the *filioque* in relation to the Trinity, concerning whether the Holy Spirit derives from both the Father and the Son, or the Father alone. In effect, as we stated, this problem marked a line separating occidental Christianity from oriental orthodoxy. This was precisely the reason for Lacan's view that Catholicism, when it incorporated the doctrine of the *filioque*, became the "true religion." This theological conflict is embedded in *Finnegans Wake* and touched on by Lucia, in the letter in question. On page 156 of the *Wake*, in the paragraph beginning "While that Mooksius . . . ," Joyce refers to the doctrinal quarrel. This is how Lucia tells her correspondent about it:

> . . . they have abolished the Filioque clause in the creed concerning which there has been a schism between western and eastern christendom for over a thousand years. . . . Of course the dogmas subsequently proclaimed by Rome after the split are not recognized by the east such as the Immaculate conception. See the Mooks and the Gripes that is West and east. . . . All the grotesque words in this are russian or greek for the three principal dogmas which separate Shem from Shaun [the twins who play a major role

in *Finnegans Wake*]. When he gets A and B on to his lap C slips off and when he has C and A he looses hold of B.[20]

The last line could almost be a reference to the missing link that prevents Borromean knotting, as if, Joyce having "said" it in his writing, Lucia remembers the allusion and draws attention to it. What is at stake is the effect of one of the three rings coming undone; this takes us back to Lacan's point about the "slip" that causes S to break free from the triple Borromean chain. Later, as we have seen, he considers this occurrence in terms of the Imaginary, where it gives rise to the subsequent reparation. Here, we can sketch in a certain assumption or intuition on Joyce's part concerning the chain and its implications. Lacan never mentions this letter; we do not know if he was aware of it or had paused over it. If he had done so, it would have helped him to confirm how much Joyce was affected, on a practical level, by "living" the knot—here mixed up with reflections on the Trinity in Lucia's letter.

As for imposed speech, it points to a striking link between Joyce and his daughter: both of them suffered in this respect. Nevertheless, there are crucial differences. As we emphasize below, it is the writer's invention of his work that is "responsible"—as *sinthome*—for opening an unbridgeable gap between the psychical problematics of father and daughter. Concerning this, we should stress Joyce's idea about the relations between his life and his work. If we look, for instance, at the same letter we examined in the previous chapter because of the joke aimed at Freud and Jung, we find him writing:

---

20. *Selected Letters of James Joyce*, op. cit., p. 367.

> My head is full of pebbles and rubbish and broken matches
> and bits of glass picked up 'most everywhere. The task I
> set myself technically in writing a book from eighteen dif-
> ferent points of view and in as many styles . . . , that and
> the nature of the legend chosen would be enough to upset
> anyone's mental balance. . . . After that I want a good long
> rest in which to forget *Ulysses* completely.[21]

The fragmentation Joyce undergoes in grappling with
these different points of view reminds us of the Morris dance
of signs he once mentioned. Writing, we can thus see, is a way
of attempting to give a certain coherence to these signs that
begin by filling his head like broken bits of rubbish, troubling
him and causing him immense fatigue.

In another letter, of 1926, Joyce sets forth his principal
ideas about language, writing: "One great part of every human
existence is passed in a state which cannot be rendered sen-
sible by the use of wideawake language, cutanddry grammar,
and goahead plot."[22] From this point on, Joyce strives to break
up these categories he lists by means of new insignia that must
be outlined. This attempt to disrupt representation takes Joyce
very far from the aesthetic credo put forward by Stephen in *A
Portrait*. Now, this Joycean disruption is crucial. How does
Lacan approach it? Joyce, he claims, strives to free himself
from the "verbal parasite," the cancer that inevitably afflicts
the speaking-being. In this sense, Lacan describes as "astute"
Primeau's recognition of the strangeness of imposed speech.
Both Joyce and the latter seek to get rid of a certain linguistic
parasite. But do Joyce's actions imply the ability to escape from

---

21. Ibid., p. 284.
22. Ibid., p. 318.

such a parasite or not? Lacan states that the writer "allows himself to be invaded by the essentially phonemic qualities of speech, by its polyphony." Does his singular writing therefore liberate Joyce or not? If polyphony reigns, one must accept all the associations and evocations carried by a word that one is used to considering as a univocal sign. The paradox is as follows: we become "free" of an omnipresent polyphony when we note of a word that it is precisely that one, and not another. When we fragment a word, begin to break it in pieces and assemble it with other words, we do exactly what Joyce does; but is this to affirm a writer's linguistic liberty or his inevitably "imposed" subjection to language? Paradoxically, Joyce precisely fails to "escape" from the imperative of the speaking-being. What Lacan tries to get across to us about Joyce highlights the singular work achieved by the writer by means of his jouissance. There is no doubt that Joyce's elaboration is unique, but this does not justify us in imagining that he was able to thrust aside the limitations that restrict us all as those who speak.

In this sense, we must return to the question of Joycean paternity: not in terms of Joyce's strictly empirical (and thus imaginary) relation to what we might term the instance of the real father, that of desire; but rather of the effect and currency of his *père-version*, in other words his *père-sonnores*. Concerning this, we have pointed out a crucial moment: in fact, between 1931 and Joyce's death ten years later, two major events marked his life—the death of his father (in Freud's view, the most transcendent event in a human life) and the definitive collapse of his daughter Lucia's mental health.

We will shortly examine some of Joyce's letters with metaphorical evocations of his father as well as his own comments about the question. This material, we think, was treated somewhat tangentially by Lacan in his seminar; so we propose a new key for reading it. We have already noted the relation between father and fatherland; indeed, if we dwell on this we may succumb to the commonplace assumption that derives the Motherland from a Mother Earth. For Joyce, Ireland is the representative of *père-sonnores*, above all relating to a very powerful "personality," a menacing, terrifying presence. What we will shortly see in Joyce's statements about his father and Ireland shows, on one side, the impossibility—due to a fantasmatic mortal danger—of his returning to his native land, even as he considers the actuality of doing so when his father dies. This is directly linked to his *père-version*: he turns to the father in both instances, corresponding to versions of the latter. This, in brief, is our psychoanalytic interpretation of John Gross's statement, which we looked at in the previous chapter: "The father and the fatherland have such importance in Joyce's work. . . ." Let us bear this in mind as we read the manifest content of the letters: if not, they will seem nothing but the devoted avowal of the mutual love between father and son.

On January 1, 1932, Joyce writes to another famous writer, T. S. Eliot. He apologizes for the delay in replying, due, he says, to the difficult time he has had with his father, who has just died:

> He had an intense love for me and it adds to my grief and remorse that I did not go to Dublin to see him for so many years. I kept him constantly under the illusion that I would come and was always in correspondence with him but an instinct which I believed in held me back from going, much as I longed to. *Dubliners* was banned there in 1912 on the advice of a person who was assuring me at the time of his great friendship. When my wife and

children went there in 1922, against my wish, they had to flee for their lives, lying flat on the floor of a railway carriage while rival parties shot at each other across their heads and quite lately I have had experience of malignancy and treachery on the part of people to whom I had done nothing but friendly acts. I did not feel myself safe and my wife and son opposed my going.[23]

The level of rationalization here is almost pathetic; apparently Joyce can only submit obediently to the orders of his wife and son! They might certainly have pleaded with him; but, again, if we interpret Joyce's words about the situation of mortal danger beyond their "concrete truth," we must conclude that, as is fairly obvious, he did not wish to return to Ireland. And this unwillingness to return, this "instinct," as he calls it, points to a marked rejection and an attachment to notions of treason or ill-speaking—a clearly paranoid *père-version*, metonymically linked to Ireland.

As for the real father, on a manifest level "everything was fine"; but the flow of associations marks the return, by way of what is split off, of the *père-sonnores*.

But this is not all: in another letter, addressed to Harriet Shaw Weaver several days later, on January17, he writes: "Why go on writing about a place I did not dare to go to at such a moment [i.e., his father's death], where not three persons know me or understand me (in the obituary notice the editor of the *Independent* raised objections to the allusion to me)? But after my experience with the blackmailers in England I had no wish to face the Irish thing."[24] We may read in

---

23. Ibid., p. 360.
24. Ibid.

this passage a constant displacement of Joyce's grief at his father's death—which, he tells Weaver, has left him in "prostration of mind"—onto a paranoid version of what is happening in Ireland. He goes on: "All my family and even my Irish friends were against it [i.e., his returning to Ireland for his father's burial]. My father had an extraordinary affection for me." Without an understanding of our key, the way Joyce talks of Dublin and Irish people, and then suddenly his father, might seem chaotic. But next he reinforces the compensatory side of his feelings: "He was the silliest man I ever knew and yet cruelly shrewd. He thought and talked of me up to his last breath." [But what proof does Joyce have of this, being so geographically remote from Dublin?] "I was very fond of him always, being a sinner myself, and even liked his faults."[25]

Here we add a digression concerning two interlinked questions. Joyce, in his own words, loved the fact that his father was a sinner. Lacan will likewise indicate that what he calls a "slip" in the trefoil knot may also be called an error or *faute*. This latter term has a double acceptation: that of "making an error" [*faire une faute*] and that of something lacking or "in default" [*faute de* . . .]. The Joycean constellation corresponds to this double meaning; thus the play or pun that allows the entanglement of the trefoil when it is not tied in the standard way. Joyce loved the faults of his father. As he puts it: "Hundreds of pages and scores of characters in my books came from him." This is why James is not only talking about his father when he openly refers to him. In the hundreds of scenes, he continues to show the extent to which he is burdened by the father; that is, endlessly seeking him and

---

25. Ibid., pp. 360–361.

at the same time denying him. The search for closeness goes even as far as finding physical resemblance, things in common. What has Joyce received from his father?

> I got from him his portraits, a waistcoat, a good tenor voice [we recall: *père-son*] and an extravagant licentious disposition (out of which, however, the greater part of any talent I may have springs) but, apart from these, something else I cannot define. But if an observer thought of my father and myself and my son too physically, though we are all very different, he could perhaps define it. It is a great consolation to me to have such a good son.[26]

As we can see here in a real sense, Joyce's vision of his life makes clear the relevance of the Lacanian notion of the articulation of three generations in terms of *la faute*, sin, error, or that which lacks.

---

26. Ibid., p. 361.

The Sinthome, *Disinvested*
from the Unconscious

We have now tackled the preliminaries necessary for us to approach the different modes of possible reparation at work in the failed trefoil knot.[1] In what sense are these reparations different? As we have indicated, Lacan points out that if we pause over the crossing-points—we will number them 1, 2, 3 (and the "reparation" entails simply adding one more strand)—it is possible to arrange the knot, in principle with no variations, so that it appears to be a trefoil. Here are the numbered crossing-points in a "successful" trefoil (Figure 34):

---

1. As indicated above, in the seminar *Identification* Lacan introduces (on May 16, 1962) both the trefoil knot and a "failed" version of it, the failure due to a "slip" in the way it is tied (a point that Lacan does not seem to have particularly highlighted). In addition, Lacan links to these knots the interior or inverted eight, which is prevented from becoming a circle by the fact that it is knotted by a second instance. Since this second instance does not follow—according to the drawing that transcribes it—the over/under alternation, the result can only resemble Whitehead's double chain, which we will return to directly.

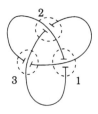

Figure 34

In Chapter 5 we discussed the reparation at point 1. We will now inscribe the remaining "slipped" crossing-points (Figure 35):

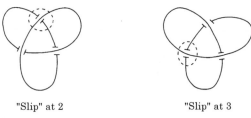

"Slip" at 2   "Slip" at 3

Figure 35

These are the equivalent reparations, including of course a second element as suppletion (Figure 36):

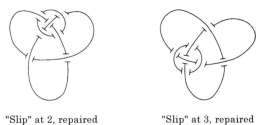

"Slip" at 2, repaired   "Slip" at 3, repaired

Figure 36

These two reparations, which are not shown as diagrams in Seminar 23, are obtained according to a well-known principle: the new line of the suppletion passes above the top line and below the bottom line. Thus, we are now dealing with an imitation of the triple knot (i.e., with three crossing-points), although strictly speaking it is a chain made up of two elements. What these two reparations have in common—which moreover distinguishes them from that of the slip at point 1— is that they are governed by the principle of "inversion," to use Lacan's term from the seminar (or "inversibility," according to another transcription); even if a more precise topological term would have been "interversion." Why is this? Because once again we should not be content with a simple semantic superimposition of these terms—which in addition would only be partial—in order to avoid everything becoming a mere play of synonymy. It is therefore a question of a topological *writing*, which consists in the following: through continuous deformation—without cutting—it is possible to draw the following results from compensations 2 and 3, and to obtain an eight and a circle. In this writing, we will represent the circle with a dotted line (Figure 37):

Figure 37

This is the first step, barely preparatory, in the operation of interversion. The second step depends—once again through continuous deformation—on verifying this principle: the circle is susceptible to being transformed into the eight and vice versa, maintaining the same crossing-points as shown in the previous diagram, and likewise the same clockwise movement (Figure 38):

Figure 38

These two instances are thus interchangeable, which is not the case when the reparation occurs at point 1. At 2 and 3, we can state that there is an equivalence of the instances at work; with 1, by contrast, we are able to preserve the heterogeneity, the nonequivalence, of the instances. We recall that the latter principle is also valid for the quadruple Borromean knot, but not for the triple. In this sense, it is hard to see why Lacan repeatedly emphasizes, concerning both kinds of knot, the nodal importance he ascribes to heterogeneity.

The above is reinforced by the fact that the structure formed by the eight and the circle—also known as Whitehead's knot or chain—was put forward a few years ago by E. Porge, following Lacan's inspiration, as an appropriate way to write the knot of fantasy. In the latter, the eight is from the outset the divided subject, while the circle is the object $a : (\mathcal{S} <> a)$, the formula of fantasy with interchangeable elements.[2] For this reason, if we take it to be true that the end of analysis is centered on the question of fantasy, the schema of interversive

---

2. Cf. R. Harari, "Identificacion interversiva," in *De qué trata. . . ?*, op. cit., pp. 181–189.

equivalence has not been exceeded, given that the terms are compatible with such an operation. And the spirit of the final Lacan, on the contrary, is to place the accent on heterogeneity, which occurs in reparation at point 1, where he situates—in this particular approach—the *sinthome*. In this sense, when, due to the *sinthome*, equivalence does not prevail, there is sexual relation: it is this that Lacan's argument leads to. We should thus ask ourselves, in that case what has become of the oft-repeated aphorism "there is no sexual relation"? Lacan's response is that there is "thus both sexual relation and no relation. . . ." But we are surprised to see this relation located in such a way: there is relation only if the *sinthome*, for "every man," is a woman. The latter here being, of course, not interchangeable with the man.

Where is the *sinthome* for every man? In what is closest and most familiar to him: his woman. However, this is not reciprocal—or else we would be making the mistake of supposing the two positions to be interchangeable, equivalent, practically equal. It is for this reason that the man is not *sinthome* for the woman. He could be anything at all, Lacan tells us, be he devastation or plague, in short "whatever you like"—but not *sinthome*. This is the result, to the extent that there is a lack of equivalence; in this sense, "it is quite clear that we need to find another name. . . ."

An attempt to trace this line of thinking in Lacan's work reveals that it is somewhat incongruous there, and that in fact he does not support it for very long. In the talks from the *Journées de l'École freudienne de Paris*, when he presents his conclusions on July 9, 1978, he reveals a different position. To begin with, he returns to the idea that the symptom is what falls conjointly, for *ptoma* means "fall." What does Lacan mean here? At the very least, to link what "chooses together" to the theme of the couple entails a little strategic trickery. In order to shed light on this point, we might turn to one of those popular phrases that is continually and spontaneously uttered: "there are never two without a third." It is thus inappropriate to think of simply progressing from two to three, just as such a progression is impossible, as we have seen, when moving from the triple to the quadruple Borromean knot. Three, then, makes two possible; and two signifies three, we might say, for if by definition there are two in the couple, since one has to do with the other, which one retroacts onto the first? This is not enough, because there is a deciphering at work here, and that implies, calls for three elements. I write two, but rigorously speaking I count the one, then the two, and lastly the act of deciphering. The symptom is of this order: that of the three that falls conjointly with the two. (We will soon return to this question of what qualifies things as Borromean).

This is the basis for an understanding of what Lacan stated not long after having given Seminar 23, around 1978. In the Conclusions we referred to above, he claims that the symptom chooses together [*ensemble*], but has no relation with the set or group [*ensemble*]. He thus calls on the ambiguity of the French term *ensemble*, once again positing the principle of heterogeneity. For what is a symptom? No doubt an occurrence that disrupts any harmony, given that it forms part of no set or series; to put it in Freud's words, it is an "internal foreign land." We have no idea why we have a symptom; it is suffered, but we know it belongs to us. The subject, as we have said, believes in the hidden meaning of the symptom, and that this meaning is linked to his own life. In other words, he does not believe that someone else has imposed it on him (in the sense of imposed speech, although the symptom shares its ungovernable quality).

Lacan declares: "A *sinthome* [and no longer a symptom] is not a fall, although it seems to be one." What does the term "fall" indicate here? It should be taken, according to our reading, as pointing to a sort of downgrading of each person's *élan* or "zest"; as we have already indicated, this is a question of impulse. The symptom clearly obstructs this impulsive register; by relating to what does not function in the Real, it shows forth how the scope of the speaking-being's freedom is restricted. As for the *sinthome*, Lacan indicates that it entails the contrary; thus, its condition is not that of a fall. And he goes further: "So much so that I consider you all out there, insofar as you are, you have every Jack as *sinthome* his Jill. There is a he-*sinthome* and a she-*sinthome*." Here the discrepancy with the claims made in Seminar 23 becomes manifest: there is a he-*sinthome* and a she-*sinthome* and "that's all that's left of the so-called sexual relation." If there is no interversive equivalence, what survives as sexual relation, all that's left of it, is for every man to take his woman and vice versa, always as *sinthome*. Thus the sexual relation, or all that's left of it, is an *intersinthomal* relation. This is the "repaired" remains of the sexual relation; in other words, each individual supports the "remaining," bound sexual relation in accordance with whatever one's *sinthome* incarnates. If the relation were supported by the symptom, they would begin to fall together, opening a space for a pathology of mutual stimulation, of falling. If, by contrast, it were *intersinthomal*, it might be considered a relation that does not "fall," or fade away.

Toward the end of his presentation, Lacan declares that "it is indeed because of this that the signifier, which is also of the order of the *sinthome*, it is because of this that the signifier functions. It is because of this that we begin to get a suspicion of how the signifier might function: through the in-

termediary of the *sinthome*." And he wonders, lastly: "How
then is the virus of the *sinthome* transmitted by means of the
signifier?.," before finishing very categorically: "This is what
I have attempted to explain throughout the whole course of
my Seminars." Note the weightiness of this statement: it offers the broadest, the most illustrative motto, as it were, to
sum up what Lacan has attempted to teach through the whole
of his lifetime. That is to say, to teach—in the sense of to
show—the virus—as a way of investing in its propagation, the
virus of the *sinthome*, in the form of the signifier. This virus
spreads, is transmitted, multiplied. And of course: it might
be stopped. In order to prevent that happening, each analyst
"reinvents how psychoanalysis might endure."[3]

If we keep in mind what has been previously said in all
its rigor, it is possible to verify, once again, how the "final
Lacan" subordinated the signifier to the *sinthome*, given that
without the latter the signifier would not have functioned
properly. Thus, the virus, the *élan* or zest, is inherent to the
sinthome. It is for that reason that we can deduce the following piece of teaching: it is only through what remains of the
sexual relation—that is, what is *intersinthomal*—that the signifier functions in the transference. On this subject, we might
recall the link between this Lacanian elaboration and an earlier one governed by the logic of fantasy. What we are examining here could be aptly termed a *logic of the sinthome*; in the
former elaboration, that of fantasy, one was placed in the
position of object, like it or not: if one ("x," regardless of sex)
takes up this position, something falls. Lacan insists, by con-

---

3. J. Lacan, "Conclusions," Journées de lÉcole freudienne de Paris,
Petits écrits et conférences, s/e, pp. 175–176.

trast, that in the *intersinthomal* relation, there is no falling-off. Fantasy, however, has this falling-off condition for, among other reasons, its characteristic that Freud discovered: that which links it to beating, or being beaten (in a fundamentally symbolic way, since this in no sense implies a masochistic act). The question of the "child being beaten" is, in our reading and our clinical practice, a defining characteristic of all fantasy.

We should emphasize again: it is a question of going beyond the domain of fantasy, through the *sinthome*, both as a goal to be attained in clinical analysis and as a cardinal point for theory to seek a foothold. As we have indicated, it is possible to identify three points in Lacan's work: that of the interpreted symptom; that of the traversed fantasy; and that of the *sinthome* as identification. There can be no doubt that fantasy gives rise to a position in which, sooner or later—through analysis—one will attempt to invert (or "intervert") the terms, and one manages to "escape" from the position of object, moving vigorously toward the place of subject. This is governed by the following myth: beginning in the position of victim, one must raise oneself up to be able to move over to the position of victimizer. If one confuses the latter with the place of subject, however, one will not be able to overcome the condition of a "beautiful soul" that typifies the early stages of analytic treatment.

Alongside the *sinthome* and its logic, then, we might wonder about the significance of Lacan's letters at this point, about what should be picked out as most important here. He is very clear: "After having spoken of the Symbolic and the Imaginary for a long time . . . , what is important is the Real." In fact, we might state—with the obvious reservations accompanying all generalizations—that the first topic that preoccupied Lacan was the Imaginary, the second the Symbolic, and lastly the Real. The Real, in principle, cannot be simply one of the circles—if we take the triple Borromean chain—because it resides in precisely the writing of that chain, in the way it is presented. And this is so because the triple chain is irreducible, for—to begin our tally of what constitutes the Borromean—it is obligatory to begin with three. The double or Hopf chain is what we term "degenerate"—nongenerative—as Borromean, for whichever one of the two elements we cut, the link is undone in a self-evident manner. Thus, to begin isolating what constitutes the Borromean, we must set out from the triple chain. In Lacan's terms, the triple Borromean is real, because it is irreducible: it is impossible for it to be different, as that would be a mathematical impossibility.

On this basis, another line of thinking becomes apparent. As we have said, the real of the chain is the writing of the triple Borromean; having said that, let us go on to isolate R as a ring. R is presented as a circle (Figure 39):

Figure 39

We would be wrong, however, to consider it as simply a circle. If it were the circumference that supported a sphere, where would that take us? To the notion of the *whole*. And the Real is not a whole. It is not a whole because it has no system, it has no law, and, moreover, because it "appears" in bits, in a fragmentary manner. Its bits do not relate back to a whole, for it is a relation *partes extra partes*, without totality. Thus, what seems to be a circle—a whole—is precisely a hole: a border circumscribing and defining a void, hence a not-all [*pas-tout*]. Why is this? Here Lacan relies once again on set theory, and indicates that we are faced with a "set." In other words, with a group of heterogeneous elements that is given coherence (more or less precariously) by a particular attributed or detected characteristic. For instance, we could insert into one set another with only one element: (A). We could introduce an element called "A" and at the same time the above-mentioned set. The two are asymmetrical and yet they can be both gathered, without any apparent inconsistency, within the circle. The latter, in sum, adds to an object, the "A," and to a set one element (Figure 40):

Figure 40

Having posited the dissymmetry and dissociation here, we come back to the notion of heterogeneity. For the whole proposes that the elements it includes are equal, and it entails closure. The set, on the other hand, shows itself to be open; this is precisely what indicates its quality as not-all. But what is that, precisely? At this point, the *pointillism* of Lacan's reasoning again gives way to a bold conceptual stroke, when he asserts: the not-all is the woman. She is not-all. A set, not a whole, where the condition of the hole is respected: this is the site appropriate for situating women. In other words: one by one. Lacan thus performs a very subtle rhetorical shift, in the best oratorical tradition, by which, starting from the not-all condition, he takes us to that of The woman. And on that basis, he highlights a characteristic of sexual difference. We, the boys, have the idea of the signifier, we "conduct" it, constantly invest in it. What are the implications of this? That we feed on syntax, on order, on the fact that events take place according to a certain predictable rhythm. And women, for their part—what do they give rise to? Something Lacan writes, using one of the jokes that distinguish his teaching, as follows: *lalangue*. What everyone knew before then as *la langue*, "language," something studied by linguists—such as Chomsky—was a particular instance of a general system. By contrast, *lalangue* clearly indicates a singular kind of process, for it is based—if we consider the very word itself—on a primary process function, to use Freudian terms: that of condensation.

The site of equivocation thus takes effect as characteristic of *lalangue*. This is based on a strikingly bold theory, for Lacan compares this situation to the emergence of derivative languages from a mother tongue. Such a division, whereby the mother tongue fragments in producing "partial" languages, emerges as a trait of The woman. This is because, not being The woman, it makes impossible—according to our reading—"The" language. Thus, women do not *totalize* language, but rather give birth to *lalangue*. They are therefore more drawn to sites of equivocation; and hence they are more sensitive to the breaking-down of language in jouissance in order to occupy *lalangue*. Such an appreciation no doubt underlies Lacan's remark about women being able to become the best analysts, if they are not the worst (in other words, if they don't overdo it).

This singular way of functioning, of not being afraid before violence inflicted in language, seems to point to the fact that the boy's castration anxiety is stronger, in relation to that transgression, than that experienced by the set of women. This set, open and heterogeneous, thus supplements phallic jouissance by means of *lalangue*. But in this very "virtue" we can locate its defect, which consists in playing with the equivocal on the basis of relations constructed on top of a complete lack of self-criticism. In such cases, it is possible to isolate a potential—and clearly sometimes an actual—lack of rigor, revealed by an erratic way of dealing with signifiers. The condition of The woman is thus shown to be nothing but a variation of the law of castration, which states that what is gained on one side, is lost on the other. But, as usual, one does not know what has been lost; one only thinks that something has been gained.

We can thus grasp the rigor of a conceptual chain that is only apparently chaotic, beginning with the circle of the Real and culminating with *lalangue*. All this is due to an implacable logic, which allows Lacan to deflect criticisms. The point of departure for this argument is marked by a new type of geometry. Precisely the following (Figure 41):

Figure 41

It is not a question of the geometry of fixed, stable forms but that of rings—in other words, of the torus. We recall that it is possible to write a Borromean chain made up of three "swollen" tori instead of three strings (also themselves tori, strictly speaking). This implies, in Lacan's view, the unavoidable need to modify the *mos geometricus*, that is, what bears on our habitual imaginary mode of naive spatial representation, a mode that we can characterize as Euclidian, intuitive, and tautologous. Lacan's way of breaking with this *mos* emerges in a didactic tendency resembling a process of hypermanic argument—although this is in no sense detrimental, for it allows him to free himself from the syntactical corset of the classical, hypothetical, and deductive methods of positivist science. Lacan begins from the theses of geometry and goes on to use his own logic to develop them. Rather than remaining trapped by methodological slogans, he is able to move beyond the pretopological *mos geometricus*.

Let us return to our Joycean enquiry, now bearing in mind the writer's "feminine" sensitivity to equivocation. To do this, we should first turn to Ricardo Piglia's commentary on William Burroughs' conception of language. David Cronenberg's film *Naked Lunch*, adapted from Burroughs' book, was no great revelation; it was well known how much the writer was dominated by various drugs, and the film gave this a fairly sinister portrayal. In this context, in the fantasmatic world produced by drug-taking, we find the reflections on language that interest us; they correspond in a surprising way to what Lacan says about Joyce. This concerns the idea of language as a verbal parasite, a proliferating cancer from which we are unable to escape.

Piglia examines the relation between madness and the novel, taking *Don Quixote* as paradigm. Thus, the knight is not only someone who drives himself mad by reading novels, but someone who uses novels as the basis for constructing other worlds. And, concerning the novelist, Piglia comments: he or she attacks reality and outlines another to replace it. As he puts it:

> This tension, already something very personal, between novel and madness relates to a well-known quote from William Burroughs, who had a very appealing idea about

the origin of language: that a virus from outer space had given rise to speech between the cavemen. Before that, men communicated using signs and blows. And then suddenly, from outer space, a virus arrived which took root in mankind: language. At first, all men were psychotics because this alien origin of language had created a world of voices and sounds which forced men into a kind of psychotic nomadism, wandering about amongst these voices and sounds of whose origin they had no idea. And then, says Burroughs, men invented religion. They thought that religion must have something to do with this new thing that had come from the outside.[4]

What is interesting here is the experience—for it is clearly something of that order—out of which the American writer has been able to give symbolic form to his imaginary with this theory of the virus.

This thematic is articulated around something explored by a writer whom Lacan refers to at the beginning of Seminar 23. In the first session of the seminar, he recommends a text by some eminent Joyceans, among them Maurice Beebe and Hugh Kenner—the latter in particular is praised by Lacan. Indeed, Kenner's piece is centered around something that recalls Piglia's remarks on Burroughs: the effect of phonation—of sounds and voices—on Joyce's writing.[5] Kenner gives only a single quotation regarding this point. However, if we take the trouble to read further in *A Portrait*, we will find much

---

4. R. Piglia, "Politicas de la conversacion," *El Cronista Cultural*. Buenos Aires, September 27, 1993, p. 3.

5. H. Kenner, "The *Portrait* in Perspective" (1955), in *James Joyce: Dubliners and a Portrait of the Artist as a Young Man: A Casebook*, ed. M. Beja. London: Macmillan, 1973, pp. 124–150.

more that relates to a theme that allows us to confirm Piglia's reading of Burroughs: namely, Joyce's particular sensitivity to sounds as the defining points of his world.

Thus, at the beginning of *A Portrait*, one child says to another, a certain Simon Moonan (Kenner remarks that the name, featuring "moon," is not an accident; in fact, we should always pay attention to the significance of names in Joyce's work):

> We all know why you speak. You are McGlade's suck. Suck was a queer word. The fellow called Simon Moonan that name because Simon Moonan used to tie the prefect's false sleeves behind his back and the prefect used to let on to be angry. But the sound was ugly. Once he had washed his hands in the lavatory of the Wicklow Hotel and his father pulled the stopper up by the chain after and the dirty water went down through the hole in the basin. And when it had all gone down slowly the hole in the basin had made a sound like that: suck. Only louder.
>
>   To remember that and the white look of the lavatory made him feel cold and then hot. [p. 11]

The sound is thus given the role of an organizational marker in a process of naming, but at the same time it gives rise to sensations that did not exist before the noise was heard. And this is already at work at the beginning of *A Portrait*. But we can find further examples; one of these is characterized in particular by its pathetic quality, which is linked to the moment of deidealization. In the terms of the final Lacan, we could describe it as testifying to, *teaching us about*, the structural lack on the side of the father. It is Stephen's father, precisely, who walks with him and tells him about his own father:

He was the handsomest man in Cork at that time, by God he was! The women used to stand to look after him in the street.

He heard the sob passing *loudly* down his father's throat and opened his eyes with a nervous impulse. The sunlight breaking suddenly on his sight turned the sky and clouds into a fantastic world of sombre masses with lakelike spaces of dark rosy light. His very brain was sick and powerless. [p. 92; my emphasis]

We see here how effects of depersonalization and unreality massively affect language. And the next line continues this:

He could scarcely interpret the letters of the signboards of the shops. By his monstrous way of life he seemed to have put himself beyond the limits of reality. Nothing moved him or spoke to him from the real world unless he heard in it an echo of the infuriated cries within him. [Ibid.]

With these "infuriated cries," the voice takes the place of a missing signifier: he is unable to respond to the external stimulus offered by the shop signboards, and the cries within correspond to a "fragmentary hallucination," as it would be described in psychiatry. He goes on:

He could respond to no earthly or human appeal, dumb and insensible to the call of summer and gladness and companionship, wearied and dejected by his father's voice. [Ibid.]

This sound that immerses him, almost making him scream, results in him partly failing to recognize "his" thoughts as his own. He repeats slowly—attempting to regain some coherent identity, it seems:

> I am Stephen Dedalus. I am walking beside my father whose name is Simon Dedalus. We are in Cork, in Ireland. Cork is a city. Our room is in the Victoria Hotel. Victoria and Stephen and Simon. Simon and Stephen and Victoria. Names. [p. 93]

Naming, then: once more the Joycean text comes back to that operation of the Father-of-the Name. This instance of nomination allows us to reconsider the earlier moment of depersonalization and unreality (relating to the external world). We thus return to the (absent) Name-of-the-Father—more specifically, here in its aspect of Father-of-the-Name. We should clearly distinguish this from the Joycean formula about "making one's name," which also refers to nomination. In short, the passage from *A Portrait* allows us to see the transcendent status of the name as an appropriate register for overcoming the fall of the signifier.

At another point, when Stephen is beginning to wonder about the possibility of exile, we read:

> He shook the sound out of his ears by an angry toss of his head and hurried on, stumbling through the mouldering offal, his heart already bitten by an ache of loathing and bitterness. His father's whistle, his mother's mutterings, the screech of an unseen maniac were to him now so many voices offending and threatening to humble the pride of his youth. He drove their echoes even out of his heart with an execration; [p. 175]

Here, we should recall our discussion of schizography and imposed speech; it is clear that exile—a term to which

we return below—is something "imposed" on Joyce as the
only possible way to try to escape from those voices. We will
choose one of the very many quotations that might testify
to this, for the extreme clarity of what it illustrates. Stephen
is speaking with the college dean, "a countryman of Ben
Jonson," and thinks:

> The language in which we are speaking is his before it is
> mine. How different are the words *home, Christ, ale, mas-*
> *ter*, on his lips and on mine! I cannot speak or write these
> words without unrest of spirit. His language, so familiar
> and so foreign, will always be for me an acquired speech.
> I have not made or accepted its words. My voice holds
> them at bay. My soul frets in the shadow of his language.
> [p. 189]

This definition of the dean's language, "so familiar and
so foreign," is remarkable in coinciding almost completely
with Freud's definition of the uncanny, the *unheimlich*: literally, something foreign at the heart of the familiar. For this
reason, "his language" refers not only to the particular instant
of the dean's speech, but beyond it to a struggle against the
entirety of that language. The above paragraph outlines a vital
program, which Joyce might be said to have followed and
completed with the care and the time it required, by putting
to work the logic of his own artistry. This is what produced
his oeuvre, conceived in order to free himself from that language that he has neither made nor accepted and that, when
he speaks it, has no relation to what is heard from that figure
of *père-version* given the name "dean." Taking this as a fundamental point, Lacan argues that what Joyce does, as *sinthome*,
"remained unconscious to him." This is clearly not a topo-
graphical reference to the unconscious as psychical instance;

that it "remained unconscious to him" simply means that he did not know what he was doing. This, as we will see, is one of the characteristics of the *sinthome*: it cannot be situated in the unconscious, but the subject remains unconscious of it. This distinction is crucial, as we hope to show.

Let us dwell further on this quote from Seminar 23: "He remained unconscious of it, and it is due to this that Joyce is a pure artificer, a man of *savoir-faire*, in other words what is also called an artist. [He] did not know that he was making the *sinthome*." Lacan then alludes to *praxis*, a term that has been employed somewhat dubiously by Marxism (by Sartre, for instance, with insistence). What is a *praxis*? A practice that is in command of the operative terms of its own agency; or more explicitly, a practice that knows what it is doing, that operates on and in what Freud theorized as *Wirchlichkeit*. Ultimately, such a practice knows how its effects can be produced, and thus leaves aside any recourse to the improvised, intuitive, or irrational. Any *praxis*, not only that of Joyce—which reaches the edge of the real, where it will trace a furrow—results from a certain "speech," or more precisely an "art-speech" [*art-dire*]. The Joycean *praxis*, insofar as it is embedded in the *sinthome*, entails the slippage, almost a pun, from *art-dire* to *ardeur*, "ardor." In everyday language, "ardor" is roughly synonymous with "heat," not in a directly sexual sense, but in that of passion, of doing something "ardently." We might say that in Joyce's *art-dire*, the subject gets hot, become ardent; let us understand this together with "he remains unconscious of what he does," for the *sinthome* results in a false hole with the Symbolic (the unconscious).

At this point our argument touches on two texts that we mentioned in the first chapter: a transcription of Lacan's opening address at the June 1975 Joyce Symposium; and a text that

Lacan published in 1979 in the collective volume *Joyce & Paris*, presenting the written, modified, version of that same conference address, entitled *Joyce le symptôme* I and II (henceforth *JI* and *JII*). Many of the ideas in these two texts will allow us to focus on some of the decisive points for understanding the distinction that we are exploring between symptom and *sinthome*.

To approach this discussion, we will begin with a short digression. At the start of one of his seminars—the eighth— Lacan remarks how fond he is of Hélène Cixous, and recommends her play *Portrait of Dora* (which was of course about Freud's patient, Dora). This literary "portrait" inevitably calls to mind *A Portrait of the Artist as a Young Man*, especially in the context of Cixous' work on Joyce. The latter work, *The Exile of James Joyce*, which had appeared in 1968, is not even mentioned by Lacan in Seminar 23, even though it contains lengthy discussions of his favorite Joycean topic, the epiphany. When he mentions *Portrait de Dora* in Seminar 8, Lacan criticizes the actor who plays Freud for seeming not to interpret the role. This actor showed extreme caution, being "afraid of overdoing Freud." The problem was, in Lacan's view, that this gave rise—no doubt despite the work itself—to what he calls a "material" or "incomplete" hysteria. How can hysteria be thus described? As we know, Lacan recalls, since Freud "hysteria is always a couple." There is hysteria, and then the one who understands it: at least two. And here we confront a decisive question, which amounts to a vital indication of how to begin drawing up a table of comparisons, with on one side the symptom—going back precisely to the hysterical symptom—and on the other the *sinthome*. We already have a first criterion: on the side of hysteria, and thus of the symptom, there are two. And this is so because we find there an unconscious knowledge that *possesses* the hysteric. This transitive knowledge, in that it is self-orienting, directed toward the outside, seeks another instance. What is it seeking? It seeks the Other—it requires the Other as site of language and it also requires someone to be specular with: the mirror image, written as i(a). To put it more straightforwardly: the symptom is a message addressed to the Other. It is for this reason that it is transitive, that there has to be at least two. In his remarks on *Portrait of Dora*, Lacan's view that the actor playing Freud was substandard conveys the idea that the production had failed to represent hysteria adequately, due to the absence of the Other.

If the key to understanding the symptom is the figure two—due to the necessary reference to the Other—we might say that in the case of the *sinthome* it is the conceptual space opened by Lacan's strange statement: "There's One" [*Y a d'l'Un*]. Let us repeat that the one here is not a figure, nor is it a whole that encloses (and is enclosed); neither is it a unity or a single element added to each preceding one in a list. We should also immediately rule out the one as understood through the imaginary phenomena of narcissism. It is not the all, as it is a question of a different One, its condition not being transitive. In other words, "There's One" entails an intransitive psychical constellation. Regarding this, Lacan states that the problem, if Joyce is taken as the paradigm, is first, before thinking about why he created his work, to shed some light on why he wished to publish it.

Here, in our view, Lacan shows great lucidity. If it is true that, in one sense, Joyce displayed great sensitivity to other people's opinions, he was above all bound up with inventing his work rather than distributing it (despite the "evidence" pointing to the reverse). One sign of this is the time he devoted to his writing: at the end of *Finnegans Wake*, we read "Paris, 1922–1939." Joyce seems to wish us to know that it took seventeen years, rather than simply following the usual practice of noting the date when the work was completed. And another unique feature of *Finnegans Wake* may also have prompted Lacan to talk of Joyce's self-adequation: the end of the book returns to its beginning. At the end of the Wake, we read, *A way a lone a last a loved a long the*, a phrase that "carries on" in the first line of the book, *riverrun, past Eve and Adam's*. What is the significance of this, which recalls a straight line being closed in on itself? Many critics have seen in this the influence of Giambattista Vico, one of Joyce's major references, with his famous historical *corsi e ricorsi*, a theme that goes back to the biblical sayings "nothing new under the sun," "everything begins again," or "ultimately, we always return."

Joyce's self-enclosure opens, in our view, some Lacanian questions. Why did he launch his words at the world and not keep them in the closure of his own Wakean end-beginning, beginning-end? There's One: as intransitive, it constitutes what Lacan terms "the One all alone." This would not, of course, be a subjective or empirical solitude, but One as a psychical formation broken off from the Other.

What is the corresponding feature of the symptom? Lacan asserts its *ex-sistence* in the unconscious, the latter understood in terms of the Symbolic. This is an important point, for in our understanding to *ex-sist* denotes "to be outside of." Again we recall Freud's resonant formulation: an internal foreign country. This is a way of illustrating the following: it is mine, I know it, it is something that belongs to me—but I cannot master it or conquer it. I no longer wish to do so, I'd rather be rid of it (as with the verbal parasite of language). Thus, it ex-sists the unconscious. But there are other ways of interpreting this. In the final Lacan we do not find, in any clearly discernible sense, the classical psychoanalytic link between the unconscious and the symptom. It had always been thought that the symptom entailed a privileged pathway for an operative reading of the unconscious; but by stating that the symptom "ex-sists," we now give it an extraterritorial location. This is not the place to pursue this point further—we have done so elsewhere[6]—but it is something to be taken account of seriously: we are *not* dealing with the symptom as unconscious formation. In other words, if we are serious about accompanying Lacan to the rich conclusion of his teaching, we will affirm the ex-sistence of the symptom in relation to the unconscious rather than stressing its position as formation of the latter. Let us note what Lacan claims in *JI*: that Joyce "is disinvested from the unconscious." In our reading, the term "disinvested" designates a speaking-being that has suspended or cancelled its subscription. Taking the idea further, we might think of someone who subscribed to a theater or music club, or a magazine, and broke off that relation at the end of a cycle, the failure to renew the subscription leading to the lapse of the contractual arrangement. Using a term such as "disinvestment" thus implies that a link formerly in place with the unconscious has been broken. This is why the *sinthome* was, for Joyce the artificer, unconscious: he did not know that he was caught up in it, or how he sewed together his own knot (and/or chain). Here, we confront something quite different from the symptom, which exists through a painful jouissance where there is no mark of a disinvestment from the unconscious. Thus, the One is inscribed as a disinvested psychical

---

6. Cf. R. Harari, *Fantasma: ¿fin del analisis?*, op. cit., pp. 199–215.

formation insofar as it has severed its original link by moving away from the upkeep of an infinite, irredeemable debt. For this reason, the formation in question is inscribed in the Borromean chain as a fourth order, distinct from the other three. In topological terms, this fourth order *is* the disinvestment from the unconscious, for the latter is indexed on the Symbolic.

Let us now turn to the question of *belief*. What does someone who suffers from a symptom believe in? In brief, he believes in meaning. He also seeks the meaning of meaning, a move that tends to slide toward interminable analysis. In truth, our picture will evidently show various different points, partially overlapping. This is why the question of the Other—the "two" in hysteria—is posed anew, given the attempt to make this Other furnish a lacking meaning. The subject believes in meaning, with which he tries to enter into a mimetic identification. We can even see this in the title of a well-known book by Ogden and Richards, much mocked by Lacan: *The Meaning of Meaning*. We might say that the title points to a paradigmatic hysterical question, for it refers to persistent dissatisfaction, to perplexity, to an enjoyable wager on the myth of infinity.

What happens, on this point, with the *sinthome*? Lacan tells us as if in passing—but not without an implicit argument—that in analysis we work to generate another form of credibility. In terms of what we have explored—that is, with the emphasis on invention—we could propose that what is produced in place of meaning [*sens*] is *j'ouïs-sens* (where "I hear meaning" puns on "jouissance"). These voices, their ceaseless interpellation, mark a limit for Joyce. In *A Portrait*, we read of those unbearable voices that force Joyce into exile. This exile, as we have argued, is not merely geographical but above all relates to language: an exile from language [*la langue*] into *lalangue*, with all its equivocations. At the same time, it is due to the hearing of these voices that Joycean invention becomes possible. The voices are neither inherently beneficial nor inherently harmful: due to the law of castration, they produce a meaning once they are heard. But this meaning derives from a singular, "imposed" hearing, not from something sought out deliberately by a being. This "being in search of something" appears, for example, in a phrase like: "You know what's happening to me, so please interpret me and make me better!"(a common form of the neurotic demand directed at the analyst). Thus, the *sinthome*, regarding the either/or of being and meaning (as it figures in Seminar 2), determines the credibility of being.

Moreover, as we know, instead of simply talking of the unconscious in the Freudian sense, Lacan proposed the condensed term *parlêtre*, which we have made frequent use of before. As well as blending "speech" [*parler*] with "being" [*être*], the term encapsulates something germane to our argument at this point: *parlêtre* is a pun on *par la lettre* ["by letter"]. An individual, we might say, *is* "par la lettre": the letter constitutes him or her. Thus, we can situate the *parlêtre* on the side of the symptom. On the other hand, as we have shown, in *JI* and *JII* and Lacan's other work of the same period, there appear terms that are "foreign" to his teaching. One, for example, that he writes simply LOM or lom.[7] What is the significance of replacing *parlêtre* with LOM, a term that is obviously a pun on *l'homme*, "man"? If, as the seminar argues, with the *sinthome* there is no trace of the symptom, then

7. *JI* and *JII*, pp. 28, 31, 33.

nobody feels himself torn apart by an effect of traumatic division. If Joyce is a paradigmatic instance of *l'homme*, what would characterize it? As Lacan explains, "Joyce, as is written somewhere, identifies with the *individual*."[8] An odd term, the "individual" designates that which is undivided, cannot be divided. Thus, Joyce identifies with the individual, and LOM is individual. Is this, as we have hinted, to bring into question the "classical" divided subject that had been Lacan's theme for so long? No, because in our view Lacan is in the process of outlining a psychical formation that is precisely distinct from the unconscious and its formations, the *parlêtre*, the S_1. And this is the principle innovation, the theoretical subversion brought in by Seminar 23 and its parallel texts: it is no longer a question of a subject that is torn, divided, broken, or barred but of a subject identified with the "individual." Lacan goes on: "[Joyce] is the one who was privileged to have been at the extreme point of incarnating the *sinthome*,[9] by which [he is reduced] to the very structure of lom ('man')." This gives us no further explanation, although it is absolutely consistent with what has just been presented. Here we see, once more, the function of a line on whose basis a new type of nomination emerges: due to this, Lacan is able to "play Joyce." It is revealing that he, or for that matter we ourselves, could only do this by deliberately imitating a style. Such a procedure would not be acceptable when we are working as analysts. Why is this? Because if we allowed ourselves to

---

8. *JI*, p. 28 [italics in original].

9. As we explained in Chapter 1 above, due to the fact that *JI* (the source of our quotation) is a lecture in a single text produced by an official transcription, we have corrected the text at various points, as here, in order to show the coherent development of Lacan's thinking.

work in such a way, we would risk introducing terms invented by ourselves alone, without considering their relevance to the signifiers of the analysand. In brief, such a stylistic procedure is valuable for didactic ends such as Lacan has in mind, but must be radically excluded from the conduct of analytic treatment.

Thus, LOM is an alternative to the *parlêtre*. Our next step is to return to a reference given above, but with a new understanding. We indicated that in the symptom, meaning emerges as a reference to credibility, to what can be believed. We can now see another aspect to this. Our question was: How does someone who suffers from a neurotic symptom act? He seeks meaning, through asking questions—and this implies, according to Lacan, that he is searching for a master. He seeks an S_1, a unitary or master signifier. But what does Joyce do—paradigmatically—instead of seeking meaning? Without any hesitation, he undoes meaning. (This, according to Lacan, resembles what women do.) Joyce respects neither syntax, nor semantics, nor pragmatics: in other words, he does away with all the variations proposed by the different branches of linguistics. He breaks apart, massacres meaning, and—far worse—he produces enigmas. Another quotation from *JI* is relevant here: "The *sinthome* in Joyce is a *sinthome* that has nothing to do with you. It is the *sinthome* that has absolutely no chance of connecting with your unconscious."

We can take this last point as the basis for an assessment of the notably different implications of the tacit theory of art here and Freud's equivalent theory. On this topic, Lacan speaks of "post-Joycean" art—meaning that Joyce marks, in principle, a distinct rupture in the very conception of art and of literature: there is an era before Joyce, and an era after him. In effect, because Joyce does not aim at "your unconscious," the reader can only feel elided, brushed aside. And if his work doesn't touch us at all, no one can claim to have "identified" with it—at the conscious level—so as to have been moved. There is no mimesis, only enigmas. *JI* puts it in the following way: ". . . without anything being analyzable, one is struck by this, and literally 'forbidden.'"[10] Joyce is forbidding, dumb-founding, in that he prevents imaginary identification. In the face of this, interpretations emerge that are inductive or in-duced, induced by this *sinthomatic* writing that "forbids" our access to its supposed clear sense.

Lacan goes on to explain that using the words "to for-bid" to mean to dumbfound or stupefy is extremely signifi-cant.[11] The production of Joycean enigmas leaves us in a state of stupefaction, dumbfounded, gobsmacked; it leads to a feel-ing that we strive to counteract by means of advancing differ-ent kinds of S_2 with a view to stimulating the production of meaning.

Undoing meaning, in sum, entails a crucial point that we should articulate with a term we used earlier. For what Joyce brings about is *absense*: playing on the absence of sense, he forges absense. It is rather like what happens when a "well-informed" journalist interviews an artist about the "message" his or her work contains. Usually, the artist is incapable of responding, only managing to mutter something like, "I don't know . . I have no idea . . . whatever you like." And he or she is perfectly right: such a question is totally illegitimate, for it implies a model of "conscious expression," according to which

---

10. Translator's note: *interdit*: Lacan plays on the colloquial expression whereby *je reste interdit*, "I remain forbidden," can mean "I am dumbfounded."

11. *JI*, p. 27.

one always knows what one does, being the absolute master of sense. By contrast, Lacan's teaching here aims to show that when LOM invents or artifices, he has no idea what he is doing, his relation to the act is unconscious. If you wish to give it a meaning, that's no problem. But it is of no interest to the artist; whatever you say, he is not implicated by it. This is the crucial point: you can give it what name you like, for what belongs to me is another story. Thus, there can be no effects of identification.

Here we touch on another point, to do with so-called "hysterical" identification. The latter emerges, paradigmatically, in the question of what it means to be a woman. However, the alternative proposed by Lacan concerning the end of analysis states that instead of the subject identifying with that question and wearing herself out trying to obtain the impossible answer, what occurs is an identification with the *sinthome*, a "being One" with it. By contrast, the question of the symptom remains always open: it can never be answered, since what characterizes it is the endless drift into metonymy.

Let us recall, in this context, the case of Dora. For her—and this was of great clinical significance—the close relationship between the K couple and her parents (more precisely, the relationship between Frau K and her father) was decisive. Dora claimed that she was being made part of an exchange, a deal; that, for instance, her care of Frau K's children served to enable her father to spend time with that woman. At the same time, she felt that Herr K was making passes at her, with the passive consent of her father. Freud's classic question to Dora, which Lacan describes as an attempt to dismantle the Hegelian position of the "*belle ame*" (or "beautiful soul"), was the following: What is the part that falls to you in producing the turmoil that you denounce? But in truth this question misses the essential point. For Frau K was not merely a troublesome rival or a contingent and substitutable presence in Dora's history; indeed, rather, she was precisely someone who seemed to be able to answer the question of femininity, who "knew" what it meant to be a woman. It is thus crucial to see that the "unbearable" triangular situation—as is *not* self-evident—persists, indisputably, because of the support given it by the three participants. Not, that is, for the cliché or wild card of homosexuality. It is not necessary to be close to the woman to "have" her; one can struggle *to be like her*. To this end, one has to maintain a proximity to the repeated encounter. The presence is required not in order to have her—on the path of object choice, to put it in Freud's terms—but that proximity serves to feed the enduring desire that without it would collapse. It is rather Dora herself that "collapses," on every occasion; in Lacanian terms, she undergoes *aphanisis*. This is what characterizes hysterical identification: it is partial, unlike the identification that occurs with the *sinthome*. The hysteric is clearly torn asunder; while the "sinthomatic," although not tranquil, is often without the surging anxiety that afflicts the former.

In *JII*, Lacan distinguishes between the other as *sinthome* and the other as body. As he puts it: "Thus, the individuals that Aristotle takes to be bodies might only be symptoms [to be read: *sinthomes*] themselves in relation to other bodies. A woman, for instance, is a symptom [i.e., *sinthome*] of another body." A woman, then, not thought in terms of "body to body," but as *sinthome* of another body: thus the lack of a sexual relation is maintained. Since there is no body in a "raw" state, its very status is transformed; for there is no preestablished link or instinct, nor a prototypical response to phylogenetic images that would trigger some event. There is no such thing as a "genotype" that would direct the search for the "right" male body on the part of a woman, or vice versa. And Lacan continues: "If that is not the case, she remains a so-called hysterical symptom." In other words, if it is not a *sinthome* it will be a hysterical symptom that constitutes the "bodily event."[12] It is here that we can see a clear difference isolated by Lacan. If the event is not transformed, there is only one remaining alternative: having not been made *sinthome* for a man, she can only be "made" into a hysterical symptom. Which, obviously, would cause her to suffer. And where does this suffering lead? As we have seen, it leads to taking an interest in another symptom. Thus, a relation of symptom to symptom, of question to question, emerges. The question of the *sinthome*, by contrast, is: if someone is asking me something, the question does not interest me; as for my answer, I can see no reason to give it. And to add yet another twist: I'm not interested in the answer because the event holds no interest for me; that event is located, in effect, outside discourse, for it does not implicate me as subject of enunciation. Let us consider the paradigmatic example above: What did you mean to say through your work? What is its subject? Were you aware that you wished to convey that? Such questions are precisely what the *sinthome* brushes aside. To identify with these questions, in turn, is to be driven by the search for the other's symptom through the subject's own symptom.

In exploring further these interrelating points, our argument will center in what follows on the different forms of jouissance. It is thus worthwhile asking, at the outset, what kind of jouissance is comprised by the *sinthome*. Lacan will

_____

12. *JII.*, p. 35.

describe this as "opaque" jouissance,[13] a quality due to the exclusion of meaning; for the sinthome, with its "heard-sense" [*ouïe-sens*], privileges what is heard over what is meaningful. In the case of the symptom, jouissance can be described using a term that goes back to Seminar 10, *Anxiety*: that of "rotten" jouissance. In the symptom, jouissance has become degraded or rotten because what it "enjoys" is meaning. Furthermore, we can add that what is at stake here is the jouissance of the unconscious that determines the subject. In many accounts by analysands of how it is impossible for them to break out of certain situations—in other words, of their supposed inability to resolve them—it is necessary to pick out the determining instance of unconscious jouissance. Determining what, exactly? Repetition—but a repetition that, in our view, does not rule out belief in a meaning that can bring things to a conclusion. This is therefore the crucial point with regard to signing it up as phallic jouissance. Belief in a primordial signifier—the Phallus—as something likely to bring a decisive meaning to the treatment of neurosis, is in fact a key hope for every neurotic. This belief sets the signifying presence of the Phallus in place and feeds the conviction caused by the Subject-supposed-to-know. What does Lacan teach, on the other hand, about the site of the Phallus in the *sinthome*? He begins his argument by referring to the "false" hole in topology, produced by the Symbolic, S and the sinthome, written as Σ[14]; as we know, something must pass through the middle for this false hole to be connected. In the following way (Figure 42):

---

13. *JII.*, p. 36.
14. Cf. Figure 15 above, p. 88.

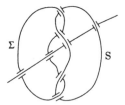

Figure 42

Here, the Phallus traverses the false hole, thus verifying it as a real hole. But the Phallus does not give rise to the ensuing jouissance, for its function is to *opacify*—that is, according to the pun, both to render opaque and to pacify. Phallic jouissance, according to what we have argued, does not pacify at all: it is rather a constant, needling pressure, bound up with the question of locating the elusive element, the "something more"—for, without a doubt, it *believes in* that element.[15] Why, then, has it been denied to it? Why has the injustice of the world fallen on its head? Who has gotten away with the greatest part of jouissance? When and how should it be recovered so that it can be fairly distributed?

In what follows we confront one of the fundamental innovations comprised by this seminar. To elucidate it, we will

---

15. This whole argument implies another transition, correlative to the move from the triple to the quadruple Borromean; in the former, phallic jouissance is located in the intersection of R and S. The body, which Lacan writes as I, would thus remain outside phallic jouissance. However, as we saw in Chapter 1, phallic jouissance extends from S to R, as an "invasion," giving rise to the symptom (still within the triple knot). In this way, phallic jouissance reaches the body, taking the logical paradigm of the hysterical symptom. But in producing the rupture brought about with the *sinthome*, it no longer amounts to a simple invasion: phallic jouissance is bodily—and not beyond the body—to the extent that the *sinthome* is characterized by mental jouissance.

turn again to Joyce's *A Portrait*—to the moment when Stephen loses his coordinates, finding himself mumbling the following words: "Victoria Hotel. Victoria, Stephen, Simon. Simon, Stephen, Victoria. Names." What we find illustrated here is the function of the signifier Name-of-the-Father, as ordering instance, and equally as a function of the Father-of-the-Name. We should locate both of these instances, definitively, on the side of the symptom, for taking on these functions makes them unavoidable notions for our understanding of the structure of neurosis. We have already alluded to the transcendent status—which is confirmed by Seminar 23— of another question: that of the suppletion of the Name-of-the-Father. And this is the exact context within which a Lacanian formula emerges, one that has begun to make a powerful impact (and that should do still more so): "One can do without the Name-of-the-Father provided that one makes use of it." This is doubtless one of the most effective of Lacan's aphorisms concerning the Name-of-the-Father, in that it precisely designates it as implying *suppletion*. (We will return to this point later in our argument.) To begin with, we should again stress the crucial point here: that is, that the Name-of-the-Father, as Father-who-Names—put to work by Stephen and Adam, but not by Evie—is a *normative*, as well as a nominative, instance. This function does not merge into that of Joycean suppletion—it is not equivalent to the erection of his proper name. Here, we refer to the singular importance of "wanting to be Joyce," in other words: wanting to be the one everyone talks about, able to incite people to talk about him (something in which, undoubtedly, he succeeded). "Normative" indicates, for its part, that which allows for the regulation of norms, accounting equally for degrees of deviation and correlative penalties.

Let us continue with this point in slightly different terms. In *JI*, Lacan evokes "a structure in which the Name-of-the-Father is an unconditioned element." Why does he define it thus? If we look at the emergence of the notion, we can ascertain—and this is confirmed by certain clinical findings—that it is dependent on the Desire of the Mother. We often discover, putting things in empirical terms, that everything hinges on the place attributed to the father by the mother. We can thus deduce the place corresponding to the Name that implicates him. To put it differently, we can postulate a sequence beginning with the Desire of the Mother (DM) and leading to the Name-of-the-father (NF). If this were so, we could write DM as a first signifier and NF as a second. The sequence would thus be as follows:

$$S_1 \; (DM) \rightarrow S_2 \; (NF)$$

But Lacan now introduces the notion of an "unconditioned" Name-of-the-Father. The "classical" Name-of-the-Father is held to be entirely conditioned. An example of this understanding would refer to such common expressions as "the mother has not given the father his place": this would correspond to the place of the Name-of-the-Father being put in the background. In *JI*, Lacan does not repudiate his earlier conception but claims to be outlining another aspect—thus he notes, a few lines further on: "The father as name and as the one who names, they are not identical. The father is that fourth element . . . without which nothing is possible in the knot of the Symbolic, the Imaginary and the Real."[16]

---

16. *JI*, pp. 27–28.

If we characterize this fourth site as what corresponds to the unconditioned Name-of-the-Father (UNF), we can deduce that without this fourth, there can be no knot. We can write this in the traditional matheme of signifiers, with UNF as S_1 and RSI as S_2, its derivative:

$$S_1 \ (UNF) \rightarrow S_2 \ (RSI)$$

RSI is the result for, as we know, the three links are free, so there's no chain. The fourth is what allows the knot to form, producing the quadruple Borromean. This fourth, the unconditioned Name-of-the-Father, is the instance of suppletion. The place of the Name-of-the-Father has clearly been altered, given a new privilege, in relation to Lacan's earlier formulations. In our view, this change has not been sufficiently acknowledged, although it has major consequences for clinical work.

With Joyce, this suppletion, as far as the Symbolic goes, comes about by means of a (self-made) proper name. The latter, of course, is not the Name-of-the-Father. Let us consider this point further: by returning to "The Agency of the letter," in which Lacan declares, somewhat peremptorily, that "the symptom *is* a metaphor." This indicates that it is a creation of meaning, as a metaphor is found in place of another element. A phrase, for example, can be "converted" into a bodily equivalent. Let us take a traditional Freudian example: a patient who, tempted to "take a wrong step"—because she is about to go for a walk in the hospital gardens with the doctor about whom she has erotic fantasies—immediately suffers a paralysis of the leg. The symptom encapsulates both a recognition of the intention and its criticism or censorship: "taking a step" with the desired doctor is thus prevented. For all its simplicity, this example is a clear illustration of the function of metaphor.

But we should also pay attention to what follows: such a metaphor is for Lacan, in a primordial sense, a reference to the place of the father. For *any metaphor only functions on the basis of an effectively working paternal metaphor*. The latter, by substituting the Name-of-the-Father for the Desire of the Mother—which, as it appears twice in Lacan's formula, once as numerator and once as denominator, is arithmetically reduced, allows the emergence, beginning with X, of the signified for the Subject:

$$\frac{NF}{DM} \cdot \frac{DM}{X}$$

Which leads to:

$$\frac{NF}{\cancel{DM}} \cdot \frac{\cancel{DM}}{X}$$

And then in conclusion:

$$\frac{NF}{\text{Signified to Subject}}$$

To sum up, the Name-of-the-Father gives the Subject its signified. It is thus, without doubt, metaphorical. What depends on the Name-of-the-Father involves an operation of substitution. Now, with the *sinthome*, metaphor is precisely what does not function: as we saw in Chapter 3, metaphor "fails" in Joyce. Therefore, the *sinthome* is not characterized by an effect of substitution, but by one of nomination. What, in this new context, does nomination involve? Different modes of reparation; and so in Joyce we find not one but several kinds of nomination. With one kind, for instance, he is able to "construct" his name; with another, he can "inflate" his ego. Let us reiterate what we brought out in Chapter 1: nomination, as opposed to metaphor, goes along with and is inflected by each of the three registers;

it can be Real, Symbolic, and/or Imaginary. And Seminar 23, in our reading, proposes—at least implicitly—that Joyce puts into effect all three kinds of nomination. (We will return to this point toward the end of our argument.)

If the symptom is metaphorical, by contrast nomination does not work according to a pattern of substitution: it is not a replacement of anything else, but sets itself up for and by itself at the site of reparation where the "slip" or lapsus has occurred. Metaphor remains within the order of the signifier, whereas nomination works by means of the letter.

A general schema with two columns can be set out at this point in our argument:

Symptom	*Sinthome*
Two: transitive unconscious knowledge: demands Other, i(a)	There is One (alone), intransitive
Ex-sists in the unconscious (referring to the Symbolic); limit	Disinvested from the unconscious, exiled, outside discourse, artificed (*savoir faire*)
Believes in meaning	"Another mode" of credibility: *J'ouïs-sens*, believes in being & S_1
Speaking-being [*Parlêtre*]	LOM (individual)
Seeks meaning in S_1, addressee of question	Undoes meaning: produces enigmas; stupefies, seeks S_2
Hysterical identification with a question (S_2)	Identification with the One of the *sinthome* (S_1)
"Rotten," phallic, bodily jouissance	Opaque, mental jouissance of the Other
Name-of-the-Father (Father-of-the-Name)	Unconditioned Name-of-the-Father (without the fourth there is no RSI)
Metaphor (substitution)	Nomination—r. s. i.

8

Prelude to the Wake *of a Faun*

At the start of this chapter we find ourselves—to put it in Euclidian terms—running out of the space needed to bring our argument full circle. To do this would be to succeed in tracing a circular inscription, in accordance with a geometry that would make our account sufficiently rounded and weighty, the epitome of formal "perfection." Such a circular conclusion, however, will elude us; on the contrary, there will be uncompleted elements, or at least elements implicitly requiring supplementary explanation. Our argument will thus, evidently, be not-all.

To continue, we might invoke a small discovery that puts to work, and gives a new confirmation to, the phrase "I do not find, I seek." As indicated in Chapter 6, Lacan gave his name to a certain type of psychosis, dubbing it a "Lacanian psychosis," as well as to the knot with five crossing-points, "Lacan's knot" (cf. Figures 32 and 33). These two moments, in our view, implicitly point to ways of rethinking the question of the proper name. The latter, as is well known, traverses and classifies certain events, including scientific procedures, instruments, and discoveries. It is in this domain that we should locate the quintuple knot mentioned above. Now, in the seminar the discussion of this knot is preceded by a reference to a quadruple knot, thought up—says Lacan—by Listing. However, in the French edition of Listing's *Introduction to Topology*, the editors Pierre Bruno and Claude Léger write the following: "*A Note on Lacan and Listing.* Lacan followed the usage of mathematicians in associating the quadruple knot with the name of Listing." In other words, he was acting on secondhand information. They continue: "The quadruple knot, however, does not appear in any text by J. B. Listing." Let us recall that this knot is not the quadruple knot, for despite being made up of four crossing-points, it does not have an equal number of elements.

As we know, the knot is defined as such by being made up of a single element, which governs its crossings in an alternating over/under pattern. It can be presented as follows (Figures 43, 44):

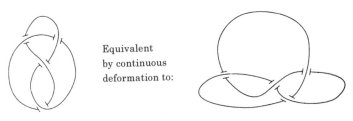

Equivalent by continuous deformation to:

Figure 43   **Figure 44**

Bruno and Léger support their argument by referring to a book by R. H. Crowell and R. H. Fox, *An Introduction to Knot Theory*, published in 1963. They specify that what can be found in Listing's work is in fact the quintuple knot.[1] That is, the knot explored in Chapter 6 above (Figure 45):

Figure 45

It thus emerges that "Lacan's knot" actually belongs, strictly speaking, to Listing. Is this a simple error, or does it reveal a certain paramnesia on Lacan's part? Without wishing to give a definite answer, the value of this is that there is consequently no "Lacan's knot," in the sense of a knot "thought up by him." Nevertheless, in our view there is indeed a "Lacan's knot": the Borromean chain of four elements. This is evidently a figure of speech, in one sense, for that chain was not his invention, even if he "appropriated" it and developed it.

Why, then, should the quadruple Borromean chain be thought of as Lacan's knot? Let us stress once again that with Seminar 23, Lacan outlines something very different from what is still indefatigably and solemnly stated in endless conference papers and articles, namely that the seminar *R.S.I.* marks the final development of Lacanian theory. Some even go so far as to "raise" the triptych of that seminar's title to the epistemological category of an invariable "paradigm" of

---

1. J. B. Listing, *An Introduction to Topology*. Paris: Navarin, 1989, pp. 92–93.

Lacan's teaching, according to the model introduced by Thomas Kuhn. In this line of thinking, Seminar 23 is proof enough of the absurdity of such claims. That is, without the fourth element it is impossible to articulate R.S.I.: this is one of the most powerful, uncompromising, and subversive propositions in all of Lacan's thought. Nothing can be understood without the fourth term; there can never be simply R.S.I., for the triptych only ex-sists due to the fourth link.

Having made clear that this quintuple knot, claimed by Lacan as his own, does not, properly speaking, belong to him (whereas, in our view, the quadruple knot *does*), let us return to what we saw in the previous chapter relating to the two contrasting columns of the aspects of the symptom and the *sinthome* respectively. Here, we should repeat the qualification outlined above: there are certain points where these aspects overlap, given that we are not dealing with a metaphysical opposition, far from it. In any event, such a procedure is primarily useful as an illustration from a didactic point of view. Thus, if we examine the various factors at work, we can state the following: the symptom, as a traditional formation of the unconscious—in which it ex-sists—is a response, as regards its origin, to the well-known mechanism of repression. Now, as Lacan teaches, there is no repression without the return of the repressed. In brief, to speak either of the former or of the latter amounts to the same thing. This undermines the illusory idea of a "successful" repression, capable of radically abolishing whatever is to be displaced. The triumph of repression must conceal a paradox, for it must consist precisely in its failure. Repression consists in failing as a condition or absolute imperative: it can "succeed" only by producing substitutes. Among the latter, of course, we find the object of our current interest: the symptom. And Lacan teaches that the

sinthome, in contradistinction to the symptom, entails a formation disinvested from the unconscious: thus, neither repression nor the return of the repressed can be ascribed to
the *sinthome*. This point must be given its full significance
in a clinical reflection, for that which returns from the repressed—that is, signifiers "fallen beneath" repression but
recycled—amounts to the only valid index for our work, and
serves to neutralize the risk of Imaginary projections on the
part of the analyst. Moreover, that which returns is what produces illness. In sum, it is a question of the recovery of phallic jouissance: what emerges is a regained jouissance, and thus
tension increases and the symptom causes trouble. As we have
said, in psychoanalysis there is a symptom only if the one who
suffers can speak of it. By contrast, a psychiatrist or a psycholo-
gist is authorized, from an external viewpoint, to posit that a
subject has a symptom. Such attributions are avoided by the
psychoanalyst; or if she offers them, they have no effect—for
analysis is not a question of the more or less relevant clinical
gaze, but of the act of questioning itself, the involvement of
the subject faced by repression and its return.

What, then, in the case of the *sinthome*, can we designate as an equivalent of the workings of repression with the
symptom? It would seem, de facto, to be *Verwerfung*, foreclosure, which we discussed above. As we indicated, Lacan
makes use of this term, as if putting to work "in desperation"
a conceptual tool. We explore this point further below when
we examine one of the last sessions of the seminar. Lacan introduces there, in all rigor, the possibility of positing another
type of *Verwerfung*, the foreclosure of something other than
the Name-of-the-Father. We will return to this question in
order to stress how in that session Lacan reformulates the topic
of metaphor.

If we return to our columns from the previous chapter, then, we see that they end with the opposition metaphor/nomination. Since this opposition, however, is of crucial importance, it deserves further consideration. We can thus state that metaphor, for the Lacan of Seminar 23, is defined as an index of the sexual relation, but that the latter—by the very action of metaphor—amounts to "taking a bladder for a lantern," to translate literally Lacan's familiar French expression. What does this mean? The expression is proverbially used to designate a completely mistaken equivalence or substitution; putting a bladder in place of a lantern, even metaphorically, seems evidently mistaken. Metaphor implies the possibility of substitution, in a register clearly accessible to all, through language. Metaphor creates meaning, but by the same token it can befuddle and create confusion in plausibly substituting one thing for another. In order for metaphor to operate, as we stated above, a decisive substitution must have taken place: namely, the Desire of the Mother must have been replaced by the Name-of-the-Father. This is a crucial clinical point because of the consequence that flows from it: because of the foreclosure of the signifier Name-of-the-Father, the psychotic cannot make metaphorical the text of his madness. The impossibility of generating metaphor—at precisely this point—becomes a major obstacle preventing the analysis of the psychotic according to the "normal" procedures. Thus we see here one of the limits of analysis, indicated by the foreclosure of the site of enunciation. Yet Lacan teaches—nay, demands—that we should not turn aside from psychosis; although, we would add, he also warns us not to produce psychosis through analysis, something that can occur when prepsychotic states are "triggered." Thus an inquiry into metaphoricity is an unavoidable ethical premise to be gone through with every potential analysand. What are the relevant clinical criteria here? If spoken to in an allusive manner, the subject must be able to relate what he hears to another current of signification. Correlatively, he must be able to tolerate a nonliteral interpretation of his own discourse, without taking it to mean that the analyst is accusing him of failure, understanding it in a paranoid mode as an attempt to undermine his beliefs. On this level, we will make clinical use of metaphor to develop our argument.

Nomination—which we will explore more particularly in the last chapter—entails the return of a term already part of Lacan's teaching, although now with different connotations. From Seminars 22 and 23 onward, the notion emerges with a new breadth and originality. We will examine how the various modalities of nomination outlined by Lacan in *Le sinthome* bear on the way Joyce gives names to things; that is, how he produces singularities by naming in the different registers. We will see that Lacan deployed, at various points, certain knots and/or chains; in our view, he did this because of questions of naming. In brief, this is where the binary opposition comes into effect. Regarding the left-hand column, it is useful to recall that repression, like the symptom, is for Lacan metaphorical. At different periods of his teaching, he supported a definition of repression as the production of a substitute; and this substitute, in turn—namely, the symptom—is a metaphor. Nothing of this sort is at work in the formation of the *sinthome* as highlighted in Seminar 23.

Let us approach things from a different perspective, which is not simple to understand. On the left we write *signifier*, the classical term of Lacan's early work; its theoretical apogee, we might say, comes in 1957 with the *Écrit* entitled "The Agency of the letter in the unconscious; or reason since Freud." For this term, taken from the linguistics of Ferdinand de Saussure, Lacan proposes a definition that is almost a joke, with its (vicious) circularity and its falsely didactic appearance: a signifier is what represents the subject for another signifier. This cannot be a definition, for its statement includes that which is to be defined. If we add numbers to the signifiers thus incorrectly contained in the definition, we obtain S_1 and S_2. We can thus make things more precise by saying that S_1 represents the subject for S_2; we have a relation of representation, of delegation. What emerges, in effect, is that if we seek to define the signifier, we can only do so by placing it in a chain. It is impossible to define only one of the two, for this requires *a minima* an articulation with the subject and the other signifier. Thus, the signifier is articulated in an obligatory, unavoidable sense; and it therefore is always situated in a structure. This is consistent with the notion of metaphor, given that the signifier slides between the chains, is substituted. As we can see, these are different ways of thinking about the same conceptualization.

What is differentiated from the signifier is the letter. Here, we have to move carefully, for at certain moments Lacan takes the two terms to be synonymous.[2] In *L'instance de la lettre*, he defines the letter as the material support that concrete discourse borrows from "language." In using the term "material," Lacan refers to the fact that the letter can be inscribed (but clearly not in the sense of simply writing a letter on paper). What does this imply? It is a question of unconscious "litter," even if the early Lacan understood this to fall under the

---

2. For instance, in one of the lectures given in the United States, cf. *Scilicet* 6/7, p. 60.

sway of the signifier. And clearly this refers to Joyce, with his "a letter, a litter." We thus conceive of a littered letter.

We do not expect anyone to feel wounded by Lacan's Joycean assimilation of letter and litter, for it is no reflection upon the domain of Letters (a discipline especially valued by the author). It is, rather, valuable in highlighting that the letter will end up being evacuated; it is excess, superfluous, refuse. If we locate the signifier in the domain of the Symbolic, the letter shows predominance in the Real, as its status as rubbish might indicate: it is indeed a product of the Symbolic, but a product that has no place there. It is rather that, in order to be perpetuated, the very structure of the Symbolic requires the elimination of this excrescence. For this reason, in our view, Lacan recommends that we take *liter*ally Joyce's description of himself as a "man of letters." In the final analysis, that is, it is letters that constitute him. It is letters, unlike signifiers, that can become part of a "Joycean" arrangement: a transliteral transaction that ex-sists the chain of signifiers.

In particular, for we will see how this takes effect with letters, regarding the question of phonemics. This is not to do with hearing words so much as with ways of "playing" with the phonemes—the earliest and the most recent—that make up a language. To do language, *lalangue*: for this one must work insistently on the characteristic traits and phonemes that constitute and define it. If, for instance, we were to ask what is Spanish, a possible answer would be: the contents of the *Real Academia Espanola* dictionary. We would find our answer if we read through all of the terms in the book. But that is not Spanish: what constitutes it, rather, are its interconnected phonemes. And it is chains of phonemes that lie at the origin of words. A language is not made up of the thousands of words listed in its academic dictionaries; there can be more or less of them, but they amount to the lexicon and not the language. From this perspective, Lacan's re-introduction of the concept of the letter is extremely important, precisely on the basis of Joyce's work: he thus aims to address the fundamental elements of language, in addition to elucidating the workings of *lalangue*.

Concerning *litter*, Lacan introduces (as we will see, in *JI* and *JII*) other perspectives, bringing into effect precisely the concepts implied by the teaching he is setting forth. Thus, he plays on the word *f.a.u.n.e.*[3] The faun has no existence outside of the signifying domain. Likewise, in the hackneyed example used in the manuals of logic: Does the centaur exist or not, or is it the signifier, we might ask, that gives it existence? Are we thus dealing with a creation *ex nihilo* by the signifier? Let us set out a response by way of the negative. Lacan speaks, in exactly the same context, of the *faun* because it can be used as a pun to link up with the letter as litter: phonetics becoming "faunetics" (the pun condensing "faun" and "ethics").[4] In phonetics, we are able to *invent*—and evacuate—anything at all; we do this with the letter, which is ultimately or primarily rooted in the *phoné*. And if we invent faunlike creatures, what should they be called? Nonexistent? This notion raises questions about the basic principle of Freudian reality: accordingly, ethics is no longer to be defined in reference to *Realität*, but

---

3. *JI*, p. 26.
4. *JII*, p. 31. This pun may not be without a further glancing reference to the letter, phonetics, and music in Joyce. In fact, the singular relation of Joycean writing to music (going back to his father John) is well known. Is Lacan not thus also alluding to Debussy's arrangement of Mallarmé's *Prelude a l'apres-midi d'un faune*?

rather to be redefined as an "ethics of the faunic." In other words: ethics aims at *invention*, due to bits of Real, fueling a heretical praxis.[5]

Furthermore, phonemics shows another occurrence of *ph*, taking us back to the Phallus. The latter term, of course, reveals its well-known predominance in neurosis, emerging as the signifier par excellence, as zero. It has, according to what we have argued, no material form, for the Phallus is what, running through our discourse, bestows signification: in the last instance, it libidinizes "everything" that we can "do," for it is what lacks. Because the Phallus has no preestablished embodiment, everything can be virtually rendered phallic. But for the final Lacan, the Phallus is not positioned simply as zero, as that which lacks; as we have seen, it connects the false hole made up of Σ and S, *but does not found it*, because it does not begin the series in the same way that zero does. According to our reading, then, to the unconditional Name-of-the-Father is added in theory a conditional Phallus. For even if it is mobile, phonemics does not amount to a sliding "search" of the Phallus, but to a (serious) form of play, of an auto-erotic nature. It is a matter of playing with sounds, of jouissance of and with fauns—far removed from the phallic logic that governs the opposition marked/nonmarked. This does not come back to the discovery or capture of phallic signification—bestowed, we recall, by the Other, for it belongs to the Other—as occurs with neurosis, where this signification is poured into the symptom. The way that the Phallus forms part

---

5. To this extent, do we not need to respond to this theoretical rupture by moving beyond the classical statement of psychoanalytic ethics in Seminar 7?

of phonemics allows us to understand why Lacan writes *ph-onation*: it is therefore now the real of the Phallus, no longer understood as the signifier that divides up sites for its subject. Let us repeat: in accordance with this new ethics—this new logic—we are producing an invention. And it is here that we find another of the "secrets" secreted by invention: it is no longer the invention of a meaning, but it now consists in—why not?—the faunic design of non-sense. And thus we encounter Joyce. The production of nonsense fueled by the jouissance of phonemics comes together with the real—the impossible—of signification, the result of what signifies nothing and is linked to the emergence of nothingness.

Moreover, in the search of the neurotic, and also in psychoanalysis itself in the earliest period of Lacan's teaching, what is sought is the individual's truth. Even if, as we have seen, Lacan states that truth can only be "half-spoken" or attributes the structure of fiction to it, there is no doubt that during this period the structure of the analytic cure relies on an attempt to attain the truth, to unveil it. We recall that, for Lacan, truth is never to be conceived of in the manner of conventional philosophy, that is defined as *adaequatio rei et intellectus*, "the right fit between things and the mind." According to a perspective reliant on Heidegger's thinking, Lacan declares that truth is *alethia*, unveiling, dis-covery of the veil that impedes understanding. This is the emphasis that we can locate in Lacan's early work, whereas it is not given the same status in, or considered as relevant to, the work of the "final" Lacan, as we have termed him. For the latter, truth will constitute a situational component, structured in a discourse. We cannot fail to note this from the way Lacan writes the different positions linked, in a fixed pattern, by the four discourses:

The above is one of the possible versions; as can be seen, truth is a site, equivalent to the three other sites in the structure. The terms occupy different sites as they rotate according to the different discourses—a topic we will not explore in depth here, to avoid embarking on a long digression. Briefly, the site of truth is one among others: neither a decisive nor a definitive site. Consequently, it is not what our work as analysts should aim at. Truth, in the crucial role assigned to it while Lacan was preoccupied with matters relating to the symptom, leaves the stage when the engagement with the *sinthome* begins to take on a growing intensity. As we know, Lacan wishes to devote his final intellectual efforts to the Real, and no longer to truth. The Real, as he shows in his seminar, neither admits nor acknowledges any form of binding. Lacan maintains, furthermore, that the Real always comes in bits, in fragments. Let us note the gap between this description and the nature of the concepts we listed in the left-hand column at the end of the last chapter; those concepts, in one way or another, manifest articulation, bond, substitution, or slippage—in the last instance, system or structure. Even situated around a hole, even if the structure is not full or lacks a *Gestalt*, these concepts imply a necessary reference to a relational logic. Our columns thus propose to put truth on the left, the Real on the right: on the side of the symptom, what is articulated and articulable; on that of the *sinthome*, bits and pieces.

---

6. J. Lacan, *Seminar XX: Encore*, op. cit.

In order to approach the next binary opposition, let us turn to something hinted at in the earliest seminars—in fact, precisely in the first, where Lacan indicates that it is necessary to go through moments of depersonalization in analysis. What does this imply? Depersonalization entails the loss of references and connections, a sense of emptiness and of no longer knowing who one is. This phenomenon is very common in schizophrenia, which can be identified through forms of depersonalization, strangeness, and/or unreality. This occurs when the ropes that moor us slip, so to speak, no longer maintain us in our being. And this is the crux: Lacan will tend to ascribe importance to *having* rather than being. For "having" is something it is quite possible to cease doing, whereas "being" will remain one of our most precious fantasies. In fact, we can see something of the way that advertising cleverly "bites on" the real of this fantasy: a recent poster in Buenos Aires declared, "To be," adding that this designated low-fat dairy products, and concluding, "because the most important thing is to be yourself." This is perfect *self* psychology: the most important thing is (to be) yourself. There is a patent belief in being on display here. By contrast, Lacan proposes that we should recognize ourselves "in what we have," given that "to have something, is to be able to do something with it,"[7] a phrase recalling the "know-how-with" we explored in Chapter 4. In the last instance, being is a defense. When we say what we are, "we believe it," for "to be" belongs, says Lacan, to the order of copulation (in both a verbal and a sexual sense, of course). It is a narcissistic or imaginary belief, although it has to be understood carefully if we are to distin-

---

7. *JII*, p. 32.

guish it from the "being" placed alongside meaning by the *vel*, as outlined in the previous chapter. In that passage, being was "elective," since the *sinthome* does not demand meaning. The distinction between these two senses of "being" is similar to that between the one that unifies and "There's One." Thus, if being in the sense bound up with identity stimulates copulation, the Real by contrast, insofar as it fragments us, disinvests us from the unconscious. By emerging in fragments, it immerses us, when we come in contact with it, in particularly productive situations. And as experienced in analysis, these situations appear sharply in the dimension of the act: having gone through the event, one is no longer the same as before. This is one of the most elementary definitions of what is entailed by an analytic act: as a praxis of the Real, analysis—no longer a search for truth—allows the analysand to traverse such experiences in several ways, and reversibly.[8] Thus, the predominance of the Real in the face of truth is one of the fundamental points that allow us to reflect on the nature of the *sinthome*.

This last point allows us to reinscribe an everyday phenomenon linked by Freud, at a structural level, to the symptom: that is, anxiety. Clearly, anxiety can be referred back to the triptych we explored in Chapter 1; but Lacan brings out another aspect of it when he reminds us that the word *Angst* entails, etymologically, a sense of being "narrow" or "constrained." Such constriction is simple to identify in bodily sensation—or more precisely, in feelings in the throat and

---

8. Of course, "early Lacan," as we are calling him, was not completely unaware of this point. In "The Function and Field of Speech and Language in Psychoanalysis" (1953), he is already situating analytic work as a search to suspend the "certainties" of the analysand. Cf. *Écrits*, op. cit., p. 241.

chest. Beyond this level of bodily phenomena, Lacan argues—in Seminar 10, *Anxiety*—that anxiety is governed by the constriction of the gap between desire and jouissance.

What is it, by contrast, that occurs when we confront the paradigmatic case of Joyce and his *sinthome*? In *JII*, we find some more wordplay around a pun on "obscene"—a quality detected in Joyce's work by many a reader. What is provoked is not exactly anxiety, but another sensation that we will identify shortly. First, let us follow Lacan's argument by considering his neologism, *l'eaubscene*.[9] We could clearly read there the word *eau*, "water," but that would be to miss the point. What we should pick up on here is that, although Lacan never makes it clear in metatheoretical terms, the "b" that follows *eau* could also be written before it, to produce *beau*, "beautiful." It is a question of the "beau-scene" or scene of beauty—and at the same time, of the obscene. For the aesthetic, as we have indicated above, is not confined to the beautiful: its jouissance also entails obscenity. This is one of the fundamental supports of an aesthetics that we can justly describe—especially after *Ulysses*—as "post-Joycean," and that there are no grounds to label hastily an aesthetics "of the ugly." Indeed, we are not, in all rigor, dealing with the "ugly" here, but with a singular *mise en scene*.[10]

We understand by this a montage of scenes that attain beauty, paradoxically, by way of obscenity. For this reason, the obscene does not provoke anxiety, but rather disgust. It is precisely by provoking disgust that Joyce does not seem to

---

9. *JII*, p. 31.

10. We might relate this scenario to the verbal parasite discussed in Chapter 6. In other words, the scenario is also afflicted by the parasite, which it seeks to get rid of due to know-how-with the *sinthome*.

concern himself with the reader. And this lack of concern for the reader, we suggest, might derive in turn from Joyce's disinvestment from the unconscious: it is this that produces the lack of empathy in reading the text, makes the text so "repulsive." It is not only the mode of the text's narration that is repulsive, but equally what is narrated. Lacan thus makes apparent to us, through the term "obscenity," the subversive significance of Joyce's work, which consists in managing to have introduced the crucial factor of revulsion into narrative. In fact, this subversive quality goes beyond narrative and touches on the domain of writing itself; it truly forms part of the general field of aesthetics or art. It is this quality, in sum, that "opens up" the *sinthome*.

By contrast, as we see over time in our clinical experience, it is not disgust that accompanies symptoms. It is thus valid to assign disgust a place after the "progress" of some "victim" to hysteria, the hysteric currently feeling disgust for the penis. But what we have here is a displacement onto signifiers that are rooted in orality, for disgust is essentially oral, linked to vomiting.[11] (Thus, we can conclude again that the Real is vomited, spat out.) But the hysteric takes as her reference the Phallus, and suffers anxiety at the prospect of being "deflowered." In our view, at any rate, disgust does not have an absolute value in itself, but is significant as an index of non-anxiety, whereas anxiety encapsulates feeling the desire of the Other. In other words, disgust or an equivalent sensation bears witness to a disinvestment from the uncon-

---

11. Few authors have been able to describe a vomiting scene with the same scope and literary panache as Kenzaburo Oé. The reason is clear: it provokes disgust. Cf. K. Oé, *A Personal Matter*, tr. J. Newman. London: Weidenfeld and Nicolson, 1969.

scious and the bypassing of the Other. Lastly, we will examine in the final chapter the function and the emergence of disgust in Joyce, around literary fantasies of his "own" body, imagined through the intermediary of Stephen.

Let us first address a different point. The symptom requires an interpretation: in the previous chapter, we argued that it demands a meaning, but in what follows we will resituate interpretation as the creation of signification. Let us reiterate: a question arises, addressed to the Other, which it enriches by creating a signification. This signification can only be phallic. So, if this decisive moment in the direction of the treatment occurs, a risk can emerge, which Lacan emphasizes from 1974: the symptom can be swollen up with meaning (or signification). Swelling up a symptom or inflating it means endowing it with an excessive weight or presence via the meanings lent it by the analyst. In Seminar 24, *L'insu* . . . , Lacan claims that there are cases, frequently among "re-analyses," where what is needed is in fact a "counter-analysis" to break down the imaginarization of the Symbolic or the reign of a pan-symbolism based on *Realität*.[12] There are well-known anecdotes about people who asked Lacan for a new analysis and were advised to seek a "de-analysis." In the end, the same desideratum as "counter-analysis" was at stake: to puncture the sphere of nonexplicated meanings, in order to allow all the over-significance that heated it to drain away. Over-significance results in nothing so much as the further constriction of the symptom. Talk of re-analysis implies that the earlier analysis, in at least one respect (which is usually not hard to iden-

---

12. J. Lacan, Seminar 24: *L'insu*. . . , session of December 14, 1976, unpublished.

tify), failed. As we know, it is the symptom, more than the analysand, that "calls us"; the symptom cries out in pain, its demand to be heard becoming unbearable.

As for the *sinthome*, instead of moving toward the creation of a signification or an interpretation—closely linked to what we explored in the previous chapter concerning the production of riddles—it offers deciphering. It can do this because it is bound up with the notion of the letter; and because deciphering implies the cipher, ciphered language, or language in need of deciphering. This is why Lacan rejects the notion of decoding, which implies the application of a preestablished, always self-identical key—whereas deciphering works with the singular, case by case. Thus, a condition of the *sinthome* is that it is ciphered. But insofar as the anxiety leading to the demand for interpretation does not arise, what emerges is not this demand but the offer of deciphering via the production of riddles already mentioned. If we place on the side of the symptom a demand, on the side of the *sinthome* we see something like, "Let's see how you manage with that." The subjective position in each of these constellations is radically different.

We will conclude our effort to extend the opposing columns by considering two modal categories. Such categories, as considered by philosophy—especially by Kantians—are diverse, but Lacan concentrated on four in particular. To give simple definitions, these are the necessary, the contingent, the possible, and the impossible. We have already touched on the way in which these are linked to the question of what is written: not in the simple sense of tracing signs onto paper, but in that of modes of inscription in the dimension of the subject. Concerning this, in our reading, it is clear that the symptom is possible. This looks, lexically, like a joke; so how is it argued? The symptom is possible, in Lacan's terms, because it ceases to be written: it was once written, and has clearly slipped away from that status. Better still, its situation is similar to that of a word that, in the course of its history, has moved from an initial meaning to one quite different. This has happened to innumerable terms, if one examines their philological trajectories. If the reader looks in an etymological dictionary, she will discover the unexpected origins of words, and often find meanings astonishingly antithetical to those currently given to a particular term. We might say that, at a definable moment in its history, the word ceased to be written. And we can make the same claim about the symptom: it was inscribed "in excess," and has been washed away by analytic treatment. It has disappeared, making room for another constellation and another destiny.

In the case of the *sinthome*, we can state that it is necessary. The *sinthome* is necessary, in our experience, not only due to the description Lacan gives of it but also because of the statements of analysands. Almost with the word "necessary" alone, people convey their singular modes of know-how-with, as, for example, "Doing that was absolutely inescapable for me" or "I cannot live unless I do it." Traditional academic philosophy has given a classical definition of the necessary: "That which is and which cannot cease being." Let us stress: "If I do not *do* this, I'll die, I'll go mad." What, then, is the necessary? Lacan gives us the following formula: it is "that which does not cease being written." If the symptom is that which ceases to be written, the *sinthome*—linked to it via the interior eight mentioned above— is that which does not cease to be written. One after the other, it turns and returns. This is why it is *necessary* to write it again, at both points. And the result may be a man of letters, in the double sense mentioned above.

The following table, now completed, is a first outline of what our argument was seeking to present:

Symptom	*Sinthome*
Two: transitive unconscious knowledge: demands Other, i(a)	There is One (alone), intransitive
Ex-sists in the unconscious (referring to the Symbolic); limit	Disinvested from the unconscious, exiled, outside discourse, artificed (*savoir faire*)
Believes in meaning	"Another mode" of credibility: *J'ouïs-sens*, believes in being & S_1
Speaking-being [*Parlêtre*]	LOM (individual)
Seeks meaning in S_1, addressee	Undoes meaning: produces enigmas, seeks S_2
Hysterical identification with a question (S_2)	Identification with the One of the *sinthome* (S_1)
"Rotten," phallic, bodily jouissance	Opaque, mental jouissance of the Other
Name-of-the-Father (Father-of-the-Name)	Unconditioned Name-of-the-Father (without the fourth there is no RSI)
Metaphor (substitution)	Nomination—r. s. i.
Repression	'Actual' *Verwerfung* (foreclosure)
Signifier (articulable)	Letter—*faun*—litter
Phallus	*Ph*-onation
Truth	Real
Believing in it: Narcissistic Infatuation	Having: being-able-to-do-something-with
Anxiety	*Eaubscenity*, disgust
Interpretation: requirement of (phallic) signification	Deciphering
The possible	The necessary

We will now begin a second comparative table that will
take into account, as we will see, the dichotomy we have just
been examining. For this, we will rely partly on one of the
last sessions of the seminar, dated March 16, 1976. This session once again foregrounds a line of thinking which at times
can be difficult to follow, for it seems to resemble a series of
free associations. However, it is governed by a strict logic that
only lacks, precisely, the Imaginary, in that it is without the
marks of unifying connections. We have to go along the "I
strand" in order, through terms like "thus," "after," "due to,"
"consequently," "in relation to," and so on, for a sequence to
take shape at a manifest level. Of course, we should not be
surprised that Lacan presents his teaching "in bits," given that
his claim is precisely that the Real itself appears in bits. Thus,
the phrases that emerge have a self-sufficient appearance, in
an aphoristic, almost axiomatic mode. The question is how
to present, give, or transmit a fragment of the Real. To this
end, and without abandoning his Joycean project, Lacan
broaches a new word-game, claiming that "Joyce is an
a-Freud." We might read this as corresponding to the Irishman's opposition to Freud, with the "a" as a negative prefix: that is, "Joyce is a non-(or anti-) Freud." Yet Lacan's next
claim is that, precisely because Joyce is a-Freud, he is *affreux*
["frightful"], returning us to the question of the *obscene*. And
then, bizarrely, Lacan talks of a-Joyce. Surely he can't mean
an anti-Joyce? No, for the "a" here is not a negative prefix,
but designates the object *a*: Joyce as *a*. And it is at this point
that we can begin our new table.

   This *a*, as the residue of structure, does not rely on or
form part of a relation. What, then, is the *a* opposed to? All
other objects, that is, those of everyday displacement, the
familiar objects that are eroticized but that, unlike the *a*, are

not objects causing desire. All these other objects entail a *relation* [*rapport*]with others. What, then, justifies talking of "a-Joyce"? For Lacan, Joyce has jouissance in and with his *sinthome* and thus does not enter into the neurotic relation that is defined by subjection to the demand of the Other. On this crucial point, Lacan sees common ground rather than discrepancy: *a*-Freud, *a*-Joyce.

Now, *rapport* is, as we know, a word with a powerful resonance in Lacan's teaching, for above all it designates *rapport sexuel*, the sexual relation. In this sense, Lacan maintains decisively that the aim of transmitting a fragment of the Real is reached by stating that there is no sexual relation. The oft-mentioned sexual relation is not inscribed—written—in anybody's unconscious. But the other kinds of object, for their part, do enter into a *rapport*. How is this? By being absorbed into language, for relations are expressed in language. (Remember that we are talking of objects in the erotic sense here, and not in that of empirical reality.) These objects, then, absorbed by language and put into relation, can only produce epithets, Lacan claims. This is a clinical point, an intriguing and perceptive one, as we will see. Epithets are a part of language made up of participles or adjectives that, rather than specifying or determining the substantive, aim to characterize it. That is to say: epithets take shape as such in the very act of adding a "plus." Thus, it is alongside the object, within its relation, that an epithet occurs. And what does it lead to? Inevitably, to "yes" and "no," taken as a fundamental dialectical couple that sets the pattern for analogous conceptions. As we observe, someone speaks about an individual, assigning an epithet to him or her. One might respond "no," that he or she is not like that; or "yes," agreeing with the speaker's judgment. This kind of exchange is of course the stuff of our daily experience. With this order entailing "yes" and "no," we encounter a classical proverb (in Spanish): "There is not a yes or no between them."[13] Of whom would we say this, if not a couple? Reading literally, we might draw from this a general aphorism, once we have put aside denial: *the epithet is a push-to-couple.* This fits completely with clinical experience. On the other hand, we can "form a couple'" insofar as—to recall our discussion above—we produce (a) metaphor. That is, we can "take a bladder for a lantern." To put this more clearly, we might say that we frequently make mistakes, and by doing so sometimes form a couple.

To explore further the figure used by Lacan, he indicates that if one inserts a flame into a bladder, it may look like a lantern. It is clearly a metaphor—but Lacan adds, "The fire is the Real." This phrase serves as a pivotal point allowing us to grasp how far the definition of this register extends, given that he then adds: "But it is a cold fire." Lacan thus seems to brush against the borders of absurdity: fire, of course, is one of the principle elements of heat. Yet Lacan continues: "The fire that burns is a mask, so to speak, of the Real." In itself, the register in question has no characteristics, for having any would imply having a meaning.[14] But it emerges that the Real—and here again we use this "strong" term—forecloses meaning (a point we will come back to shortly). Thus, the Real has a lower boundary: which is, precisely, cold. It is absolute zero, death,

---

13. Translator's note: The expression indicates perfect agreement without debate.

14. Once again, there is a clear link between this point and the ideas of negative theology. For the latter, any attribute assigned to God—however superlative—only has the effect of reducing his stature, which is unattainable, ineffable. And unspeakable, of course.

the unthinkable. By stating that it is burning, we are already producing a metaphor, injecting a certain meaning into it. And there are no grounds for claiming that this fire is flaming, because this simple predicate already takes us into the domain of reality. The Real is located, we recall, beyond reality, and thus it does not correspond to an opposition like that of hot and cold. Yet Lacan's next statement is even more surprising, concerning the possibility of "having" a bit of Real: he says that "light is not more obscure than the shadows." We note the paradox: one might have said "not more clear" to express an absurdity that was based on essentialist definitions. Or is Lacan's phrase simply a useless tautology? In our view, he is showing here what can be done with signifiers—for, to be strictly accurate, the phrase ends: ". . . than the shadows, and vice versa." With this substitutive inversion, together with the use (or abuse) of the exchange of epithets, Lacan aims to illustrate how much we are bound up with metaphor, in an unexpected way; without knowing it, we function on its terms. And this "spontaneous" function—in other words, one governed by metaphor—seems to comprise the sexual relation. Expressions like "they were made for each other," "they make a lovely pair," or 'they were born to meet one another" might support an argument against the absence of the sexual relation. In an indirect manner, the same could be said of the dimension of the unconscious—that a.b.c. of psychoanalysis—which the "final" Lacan tends to approach from the perspective of trickery. Thus, in a blunt phrase, Lacan describes language as "a side-track completely like a bladder [?!]." That is, language lies, not in the sense of telling a falsehood, but rather in that of the *ment* in *ce qu'on dit ment*, as mentioned above. The speaking-being lies without a trace of bad faith, without explicitly formulating a lie; by the mere fact of using metaphor, it is caught up in a dimension of lying. And it is this function of the *ment*, claims Lacan, that determines that every speaker believes he exists. Here, we see the point of the above-cited remarks about the illusion of "being oneself." But what happens with the unconscious? Its course being governed by metaphor, the unconscious "is only given in traces, and traces which not only cancel themselves out but which every instance of discourse tends to cancel out. . . ." This statement underlines yet again the definitive nature of the "cut" effected by the final Lacan: it reveals in practice his skepticism about the possibility of traces in the Real being left by the unconscious. Like the symptom, these traces are possible and not necessary, so they likewise form part of the *mensonge* ["lie"].

It is here that Lacan returns to Joyce. The famous Dubliner never stopped launching his criticisms of history, lambasting it as merely a heap of big words that impeded our progress and hampered us with inestimable prejudices. Such a conception undoubtedly emerges from the quotations from *A Portrait* we discussed in the previous chapter. But Joyce's response was to write *Finnegans Wake*—which, like all dreams, is a "nightmare." However, since there is "no particular dreamer" but the dream itself, Joyce slips at this point—implicitly and imperceptibly— toward Jung, his attempt to ward off history sliding toward the "collective unconscious."

Following this there come a series of definitions that we can gloss succinctly. First, Lacan rules out history—not in an allegedly structuralist mode, but because when we turn to history, we immediately fall into myth. And if we are able to transcend myth, we will discover fantasy. We can thus stipu- late a sort of gradation: "behind" each great event identified by speakers as having been "historical," we can sketch in the corresponding myth; and it is around this myth that history has come to be organized. In this context, the myth recognized by Joyce goes back to Giambattista Vico: a circular understanding of history. Lacan emphasizes that, for Joyce, "Vico is a dream." Accordingly, Joyce believed absolutely that history followed a circular pattern, returning to the same point again and again (a belief shared by Spengler).[15] And this notion of turning around, of the circularity of history, is indeed nothing but a fantasy. To sum up, then: fantasy, myth, and history are located in the dimension of what we can call the *Ment* ["lie"]. These three concepts thus entail the dream of the *Wake*—and not its nightmare.

The moment has come to include a brief description of Joyce's final, nodular work, in order to arrive at a clearer understanding of some of Lacan's claims. We will follow the pioneering work of Joseph Campbell and Henry Morton Robinson in *A Skeleton Key to "Finnegans Wake"* (see Chapter 4 above). This study was published in 1944, five years after the appearance of the *Wake*; we will draw on one section of it, entitled "Introduction to a Strange Subject." We will accompany the authors by reading a paragraph that is relatively long, due to its importance and its didactic value. Of course, our reading relies on the continuing development of the table; in particular, we think it illustrates why we place in the left-hand

---

15. In recognition of the frequent, irrefutable instances of the unpredictable—of the impossibility of predicting, a master historian like Georges Duby gives a recent book the modest title *L'histoire continue* (Paris: O. Jacob, 1991). Yes: history continues . . . but we know not how, or where to. For a deeper exploration of the relations between psychoanalytic teaching and "micro-histories" (compared with the epic history of wars, liberations, and so on), cf. R. Harari, "Psicopatologia?," in *Intensions freudianas.* Buenos Aires: Nueva Vision, 1991, pp. 45–67.

column the reference to the dream in the *Wake*. Campbell and Robinson, then, write:

> Running riddle and fluid answer, *Finnegans Wake* is a mighty allegory of the fall and resurrection of mankind. It is a strange book, a compound of fable, symphony and nightmare—a monstrous enigma beckoning imperiously from the shadowy pits of sleep. Its mechanics resemble those of a dream, a dream which has freed the author from the necessities of common logic and has enabled him to compress all periods of history, all phases of individual and racial development, into a circular design, of which every part is beginning, middle and end.
>
> In a gigantic wheeling rebus, dim effigies rumble past, disappear into foggy horizons, and are replaced by other images, vague but half-consciously familiar. On this revolving stage, mythological heroes and events of remotest antiquity occupy the same spatial and temporal planes as modern personages and contemporary happenings. All time occurs simultaneously; Tristram and the Duke of Wellington, Father Adam and Humpty Dumpty merge in a single percept. Multiple meanings are present in every line; interlocking allusions to key words and phrases are woven like fugal themes into the pattern of the work. *Finnegans Wake* is a prodigious, multifaceted monomyth, not only the *cauchemar* of a Dublin citizen but the dreamlike saga of guilt-stained, evolving humanity.[16]

Further on, Campbell and Robinson refer to Vico, to the four stages of the Viconian conception of history, a history

---

16. J. Campbell and H. M. Robinson, *A Skeleton Key to "Finnegans Wake."* New York: Harcourt & Brace, 1944, p. 3.

that is absolute, global, capable of accounting for everything. Here, crucially, in our view, we can see how Imaginary and Symbolic nomination works in Joyce, given that his book aims to be a representation of nothing less than the whole of humanity. A "little" ambition, in fact (we will come back to this point below).

To continue with our exploration of the series of oppositions, we note that Lacan adds to the line we have termed *Ment*, the adjective "meaningful" [*sensé*]. The line is thus full "of the risk of misunderstanding." Here, he sets forth another of his mild but significant criticisms of Freud: for it is the latter who produced something "meaningful." Thus, in relation to what he himself is seeking to propose, Lacan declares (not without a slight touch of irony?) that for him this "takes away all hope." Accordingly, we are now able to place hope on the line of the *Ment*; and conversely, in the opposite column that begins with *a*, we can locate *doing*. For it is better not to hope for something, says Lacan, but to do it "really." It is very likely that this point is made with a view to one of the habitual alibis of the obsessional neurotic: that rationalized as "cherishing hopes." Here, we are not claiming that this is inherently harmful, but it might add an interesting argument to the problem identified by Lacan as "procrastination." This is something that emerges every day in psychoanalytic practice, and it consists in "why do today what you can put off till tomorrow." The tomorrow in question, of course, will never arrive; it is effectively a limitless wager, aiming to conjure away castration. Rather than hoping for something, then, doing it. Or in different terms, rather than the hope of *Realität*, the realization inherent to *Wirchlichkeit*. To conclude—Lacan, rather than Freud?

Let us now return, as we reach our conclusion, to the table we are in the process of constructing. On the right-hand

side—which we will dub *Cold fire*—we locate the *a*, standing in for the sexual nonrelation, as bound up with the Real.
It is for this reason that the *a* harbors the dimension of unknotting. On the opposite side to *a* are located the other
kinds of object, bound up in relations in and through language. The latter, moreover, lead to three things: epithets,
yes/no, and (implicitly) the couple. This "integration," these
three variables, are rejected by Lacan, who argues that in
analytic treatment it is a matter of attaining a bit of Real.
The three moments listed above, as we can see, speak of
integration, of harmony, of making one out of two, of an-
drogyny, and so on. By contrast, Lacan postulates the "fragment": not only the noncouple, but not even the "one." It is
clear that the order that the "final" Lacan aims to grasp—
that of the fragment of Real, of a fragmentary knowledge of
the originary unconscious of invention—is opposed to all
the many aspects of the illusory belief that "there is" a relation. That illusion is workable, as we have shown, due to
the function of metaphor. On the other hand, the production of metaphor is what leads to meaning. Yet in this seminar,
Lacan contributes something new: "We must break through,
so to speak, to a new Imaginary in relation to meaning." Let
us pause over this word, for it picks up on what we have
already noted concerning Freud's "'meaningful' quality:
sensé ["meaningful"] is obviously linked to *sens* ["meaning"].
If Freud is meaningful, Lacan wishes to introduce a new
Imaginary in relation to meaning. But how is he to accomplish this? Clearly, by foreclosing meaning: we recall his
statement that the Real forecloses meaning. What does this
entail? We need to attempt a new reading of the diagram of
the triple Borromean chain. We recall that, in this diagram,

meaning is located where Imaginary and Symbolic overlap (Figure 46):

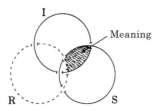

Figure 46

The Real forecloses meaning for, if one traces the ring of this register—here given, as a trivial knot, in a broken line—meaning remains outside of it. In Lacan's words, meaning ex-sists—remains outside of—the Real, and vice versa. But he chooses to use the "hardest," most conclusive term possible: foreclosure, which goes beyond ex-sistence. Here, we have one of the places where we can read most easily— as we will see in more detail in the next chapter—the way in which certain operations of foreclosure open up in language, without leading to psychosis. We should repeat, in this context, our criticism of the (many) theorists who allege that, following the consistency of his arguments, Lacan found himself positing, in a distorted manner, a "mad Joyce," the victim of foreclosure. According to the trajectory we have outlined, the error of such a claim is self-evident. The foreclosure of meaning is compatible with a new Imaginary that is recuperated by meaning. As we have argued, analysis, insofar as it is therapeutic (one of its distictive qualities), does not rely on the production of new meaning. In Seminar 2, Lacan's position was already similar: he argued that

as analysts we should give to each analysand the possibility
of coming to be articulated around our common, fundamental nonmeaning. And this comes back, yet again, to the beneficial depersonalization we discussed above. Because this
is a matter of finding a way in which the "scrounging" of
meaning characteristic of the neurotic—that is, his bestowal
of a fixed, univocal sense to different events in his life—can
be cast into doubt, "forbidden." To be clear: the idea is based
on the birth of a new Imaginary in relation to meaning,
which, determined by foreclosure, is located in opposition
to the metaphorical production of meaning.

Our next move is to write the unconscious on the side of
the *Ment*, together with the "trap" entailed by "being." In one
session of the seminar, Lacan addresses the unconscious—governed by the metaphorical dimension—in terms of three pos-
sibilities. There is, he tells us, a way of being able to do what
we are seeking after, to grasp the fragment of Real, and it is
founded on our position as analysts. In his earlier work, he
had stated this as occupying the place of the Other, the site of
speech, of the articulation of signifiers, given that the unconscious was to be reduced to the discourse of the Other. But at
this later logical moment of the seminar, in *Le sinthome*, he
states that the analyst becomes a semblance of the object *a*.
Perhaps this "semblance" is the sole way that we can succeed,
as analysts, in realizing the experience designated by *a*: embodying it as an "apparition." By becoming a semblance of *a*,
it is possible, says Lacan, to rediscover a certain "bit" of the
Real. Yet a self-critical note must be sounded here: What is
the meaning of "rediscover"? It might seem to go back to Vico,
to the circle or cyclical motion. For this sense, however, Lacan
proposes the direct term "to find." This, at any rate, is a dif-

ficult point, for Lacan—following Freud's lead—taught that every discovery of an object entails a rediscovery. But now, in order to counter this circular conception, he chooses to reject the notion of rediscovery. Rigorously speaking, this recalls what he had proposed about nonprogress, the illusion of progress. Concerning this, it cannot be denied that there have been numerous advances in many domains of existence; but, as we know, what is gained on one side is lost on the other: the law of castration. Yet our illusion, our "belief" persists: infatuated, we will not give up our claims of having made progress. There is no such thing as progress: with this formula, Lacan clashed head-on with the young "revolutionary" ideologues of May '68 in Paris. He argued that they wished to knock down one master so as to produce another, for in his opinion it was certain that they sought a master, and perhaps one even worse than the master they were fighting. Today, we do not need to embark on long discussions to confirm the accuracy of his predictions.

To sum up, then: if I claim to "rediscover" the Real, this indicates, as the one and only factor in support of that notion, nonprogress. If there is Real, strictly speaking, this can only be with reference to death, to the trace of death (understood, of course, in the Freudian sense of death drive). For once again it is a question of thinking about a limit. Yet despite his claims about the illusory notion of progress, Lacan continued almost right to the end of his life to produce new and fertile concepts, apt to relaunch a whole series of problematics. For example, we find him here—he who had argued with such rigor against the erroneous expression "death instinct," and who had proposed *pulsion* ["drive"] instead—now retranslating the Freudian term *Trieb* as *"dérive"* ["drift," "derive"],[17] when the old term was already being held sacred. It seems bizarre, obviously, to speak of a "death derive" or a "life derive." For the time being, then, we will continue to use the classical *pulsion* ["drive"]. On the side of the *Cold fire*, we situate the death drive, since death is unthinkable; it is, in fact, "the Real insofar as it can only be thought as impossible." Why is this? A first response might be to point to the simple fact that no one has ever died and then given an account of it. Our psychical apparatus is made up of representations, traces, imprints. It is not enough to witness the death of someone, as the death of another can never be equivalent to our own death. There is no trace of death in any speaking-being, since its signifier is lacking. When an analysand speaks of death, one must try and discover what it is he is actually referring to. The usual Freudian response, yet again pioneering and accurate, was to refer to castration anxiety rather than to some supposed anxiety about death or some such rationalizing explanation.

The three Lacanian responses we have looked at—semblance of *a*, there is no such thing as progress, death drive—are also articulated around yet another point. We have noted that the triad of the *Ment* formed by fantasy, myth, and history was the dream of the *Wake*. On the other side we find the nightmare, representing one of the sites where the Real impacts most precisely. Next, after the nightmare, Lacan points to a transcendent clinical pathway. For what is the meaning of his claim—ostensibly mistaken—that "every dream is a nightmare"? In our

---

17. Why should we not posit that this translation "derives" from a translinguistic pun à la Joyce, whose starting point would be the common English translation of *Trieb* as "drive"?

view, this is not reductionist but hierarchical, for Lacan is sug-
gesting that we pay more attention to the nightmare than to
the dream; effectively, because the former confronts us with a
dimension other than that of wish-fulfillment (Freud's definition, we recall, of the dream's "aim"). The nightmare thus reveals an unbearable build-up of jouissance, in the face of which
the only option is to wake up and interrupt the dream. In this
order, on the basis of the Real, all dreams are nightmares. Thus,
Lacan is indicating a way of prioritizing dreams: to lay more
emphasis, in our analytic listening, on nightmares than on
ordinary dreams. For the latter, conceived as wish-fulfillments,
move forward swiftly and imperatively in search of meaning.

The final items in the left-hand column, so far, are good
sense and hope. What do we write opposite these? In opposition to hope, we have already inserted "doing." This implies another, "technical" point: it concerns a critique of the
conception of "timing," that is, of waiting for "the right moment" to interpret in order to avoid some disastrous error.
Such a position, however, has an appearance of truth, for it
is undeniable that every analyst has to hope. Yet in a practice that borders on the obsessional—the "safeguarding" of
the setting, each session identical to all the others—the question of hope, in other words of waiting, has a major and
distortive influence. What is opposed to this is a praxis that
relies on what the analyst does, on his know-how-with. A
clinical lesson flowing from this seminar is its emphasis on
sinthomatic action, as the antithesis of the oft-mentioned
"insight," those phrases like "at last I understand" that are
often mouthed by the analysand while his "actions" remain
lamentably tame and safe. This can be easily confirmed in
numerous reanalyses in which the analysand, having gorged
on meaning, claims to "know" all about the interpretations

of her previous analyst, even if the symptom remains imperturbable when she has been through a very long "practice of hope." A practice, we might say, of "one fine day," since desire . . . well, it can always wait (according to the obsessional pattern).

By way of conclusion, and in order to put in place the right term opposite good sense, we will turn to yet another example of Lacan's wordplay. In order to understand this, we need to place it briefly in its context. Lacan is alluding to *Encore* (Seminar 20), and to certain complicated "mathematical" letters it comprises—for instance, designating the symbolic Phallus (Φ), or the signifier of lack in the Other S ($\cancel{A}$). These letters, he states, are not identical. But what is interesting is what comes next: Φ of course denotes the *phi* of the symbolic Phallus, but it is also "the first letter of the word fantasy." Moreover, he adds, this letter situates "the relations of what I will term a function of phonation." This point, which Lacan makes as if in passing, is of crucial importance, for it implies that fantasy has not only a visual dominant but also an auditory dominant, by means of phonation. There is no doubt that this constitutes an overarching transformation. In Seminar 10, Lacan had claimed that the place or "scene" of fantasy was fundamentally scopic. In the present seminar, by contrast, he emphasizes the "invocatory" aspect of fantasy by basing his argument on phonation, which also constitutes— in the line mentioned above—"the essence of Φ." Next, perhaps half-jokingly, he states: "There you are, everything I tell you there [in *Encore*] is merely meaningful [*sensé*]. . . ." There follows the above-mentioned criticism of Freud's good sense, and Lacan's avowal of his own efforts to bring about something different. What is his name for such an undertaking?

He calls it *folie-sophie*, punning on "philosophy" and "folly" or madness [*folie*].[18]

Lacan is well known for his interest in etymology: that of philo-sophy derives from the Greek for "love of wisdom." And this last term takes us back to the Book of Wisdom in the Biblical Apocrypha, attributed to Solomon, where we can find certain indications about the relation between madness and knowledge. In particular, we should turn to Chapter 15, entitled "The Evils of Idolatry"; reading this passage, for us, is of course simply a way of locating or isolating a point. But why does Lacan refer to it, and also recommend us to read it? He remarks that Catholics often look unfavorably upon reading the Bible, or even actively seek to prevent it; whereas he himself encourages people to take up the book. Let us therefore do so. We immediately come across the same example used by Heidegger and taken up again by Lacan, concerning the historical paradigm of artistic creation already mentioned: namely, the potter and his artifacts. Thus, we read in the *Book of Wisdom,*

---

18. The Argentinean poet, novelist, and essayist H. A. Murena (1923–1975) wrote a novel, published posthumously, whose title was, precisely, *Folisofia* (Caracas: Monte Avila, 1976). We might say that the author "invents" a language there: above all, "taking up" the language of the Spanish picaresque novel. He thus works with old Spanish and its orthographic uncertainties, exaggerating and deforming it and borrowing from other languages, principally Italian and French. All of this is done in a context marked by a scabrous, Rabelesian humor. Without wishing to venture into risky conjectures, we would simply point to the correspondences and overlaps here, both with Seminar 23 and with Joyce's writing: a coincidence of signifiers—folisophy, of dates—1975–1976, of the "assault" on "proper" language, and all of this by means of archaisms, translinguistic tropes, mocking wit. . . .

> For when a potter kneads the soft earth and laboriously
> molds each vessel for our service, he fashions out of the
> same clay both the vessels that serve clean uses and those
> for contrary uses, making all in like manner; but which
> shall be the use of each of these the worker in clay decides.[19]

For Lacan, this refers to creation *ex nihilo*, undoubtedly,
but also to a quality he identifies in Joyce: heresy. Joyce was
a heretic, in Lacan's view, because he was was capable of
choosing, which from the Greek *haeresis* forms the etymological root of heresy. What, then, would constitute the wisdom
of the creator? The act of choice, of course. Yet our supposed
Solomon continues:

> With misspent toil, he forms a futile god from the same
> clay—This man who was made of earth a short time
> before.[20]

This points to the possible fate of the created object; and
here Lacan does not hesitate to envisage, or even to propose,
a path that is "mad," that is bound up with madness. The Bible,
for its part, of course condemns heresy as the moral insanity
of the potter, leading to his gift—his only *savoir-faire*—being
used for wretched ends. Let us bear in mind, though, that
in Lacan's view the Joycean problematic is not reducible to
madness. But this is what he is thinking of when he regrets
not being more psychotic, for if he were such, he states, he
would be more rigorous in his conceptualization. In other
words, he would be mad à la Schreber: logical, strict, precise,

---

19. *The Oxford Annotated Apocrypha*, Oxford University Press, 1977,
pp. 120–121.
20. Ibid.

even using mathematical reasoning to grasp bits of Real without involving the dimension of *Ment*. Here, we find madness and wisdom bordering on one another. But this has nothing to do with believing that Joyce was mad.

The table takes its final form as follows:

Ment ["Lie"]	Cold fire
All other objects ↓ Relation ⟵ language ↓ Epithets ↙ ↘ Yes No ↘↙ Couple (sex and language)	*a* | Does not enter into a relation, unbound Fragment of Real
Metaphor (sexual relation) ↓ Unconscious: "to be" ↓ Fantasy ↓ Myth ⟶ Dream of *Wake* ↓ History	New Imaginary in relation to meaning Semblance of *a*, nonprogress: find and turn Death drive Nightmare
↓ Hoping ↓ Good sense	Doing Folisophy

9

Foreclosures, False Holes, Suppletions

In this chapter, we will leave aside questions that are specifically bound up with Joyce, in order to focus on some conceptual elements that so far have been missing from our argument. This will allow us to outline the thesis of the next—and final—stage in our argument. This will constitute drawing up a final table, in an attempt to schematize the argument developed by Lacan, in accordance with his nondeductive method, in every session of his seminar. In the course of the seminar, various propositions are interlinked; our task will be to find their underlying coherence, for they are not at odds with one another, far from it. Hence, in order to complete the table of the present chapter, we must return to a notion that is rearticulated by Lacan many times; hitherto we have referred to it only tangentially, as it were, and hence we will now attempt to explore it in depth. We refer to the radical concept of *Verwerfung*, or foreclosure, in Lacan's teaching.

We have already argued, following a certain popularization of Lacan, that *Verwerfung* can be defined as a central notion allowing us to disciminate between a psychotic and a nonpsychotic. In this way, it would name the process generating the distinctive nature of psychosis—according to a reading that is rudimentary and, in our view, mistaken. We will attempt to consolidate this claim in what follows. To this end, we will take as support the ideas that emerged in an interview with a well-known Lacanian analyst, the late Claude Conté.

Even while still quite young, Conté had been able to follow closely the development of Lacan's work. In an interview published in the review *Analyse Freudienne*, he spoke, among various other topics, about foreclosure. He makes the same case as we are seeking to present here: that is, he refuses to use the notion as some revelation of a "verdict of incurability" for a particular subject. For Conté, such an understanding of foreclosure is astonishing, and corresponds not so much to Lacan's teaching as to the false ideas of certain "Lacanians." Concerning this, he warns against a widespread hijacking of Lacan's statements about how to use the concept. The master, he explains, maintained that "there are certain foreclosures that are more specifically psychosis-inducing," but he never abandoned using the term in relation to neurotics, and even concerning "those we meet in the street." Conté continues by setting out in detail what we have claimed in earlier chapters: namely, that it can be rigorously shown how *Verwerfung* has effects far beyond the structure of psychosis.

Let us repeat: according to Lacan, Joyce suffered a *de facto* foreclosure. We might wonder what *de facto* means here, and if it implies another kind of foreclosure, *de jure*. In the next chapter, we will explore this point more deeply in terms of Joyce. For the present, we will focus on understanding the significance of Lacan's claims in the seminar about the permanence and characteristics of other kinds of foreclosure, distinct from that of the Name-of-the-Father. And it is within this framework that Conté's remarks should be situated. We will outline the general terms of the brief narrative he sketches. First, we have the emergence of a basic foreclosure that is linked to language as such. What constitutes this? Our explanation needs to begin with one of Lacan's most important formulations. In this foundational proposition, he radically distances himself from epistemologists, analytic or linguistic philosophers (and ultimately from all those who attempt to posit linguistic stages or levels, through which it would become possible to differentiate, for example, a concrete from an abstract language: in other words, those who claim to be able to distinguish between language and a discourse about language). Such a language about language is often called meta-language, in accordance—whether avowedly or not—with the Aristotelian tradition, with its distinction between physics and metaphysics. In the same sense, theory is distinguished from meta-theory, mathematics from meta-mathematics. The scope of meta-language thus emerges in a consistent way. For Lacan, there is no such thing as meta-language, although it constitutes one of our dearest-held beliefs. The Lacanian notion of the lack of a meta-language is taken up by Conté, who conceives of it as the effect of a foreclosure. Something is radically lacking there; the gap in question is irreducible, for everything that can be said in language corresponds, inexorably and irreversibly, to a single level. And this is the case because there is no superior language able to account for the imperfections of "natural" languages. There are thus no stages or strata of language: all of this is implied in the formula "there is no meta-language." We will find a good number of Lacanian "there is no" [*il n'y a pas*] formulas that are founded on various kinds of foreclosure. We can see that Lacan begins or concludes a series of points—especially those of an aphoristic quality—by means of an *il n'y a pas* or an *il n'existe pas*. These descriptions are, precisely, bound up with foreclosure. In this sense, as is claimed about the psychotic in relation to the Name-of-the-Father, we can state that other structural constellations show the same feature: a central, irreducible, and irredeemable lack. This is what defines foreclosure.

Concerning the same point, insofar as it is dependent on language, we can locate another aspect of foreclosure. What is it that any psychoanalytic ABC teaches, whether or not Lacanian? Obviously, that a signifier cannot simply represent itself, and nor can a subject. A constant substitution is therefore necessary: no signifier can simply close in on itself. When we isolate a signifier, S_1, it cannot turn back on itself, but because it forms part of a chain it must turn toward another signifier, S_2, to be represented. This law is irreversible, and there is no alternative to its structural condition. This law of representation is the basic principle of the register Lacan dubs the Symbolic: that denomination takes shape out of the endless slippage of the representational chain. Yet what is the Symbolic based on? It is clear, according to Conté, that the basis of that order must be foreclosure. For it is foreclosure that does not allow—we see yet again the way it is always linked to "not"—the signifier to represent only itself. Thus, at the very heart of the Symbolic, defined as the condition and function of language, we find the effects of foreclosure (this is Conté's way of organizing material with precision, and we find it persuasive). Continuing his shrewd and rigorous argument, Conté next endorses Lacan's statement that psychoanalysis reintroduced the dimension of the subject's being. How did it do this, and what had occurred beforehand? We can say that, before the advent of psychoanalysis, that dimension had been foreclosed by science. And this was a result of failing to conceive of the subject as divided, supposing it to be an invariable factor, something whole and full. Science posited the subject as not split between its speech and its knowledge, whereas the division of the subject—written by Lacan as $\mathcal{S}$—inscribes it as the victim of a loss. Effectively, what the speaker says does not express everything he might be able to say; and what is more, he will never be able to say this. The whole question is here: this will be our conclusive reflection on the operation of foreclosure. There will always remain something final, or primal, that is unsayable: this very inexpressibility amounts to a primordial feature of foreclosure.

Here, we come to a third point, which we can term the foreclosure of the subject's being—in other words, its division—by science. Indeed, the very definition of science—we refer to the positivist sense developed by a Karl Popper or a Mario Bunge—works against the place of the subject, insofar as the latter entails a factor or variable that subverts the apprehension of "objective" phenomena. This is why the incidence of the subject must be blocked out, in accordance with the ambition to attain a total "objectivity" by means of technology and measurement. Technological instruments, it is immediately clear, can offer us a sort of endlessly reproducible method, so long as we can keep constant the other variables in play. To put it briefly: the subject, by definition conflict-ridden, always tends to put a spanner in the works, or at least as long as it operates in a totalizing, interchangeable manner. Thus, Lacan himself conceived of the pattern of such a suppressive "ideology" as an effect of foreclosure. And such a foreclosure precedes psychoanalysis, for it was brought about by science in relation to the divided subject. But for Lacan to speak of foreclosure here does not imply that science is madness, psychosis, or something of that kind. Strictly speaking, Lacan is condemning and relativizing a cultural tendency that begins in the 17th century and persists, in an emptily idealized form, right up to the emergence of psychoanalysis. We should add that it is the logical structure of science that forecloses psychoanalysis: the "no" it utters is determined by that structure, beyond any ephemeral imaginary situation.

Let us move on to another *il n'y a pas*, one that introduces arguably the last important concept produced by Lacan's work in his final seminars: that is, the lack of an inscription of the sexual relation. This sexual deracination or radical absence of preestablished sexuality is the condition of "there is no *rapport*." As we have sought to show above, there is no compatibility, no right way to form a couple. This is irreversible and unavoidable: it is a constitutive absence of the speaking-being. Conté equates foreclosure with "there is no sexual relation."

As we begin to get a clear sense of this tonality, we could ask whether another of Lacan's *il n'y a pas* formulas might be linked, as such, to the absence of the sexual relation. We are thinking of The Woman, where the definite article is barred. If the latter were not barred, The Woman would exist as a universal category; thus, by barring the article, Lacan writes the nonexistence of such a category.[1] Obviously, women exist, one by one; in other words, there is no Woman, only women.[2] This corresponds, in the terms we have used, to

---

1. C. Conté, "Entretien," in *Analyse freudienne presse: Hommage à Claude Conté*. Paris: Hors serie, January–February 1993, p. 18.

2. This point, let us recall, should be read in parallel with the notion of *lalangue*, language disjoined from the distinction between universal and particular (proper to language as *la langue*).

the absence of a signifier through which The (unbarred) Woman could "identify herself" because it would represent her. A series of Lacan's succinctly expressed claims flow from this: among them, the notion of a relation between feminine jouissance and mysticism. Or the following idea: that women, due to lack of such a signifier, are in a sense displaced, disoriented, "half-mad" ("half" here indicating "not all"). This, as we know, amounts to a way of praising women's greater empathy in relation to the unconscious, if and only if that very sensitivity does not set off deliriums with a fascinating, alluring "psychological" appearance. This last risk may have notorious effects in various psychological and mental health domains, where women claim to have constructed a signifier that belongs to them, with which they identify. And thanks to such a signifier they can sometimes form groups of the kind that Lacan described memorably as *psychofatuos*. To sum up, then: the irremediable absence of "The" Woman, of a universal category to name woman, is of the order of foreclosure.

At this point, we should specify that Conté is not putting forward a hierarchy or a chronology. He is simply attempting a structured reordering so as to be able to evaluate correctly the insistence of a problematic, and how it can be articulated in terms of a central kernel or key concept: foreclosure.

There is one crucial aspect of foreclosure that Conté does not take into consideration—which is introduced, precisely, in Seminar 23, as discussed in the previous chapter: how the Real forecloses meaning. We recall that this formula flows from the writing—and the reading—of the triple Borromean chain, in its traditional diagrammatic form; where, if the edge of the ring marked Real is traced, we can see that meaning remains outside it. This exclusion of meaning should equally be termed foreclosure, as Lacan proposes explicitly on the basis of his nodal topology. Moreover, we can give this last point a new twist by returning to the puns on jouissance, *j'ouïs-sens* ["I hear meaning"] and *jouis-sens* ["enjoy-meaning"]. If meaning is foreclosed at the expense of what is "faunetic," another term—that becomes a concept—included in *jouis*, is thrust aside: the *oui*, "yes." In fact, we have to recognize the foreclosure of "yes" in extreme cases—which as such are always illustrative or paradigmatic—as shown in the negativism of many psychotics, who systematically choose "no." We can see the working of something like this in the "but not that" of the *sinthome*. There is also a "no" at work there; in this context we recall the ethical position of Socrates, in our view determined by the foreclosure of "yes" in what bears on his *sinthome*. This is one of the supplementary alternatives that we wish to include in this chapter in our articulation of foreclosure. In postulating this, we are claiming that "yes" remains outside the order of meaning. Let us not forget something fundamental: the neurotic condition consists of an extreme facility in saying yes, acceding too easily to the demand of the Other. The foreclosure of "yes" from meaning thus undoubtedly entails a proposition that is—in the best sense of the word—therapeutic.

The following table gives an account of what we have discussed so far concerning foreclosure:

Foreclosure . . .
1. Of language
   a) there is no metalanguage
   b) the signifier cannot represent itself alone
2. Of the being of the $\mathrm{\$}$ (by science)
3. There is no inscription of the sexual relation
4. The Woman (The Woman does not exist)
5. Of meaning, foreclosed by the Real
6. Of "yes," in the *sinthomatic* "but not that"

These foreclosures are therefore alternatives to that of the Name-of-the-Father. The consequence of this is what we have already indicated: we always stumble on some final "unsayable." That which is impossible to say is what causes us to talk constantly, aiming finally to be able to say what—for structural reasons—we will never manage to utter. Lacan's teachings about psychosis should be understood in this light. The psychotic forecloses the Name-of-the-Father, but the clinical effect of this is a foreclosure of speech. Speech is different from what is said; or rather, speech belongs to the order of enunciation, while what is said belongs to the order of the enounced. The subject of the unconscious is the subject of enunciation, in other words it participates in the order of speech. And it is the latter order that is foreclosed in psychosis. The psychotic is full to the brim with statements that have been "imposed" on him, as we have put it. There is no doubt that he can talk endlessly; he can even tell jokes and laugh at them (using metaphor). Hence, statements about the Symbolic becoming inaccessible and so on are nothing but a conceptual error. It is in no way a question of that; it is rather that the lack of a primordial signifier, the Name-of-the-Father, forecloses his position in speech. And this, as we show in Chapter 8 above, concerns precisely the operations of metaphor, of association. These are rendered difficult, when they are not completely obstructed, thus preventing the use of normal psychoanalytic procedures with psychotics. But this is not to imply that all types of foreclosure simultaneously bear on speech. In this sense, we find—for we have looked for them—foreclosures in neurotics, and as Lacan hints also among scientists, who in order to establish their discipline must foreclose the divided subject.

Let us take up the thread of Lacan's remarks concerning some open questions raised by the Real, with which he becomes increasingly preoccupied in his last seminars. Even if we can see immediately that these are open questions, there is a strong sense that Lacan's urgency compels our attention. In fact, if we read with sufficient attentiveness his way of linking, in order literally to articulate, these questions, we can sense the explanatory weight of an extreme symbolic instance. Lacan prepares a pedagogical strategy by rigorously adhering to a pun using the rhetorical trope of chiasmus.[3]

Let us take an example from everyday life: a bit of wordplay wisely deployed on the road-signs of Uruguay, which aims to prevent traffic accidents caused by speeding. One sign reads: "It is better to lose a minute of your life, than lose your life in a minute." The aim of the message, its instigation to behave in a certain way, explains how it goes about attaining that aim: that is, by "registering" in the mind of the driver an inhibition through suggestion. It does this by means of wordplay: the words occurring in the first half of the message are inverted in the second half. An effect of meaning is thus produced that, bearing on the workings of the unconscious, seems at times – through structural similarity – to border on the joke. Lacan proceeds in the same manner, increasingly reliant on wordplay. Let us follow one of his tropes, a chiasmus.

He begins by stating, ". . . in what I have termed the Real, I have invented something." We are familiar with the importance of invention, which we discussed at the beginning of our

---

3. On this topic, Umberto Eco's account of the Joycean pun is worth our attention, for he likens chiasmus to the condensation producing portmanteau words. The whole rhetorical tradition, as well as contemporary rhetoricians, reject such an understanding, for a chiasmus is not a composite trope. Cf. U. Eco, "The Aesthetics of Chaosmos," *The Middle Ages of James Joyce: The Aesthetics of Chaosmos*, London: Hutchinson, 1989, pp. 65–70; B. Vickers, *In Defence of Rhetoric*, Oxford: OUP, 1989, pp. 387–404.

study in the context of Joycean artifice. Invention here has the sense of *in-venire*, by which it "imposes itself" on the subject. The one who invents, working with fragments of what is disinvested from the knowledge of the unconscious, does not go to work in a sustained or controlled manner. Rather, a constellation of "imposed words" suddenly emerges, producing mental jouissance in the one who invents as he "litters" them. Lacan's reference to his own invention recalls the moment when he recognizes having "got lots of so-called Freudian things going." The point is that with the latter remark he is not talking of invention, whereas he specifically uses the term in connection with the Real. He begins, in the next line, his serious game, claiming to have invented the Real. This is not, he stresses, simply a matter of pronouncing the word; in fact, of course, "the real" is a formula as old as humanity itself. What is it, then, that constitutes Lacan's invention? The act of writing the Real as part of the triple Borromean chain: he is thus able to *say* that he has invented or written it, because he has placed R in a position of dependence on, and articulation with, the other registers.

In sum, then, Lacan invented the Real. Accordingly, he defines the Real as that which constitutes his *sinthome*. And he adds that the latter "is equivalent to" R (a point that we will have to explore further). Thus, we have a series of puns: through transitivity, we might say, all invention can be reduced to Σ. Moreover, the R of Σ, the real of the *sinthome* is imposed, in other words in-vented.

The following relations can thus be set out:

Lacan invented the R; R is his Σ;
Σ is equivalent to R;
All invention is reducible to Σ;
The R of Σ is imposed (that is, invented).

As these terms interchange in this combination, they generate new effects of conceptual teaching. This productive to-and-fro deserves the name that was later proposed for it: a T(r)opology. First, because the wordplay here is precisely a matter or tropes. If we speak, for instance, of the invention of the Real, but the Real—as *sinthome*—is precisely that which allows invention, we are deploying a trope. A trope is a figure of speech, of language, of thought (according to the various classifications of rhetoricians) that consists in this kind of logical trick or game, strictly transcendent. This is how Lacan bestows the status of invention on working with tropology. Obviously, the parenthetical "r" in the neologism allows it to be read simultaneously as "topology." The path followed by Lacan, his *dérive* ["drift," "drive"], is equally topological as tropological. He works with knots and chains, but a reading of the text of his seminar reveals how the different aphorisms fit together: their series is not random, for they are produced through combinations that seem complicated, but are ultimately reducible to a fundamental logical and linguistic figure: the pun.

The increasing emphasis on the Real gives a renewed edge to Lacan's subtle criticisms—although they are often not so much as that—of Freud. We thus return to a point at stake throughout Lacan's teaching: namely, how he was obliged to distance himself from Freud—only at certain points of course—because of weaknesses or limitations in the thought of the inventor of psychoanalysis. Now, in the penultimate session of Seminar 23, Lacan states that Freud only took into account the Symbolic and the Imaginary, and that he himself had to incorporate the Real. Let us bear in mind what we explored in our opening chapter: we saw there that Freud was criticized for "making use" of four registers, while in Lacan's view three were sufficient. Freud would thus have been guilty of what epistemologists refer to as a superfluity. Lacan, by contrast, argues for the addition of the third term, R—as *sinthomatic* response, "to the second degree"—to what Freud dreamt up. On the other hand, he would add different attributions to the unconscious: supposition (of knowledge), dreaming-up, hypothesis, discovery—and he even severs its narrow connection with the body, in other words with the Imaginary. Having said that, Lacan never states that the unconscious is Freud's *sinthome*, whereas, as we have seen, he defined the Real as occupying that position in his own case. And following the logic of his notion of Joyce the *sinthome*, should we not therefore give him a new name: Lacan the Real? In other words, after mentioning the Freudian thing, does Lacan not inscribe his own name by including the R?

There is no doubt that, with R, Lacan sought to distance himself from what Freud dreamt up. Why this term, "dreamt up"? Because that is precisely the manner in which Freud had "ideas." His ideas are never sufficiently detachable—and this amounts to a severe critique—from the body. And the body, where S and I come together, is what those ideas refer to. But if Freud never escapes such a level of reference, Lacan claims conversely to have resituated it in a Real that is conceived of without order or law. The immediate consequence of this condition is that the Real is composed of fragments, shards, bits. The important word here is "bit" [*bout*], which should not be understood as some extremity. By saying "an extremity of the Real," in fact, one is referring associatively to a segment, and to think the Real we should be attempting to think not in the Euclidian terms of segment, totality, unity, but rather in terms of infinite lines.

Let us continue to approach this vital point of Lacan's conceptual break with Freud. We next find Lacan criticizing the "Project for a Scientific Psychology" of 1895, the text in which Freud sets out his first definitions of the psyche. We read in that text that the function of the psyche consists in the assembly of impressions recorded by the neuronal-psychical apparatus, and each type of function is given a different letter. Thus, Freud is working with impressions and letters: the former are conceived of as mnemic traces, marks left on the brain, and immediately afterward he introduces the combination of letters. This seems fairly debatable to Lacan, for "there is no reason why an impression should be figured by something as remote from it as a letter. . . ." Once again, this does not indicate an epistemological judgment but is governed by the question of "faunetics": for "there is a world of difference between a letter and a phonological symbol."

Lacan's critique becomes clear when it reaches the next point. In order to be able, he declares, to support what Freud dreamt up of the unconscious, we must come down a degree from the *sinthome*. In other words, Lacan claims that his own work has attained a "second degree"; to that extent, the dreaming-up of the unconscious is reductive, incomplete, impoverishing. What is the immediate clinical consequence of this position? To be sure, that the praxis of analysis does not consist simply in interpreting the unconscious, but must aim to "touch" a fragment of the Real. Thus, we have a nodal concept: *Lacanian treatment must be another "thing" than Freudian treatment*. Without spelling this out as such, Lacan seems to imply this when he speaks of having to come down a degree to be "compatible with the dreaming-up of the unconscious." To put this in more direct terms, we could say that Lacan's clinical work has gone a degree further, since it is able to address no longer merely this "dreaming-up," but the "reality" of the unconscious. And we can make out an implicit aim of Lacan's here: only if he does not come down a degree will heterogeneity be preserved; while if he does so he will find himself in an undesired homogeneity. In our reading, Lacan's point here again confirms the effects that can be produced by the quadruple Borromean knot: a heterogeneity that remains impossible in the triple knot. But why, having said this, do we speak in terms of degrees more or less? To explain this, and for the third time in his seminar, Lacan takes support from the notion of the false hole. We have already discussed the latter in Chapters 3 and 7. Taking as an initial reference, then, our earlier discussion of Σ and S, it seems that I is the "term" that "confirms" the hole—as follows (Figure 47):

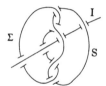

Figure 47

In this way, if it is to remain within—to be homogeneous with—the unconscious (S), the second register (Σ) must come down. What is knotted is ultimately both registers, S and Σ. Moreover, the false hole is pierced through by the Imaginary (I). If this is the case, according to Lacan's triptych—once again we are dealing with a triptych—Σ is equivalent, as we have indicated, to R. Consequently, at this point Lacan explicitly ascribes to Σ the characteristics of the Real, as its equivalent.

If we look back at Chapter 3, where we discussed the first introduction of the false hole in Seminar 23, we will see that things are figured differently there. At that point, Lacan sets forth a quadruple Borromean chain, consisting of the terms R, S, I, and Σ, in which—just as in the antepenultimate session—

Σ and S produce a false hole. Yet Σ has a different value here, for as Lacan states, when he introduces it this new register is symbolic, including the S_2 alongside the symbol. Thus, if S_2 is divided there would be an internal split *within the Symbolic*, whereby Σ would be one of the elements in the false hole. Thus, we may observe that there is a gulf between the first conception, where Σ is the product of a division at the heart of the Symbolic, and this new conception where Lacan posits an equivalence between Σ and R. If this were to lead to attempts to discredit Lacan's work, however, in our view such a response would be too hasty. For what we see at work here is Lacan's Work-in-Progress: we are faced with apparent contradictions, with hesitations, with formulations that are defined, retrospectively, as provisional. Does all this simply point to confusion? Is this the work of someone who has lost his way?

Before tackling these questions, we still have to examine the third appearance of the false hole, which occurs in the eighth session of the seminar (having begun with the tenth session and returned to the first, we finally end up at the eighth). There, Lacan declares the following: "It is insofar as the *sinthome* constitutes a false hole with the Symbolic that a praxis becomes possible." This flows from speech (from the art of speaking, *l'art-dire*, which we made rhyme with "ardor," *ardeur*), and thus it must form a false hole with the Symbolic. The formulation seems similar to what was said in the first session. But is Lacan really saying the same thing? In our view, we are dealing with a subtly different conceptualization. This time, he says "the Symbolic" but without adding, as he had earlier, that it is divided in two. With this in mind, we should look again at the whole discussion. On the first occasion, the Symbolic is divided into symbol and Σ; in parallel, R and I remain separate. By the eighth session, Lacan is indicating that

Σ forms a hole with the Symbolic, no longer with the symbol. Thus, the Symbolic is now presented as "complete," non-divisible; and again, R and I remain apart. Are we therefore dealing with the same problematic? The reason why this is dubious is that in the first formulation the Symbolic was divided and contained Σ, while in the second, Σ is located outside of the Symbolic. This, in our reading, immediately marks a striking difference. In the final instance, by the tenth session, Σ is, clearly, equivalent to the Real, forming a false hole with the Symbolic; while I is left separate. We might conclude from this that the place of the *sinthome* seems to be omnipresent. In fact, it cannot be located in a rigorous manner, using a precise and fixed definition, *vis à vis* what Lacan is aiming to grasp of this singular formation. But might it not be that one of its locations is incorrect? Are they not mere reifications? Should we argue that the last position is insurmountable? Does Lacan not state that we should privilege the register R, and hence orient all his efforts toward that? Perhaps we might be able to conceive that the *sinthome* can be articulated in different ways; and that, in order to grasp the detail of these ways, to specify the position of the *sinthome*, one must read the various nodal writings produced by Lacan. For the moment, let us maintain the enigma: in other words, the enunciation lacking—for the time being—a statement [*énoncé*]. What can be established is the following schematization of Lacan's trajectory:

Session	False hole between	Ex-sisting
1	Symbol and Σ, containing S_2 and forming part of the Symbolic	R and I
8	Σ and Symbolic	R and I
10	Σ ($\approx$R) and Symbolic	I

The way in which Lacan situates the *sinthome* in terms of the false hole at the different moments of his seminar contributes to the distancing of his work from that of Freud. But this distancing is always centered on ways of tying the knot: on how Freud "tied" it and how Lacan himself did. The subsequent critiques bear not only on Freud, though, but also tacitly on the "first" Lacan, as we have called him. Having maintained for almost all of his teaching (along broadly Heideggerian lines) that we are inhabited by language, that we are spoken by it rather than speaking it, that language constrains us into absolute dependence on it—having supported such a position for more than twenty years, Lacan's work now takes a turn that radically undermines it. In the course of this seminar, in fact, Lacan puts forward a very different point of view on what occurs when someone says that (it is his belief that) he has chosen a language. Who can really do this? If it is a question of the mother tongue, the one with which our mother spoke and sang to us, how can we speak seriously of choosing the language? So, as we wait with slight amusement for the obvious response that no one can do this, we come to the opposite extreme: namely, that "we create it [language]." We create it in the sense that each individual gives language a meaning or impetus, a little nudge, without which it would not be a "living" language. In other words, Lacan implies that there is a degree of freedom in the way that each speaker organizes the marks of the Other, according to a condition that is now named "particular" (not singular, note: for here we are at the heart of the general, although it is given a final touch, which is particular). This is why there is no collective unconscious, if not at the expense of particular kinds of unconscious. The latter point clearly entails a criticism of Jung, and of Joyce no less; for the whole aim of Joyce's project was the discovery of a Viconian history-as-reminiscence. The latter notion implies that whatever is now happening has already occurred, for it is the mere reproduction of the identical. Such a conception can be seen to encapsulate a purified Platonism: the imitation of the celestial world of Ideas, permanently recurring, and thus taking various forms in everyday life, although remaining immutable in the *topos uranos*. The notion of creating language by means of little nudges is a position, like many taken up in this seminar, which appears contingent, with no sign of its transcendence. Despite this, it marks a radical shift from the firmly held position about language holding us, rather than our holding language. In our reading, Lacan learned this from Joyce, or more specifically from his work. The reactive "nudge" of each individual faced with the heavy, alienating inheritance of language is what literary theory knows as style. It is this through which, in the reading of a text, we recognize its author: in his or her way of reordering the linguistic "heritage." Hence it is not enough to indicate here inheritance, subjection, and so on; at the same time, we must also posit a degree of freedom (a term that is fairly difficult to deploy among analysts). Let us say that the little nudge, and the freedom it implies, comes to condition "making sense." Thus, in our view, we have a notion that represents the logical reverse of the foreclosure of meaning by the Real. In other words, by foreclosing meaning that is congealed or frozen, I am able to engender new, unprecedented meanings, which cannot be inscribed as such, in *lalangue*.

An aphorism that we have already examined is connected with this problematic. We should now consider it with more attention, for it immediately condenses a large part of the teaching of Seminar 23. Likewise, this aphorism is located on the line of critical differences with Freudian thought. Lacan introduces it with a claim that in order to "hold on to" the "hypothesis" of the unconscious, we must "suppose" the Name-of-the-Father. If this were the case, there would be no way of being able to dispense with the latter, without directly dispensing with the unconscious. But is this not the *desideratum* of the final Lacan? His response, his schema—his premise, we might say, and why not, even his therapeutic diagnosis, which is also shaken up by Joyce's work—is cast forth in the following aphorism: "One can dispense with the Name-of-the-Father on condition that one makes use of it." It is one of those aphorisms that, as we have already indicated, must be allowed to follow its course, producing inexorable, expansive effects. Lacan is speaking, implicitly, of his understanding of Joyce: there, it is a question not of the foreclosure of the Name-of-the-Father, but of the act of dispensing with it on condition of making use of it. That is, by dispensing with the Name-of-the-Father function, one might be able to reach the level of naming, of making a name (for oneself). Here, Lacan is not referring to the Name-of-the-Father or to the Naming Father (or Father-of-the-Name); neither is he alluding to the father who says "no." He is addressing, in an absolute sense, one that, like Joyce—but not only Joyce—seeks to make a proper name for himself. And we might add that, according to what we have already established, what we should be able to achieve with analysands (in a sense no longer bound up with Joyce, given that he was never analyzed) consists not only in making a proper name for oneself, but in being able to reduce it again subsequently to the status of a common noun [*nom*]. The proper name or noun, then, allows one to dispense with the Name-of-the-Father. Yet this entails a risk: that of "believing in it," or to put it differently, that of "being" (in the previous chapter, we discussed the implications of this emphasis on being as opposed to having). To "believe in it" comprises constructing an identity, an ultimately psychological struggle; this constitutes one characteristic of Joyce in one of his modes of naming (as we will explore in the next chapter). Concerning this, and given that we have touched on the lack of an analysis in Joyce's case, we must make a short digression to investigate further.

Critics often wonder whether writing took the place of analysis for Joyce. As we read, or rather hear, that writing, there seem to be many confirmations of this. It goes without saying, on the basis of what we have examined in Seminar 23, that Lacan endorses no such notion. Certain groups of artists frequently come up with the incorrect idea that what they do amounts to self-analysis. There is a fundamentalist version of this, according to which for some people practically "the" condition of being an artist is not analyzing oneself: to do so, they imagine, would be to destroy their inspiration, the driving force of their work. This is a common rationalization that, in our praxis with such analysands, is shown to be a new and sophisticated modality of resistance. To be clear: in itself, an artistic practice can in no way replace analysis. Obviously, if an artist begins an analysis, it is because something has become a symptom for him or her, something that in one way or another is an obstacle to, an inhibition of creativity, productivity, artistic heresy. In this sense, due to the deception at stake, it could be argued that Joycean writing was the equivalent to a self-analysis for its author. But if analysis does not entail engaging with an artistic task, neither is the contrary true. As for what can be expected from a self-analysis, let us recall the immense effort required to dislodge the place of the Ideal Father on the part of Freud, the one who carried out the only genuine "self-analysis." But even that, as Octave Mannoni and others have shown, was not so much a self-analysis as an "originary analysis" that occurred between Freud and Fliess, his close friend at the time. In the correspondence between these two (now published in its entirety), it can be seen to what extent an analysand's discourse unfolded there. This "analysis" can even, it is certain, be termed "wild": for every analyst is taken aback by the occurrence of transferential bonds directed toward someone that seems not to deserve them (and why not: as a defense against or dispersal of derangement). This is to show, then, how Freud related to the Subject-supposed-to-Know.

Returning to Joyce, the question of making a name for oneself by dispensing with the Name-of-the-Father amounts to "being" what Lacan terms—somewhat equivocally—the son of discourse. What is equivocal is the choice of a term, to produce an instructive effect, which is not exactly felicitous: "son." The condition of a son is to continue to be supported. If it is the son of discourse, not of the signifier, that cements the subject's belief, another order of credibility may consequently be established, according to what is proposed in this seminar. We analysts should therefore support another order of credibility among our analysands; in other words, we have to bring about the laying-down of the fantasy of omnipotence that is usually linked to the Name-of-the-Father, by virtue of the unbounded love declared for it. In this dimension, we are all believers and, to that extent, the support of eternal love for the father—taken in all possible senses—entails the whole difficulty of constructing the proper name.

This point in Lacan's teaching consequently seems crucial, as it marks the conceptual transition from the paternal metaphor—based on the Name-of-the-Father—to nomination or naming. In other words, it marks the movement from the eternal love for the father—the root of the paternal metaphor—to the phenomenon of suppletion. In speaking of the latter (and nomination is one, of course), we are referring to a nonmetaphorical process, not characterized by the defining mark of metaphor, substitution. *Suppletion does not consist of a replacement, but the addition of something new.* For instance, when I am attempting to sew, to repair a trefoil knot at a crossing-point where a "slip" has occurred, I cannot avoid doing so by adding to it, so I invent, I use artifice (or rather, "I artifice," understood as a transitive verb). This, to be sure, is quite different from supporting the Name-of-the-Father through a love that is unconditional, eternal, and in this sense paralyzing in its closing-down of horizons. This is why, if it is a question of being subject to the Name-of-the-Father on condition of being able—if we now turn the phrase around— to dispense with it, this is possible by means of something very similar to the "little nudge" given to language. Effectively, it is possible to give language a little nudge on condition that one dispenses, for instance, with strict syntax, precise vocabulary, dictionary definitions, and in particular the foreclosure of puns (above all, translinguistic puns). This moving away from the imperious rules of language—which led Barthes to dub it "fascist"—is the origin of the phenomenon of suppletion. There is no question of substitution, for that term implies mournful nostalgia for what has been substituted, which is now held to be irreplaceable. The Name-of-the-Father entails precisely that: the hope it promises resides in waiting; and this is clear without even moving into the sphere of religion. We do not have to invoke God; it is enough to note the creation of a neurotic signifier, the Subject-supposed-to-Know. As we know, the latter should be gotten rid of by the end of analysis, for it embodies the belief in someone who knows what I do not know about or by myself. Thus, this product and producer of neurosis is at the same time responsible for the establishment and support of analytic treatment. And there is no doubt that it is this that must be dismantled at the end of analysis, for if not the treatment would not have "touched" the belief in the Other, conceived of as consistent, integral. The end of analysis must include an event that "dethrones" this supposed subject, as its persistence counteracts the beneficial assumption of the nonexistence of the Other.

In suppletion, then, it is a matter of *doing*. This takes us back to the question of artifice. The trajectory here might be summed up as follows:

Is taken up by

Eternal love for the father ⟶ Suppletion
Paternal metaphor (substitution) ⟶ Nomination

We might also articulate the aphorism in question with Lacan's notion that the Real has neither law nor order. This is why no type of intersection can be defined within R. At this point, it is our view that we can gloss one of Lacan's remarks, an aside aimed at those who have followed his work for some time. At a given moment, a participant in the seminar asks Lacan whether or not the point, the dimension of the point, is of the Real. Lacan's response is negative, as a point is defined by the intersection of three planes. If it is a question of intersection, the point cannot belong to the Real. What is incapable of figuring the Real is clearly bifurcation or ramification: there can be nothing of the kind in the Real, it cannot be written with a "Y." And that letter takes us back to one of the major texts of the first Lacan, where he showed how the subject was alienated, determined in and by the order of language. This was the subject of *aphanisis*, vanishing, divided—the one helplessly in thrall to language. The text in question is "The agency of the letter in the unconscious; or reason since Freud." There are many that believed—and perhaps some that still believe—Lacan's entire oeuvre to be summed up in this text (which is certainly quite didactic). There, alluding to rhetorical tropes, and in a tone that is not without certain unacknowledged literary flourishes, Lacan brackets his work with the "Y." But before we go further with that text, let us recall the sequence of critiques in Seminar 23 aimed at metaphor. For by using metaphor, of course, we can manage to state anything at all. We could even imagine the greatest conceivable contradictions in the belief that through them a reality will take shape, given that one term will necessarily be *substituted* by its opposite. We know what is at stake here, even if Lacan does not make it explicit: the claim that capitalism gives birth to its own gravediggers, so that the communist revolution must necessarily succeed over the whole surface of the globe. The Hegelian contradiction, raised up or sublated—"turned on its head," in his own phrase—by Marx, is a nodal example of how with words or speech one can maintain anything at all by giving it an appearance of credibility. This striking, if implicit, critique of the central dialectical notion that contradiction has an inevitable "realist" power, preceded by more than one decade the collapse of the Communist regimes. But the ideology of those regimes was already exposed in Seminar 23 as a pernicious effect of metaphor.

At any rate, in "The Agency of the Letter" of 1957, Lacan locates the "Y" as one way of verifying the effects of rhetorical processes, even if the letter serves there merely as a support of rhetorical productivity. How does he begin this point?

By mentioning the tree, as an allusion to the one famously introduced by Ferdinand de Saussure to account for the link between the signifier (or acoustic image) and the signified (or concept). Here, Lacan takes the risk of stating what associations are produced in him by the word "tree," *arbre*: he links it anagrammatically to "bar," *barre*. He thus aims to stress the importance of the bar separating the signifier from the signified, on which he will center his first meditation. According to Lacan, what interests analysts in the Saussurean algorithm is the thickness of the horizontal bar. On this basis, he writes the following:

> Let us take our word "tree" again. . . . For even broken down into the double spectre of its vowels and consonants, it can still call up with the robur and the plane tree the signification it takes on, in the context of our flora, of strength and majesty. Drawing on all the symbolic contexts suggested in the Hebrew of the Bible, it erects on a barren hill the shadow of the cross. Then reduces to the capital Y, the sign of dichotomy which, except for the illustration used by heraldry, would owe nothing to the tree however genealogical we may think it.[4]

For all Lacan's irony about the presence of "Y" in the genealogical tree—although he privileges its heraldic inscription—he nonetheless accepts it as the index of copulation, that which founds lineages and ancestries. Having said that, in our retrospective reading, it is the "Y" that allows the figurative condensation of the preceding statements. For it is a matter of taking any given word and bifurcating immediately, follow-

---

4. J. Lacan, *Écrits: A Selection*, op. cit., p. 154.

ing a chosen direction: and subsequently the process is repeated at will, until an endless proliferation of senses unfolds; and as our discussion has shown, these senses can even enter into completely contradictory "dialectical" relations. This is the basis of metonymy, which in turn is the basis of metaphor. Thus, if in 1957 Lacan adopts the "Y" as a figure of typical rhetorical processes, raising up its level of effectiveness, by 1976 he is constantly warning of the risks entailed by that effectiveness, which *Ment* ["lies"]. This does not amount to the retraction of any one point, but rather bears witness to Lacan's growing interest in the Real. This is the decisive point, corresponding to a double reading or polysemy of the "Y": firstly as bifurcation or dichotomy, and then as intersection. But what is surprising is that these two positions are designated by the same letter; their difference is a product of particular readings: from the bottom to the top, or vice versa. In other words, the "Y" does not transmit the irreducible density of the Real, but rather a relativism of imaginary points of view, which is a long way—through its convincing dialectical-contradictory twists and turns—from the identification with the One of the *sinthome*. The latter thus appears here to be defined through its inflection by the bias of the Real.

This is why we should raise questions once more in relation to the Real. What is its signification, ultimately, beyond the words itself or the act of writing it in Borromean chains? What are its precise clinical incidences? In short, what is Lacan getting at in such formulations? In order to attempt a response to these questions without adding yet more riddles, we will explore part of the first chapter of a book by the linguist Jean-Claude Milner, *Les noms indistincts*. In this text, Milner, a follower of Lacan, sets himself the task of separating out R, S, and I. In relation to R, he states that "nothing of R can be gleaned from either I or S": R is thus irreducible. It is impossible to deduce, because there is no place for it, a transferral of the essence of the Symbolic or of the Imaginary to the Real. The first point, then, is that the Real is irreducible.[5] And Milner adds: "[The Real is an] unbridgeable gulf that, for good or ill, will be written in S through a negation. . . ." What does this mean? What are the characteristics of the Real? We might list them as follows: it cannot be written, it cannot be spoken, it is alien to any distinctions. This lack of any distinctions implies that there is neither law nor order in R, which as we know is one of its decisive qualities.

If we try to make progress by formulating theorems, we might maintain—according to Milner—that in R "there are no totalities." And he adds still further negative characteristics, among them "there are no relations," which in our view constitutes another telling aspect of the absence of law and order. This is why we affirmed that the point is not of the Real, insofar as it is defined by the intersection of planes. Intersection is clearly a form of relation. On the other hand, in R neither are there any semblances, properties, or classes: nothing but "noes." There are no semblances, since the latter belong to the Imaginary. There are neither properties nor classes, as these form part of the symbolization of the Imaginary. On the basis of these negative qualities, Milner concludes that R is located outside of space and time, and outside of the event. Concerning what is outside of space, "certain topologies produce a metaphor"; as for what is outside of time, the instant

---

5. This "hard" point in Milner's argument only becomes possible after Seminar 23. If we look back to Figure 7, taken from the previous seminar, we see S invading R, giving rise to the symptom in the latter domain. There was thus no "pure" R before *Le sinthome*.

confirms or verifies it; while what is outside of the event corresponds to the "pure encounter." On this last point, we can
outline a different view by following some ideas in the work of
Alain Badiou, a renowned philosopher who began as a student
of Althusser's, as a historical materialist, and was also a participant in Lacan's seminar. Badiou's work is original and wide-
ranging. In his book *L'être et l'événement* ["Being and the Event"],
he works in particular with Lacanian concepts in an attempt
to establish the foundation of the notion of event, which is
linked to the unpredictable. Badiou reworks the notion of
chance, in the sense effectively developed by Lacan. The unpredictable is of course that which falls outside of all predictable orders: it is thus supernumerary, as Badiou puts it.[6] This
is not the place to explore in detail Badiou's fertile ideas, but
Milner's concept of "outside the event" can be reformulated,
in Badiou's terms, as belonging to the order of the event. The
Real is eventual because it lies outside of anticipation (which
is imaginary) and discernment (which is symbolic), in partaking of the condition of the undecidable. And the undecidable,
we would add, is founded on *paradox*—like that of the present
work's title—and not on dialectical contradiction.

Milner continues: "As opposed to S which discriminates
and I which binds together, R is therefore the indiscriminate
and the dispersed as such. . . ." And he takes up a position in
support of the Freudian Thanatos, as distinct from Eros: he
favors the death drive because it bears that which unbinds or
unknots, while Eros designates that which knots together.

These things were further confirmed, before the appearance of the concepts we have discussed—ostensibly so abstract

---

6. A. Badiou, *L'être et l'événement*. Paris: Seuil, 1988, p. 199ff.

and hard to grasp—in analytic treatment. Essentially, Lacan is referring to effects of dispersal, which should be read in the first instance as the undoing of the knot and/or the chain. On this topic, we are reminded of a point that, for our part, we noted many years ago:[7] namely, that analysis, *analýo*, means "I unknot." Thus, psychoanalysis is not a matter of breaking into pieces nor of undoing, but of unknotting—which comes about through effects of Thanatos. But we should therefore ask whether our function as *analýsts* is that of unknotting, untying the knot and/or the chain. And the response is that it is indeed a matter of unknotting, to allow for new kinds of knotting. As we have put it, there is no un-knotting [*dénouement*] without re-knotting [*re-nouement*], in every sense of that expression. There would be no conclusion if something was not reknotted; but unknotting is required for this to become possible. And that is what analysis means. Already, with Freud, the term is marked out: "analysis" does not amount, in short, to reinforcing anything, but to unknotting. And in this unknotting, at the very moment of its occurrence, arises an affect that Milner, with great clinical insight, shows as belonging to an encounter with the Real: horror. At this point, Milner takes advantage of an idea put forward by Lacan that hitherto has not been paid much attention. This was to describe the analyst's *praxis* in terms of the horror he feels concerning his act. If someone is resistant to analysis—a misconception that many choose to conceal—that person is an analyst. Beyond anything he or she may claim, the analyst feels—very often, every day—a horror of the analytic act. In

---

7. R. Harari, *Texturas y abordaje del inconsciente*. Buenos Aires: Trieb, 1977, pp. 214–216.

other words, a horror of what he or she is to say or has already said. This structural situation can be identified fairly easily in personal experience, in supervisions and exchanges with colleagues. For example, in many supervision analyses, having worked on a case, the supervising analyst comes to wonder suddenly, with stupefaction, what he or she should do with the work thus completed. The horror of addressing the analysand—at the appropriate signifying point, of course— is nothing but the horror of the Real. That horror comprises indeed the "invitation" to withdraw the capital letter from analysis; in other words, it is what will lead the final Lacan to claim that our *praxis* is the *praxis* of the Real. As expressed in Milner's terms, this leads to a phrase designed to shock: analysis is a *praxis* of horror. Regarding this, let us recall Lacan's description of Joyce as an *affreux* ["frightful"]. We can now modulate this, and say that Joyce was frightful because he worked with the Real. What he worked with was no tranquilizing Symbolic, no narcotic—for his pathway was that of nihilation. Milner continues: "[This] horror is the name that is given, for better or worse, to that which in a being marked by S and I answers to that which has no name and no form."

That, then, is horror. It was Bion who posited a limit experience, described as "nameless terror"; such a definition presupposes the possibility of a terror that in the end can be named. This is not, of course, what is designated by Milner's conception of horror; but at any rate, we would note how in both formulations the dimension of the name is lacking. This is once again to lend support to the pacifying effect of the signifier. And the linguist goes on: "[Yet] it is not that, a moment later, some more constant and more bound feeling does not cover what surges up. . . ." Hence our distinction between horror and terror, for the latter, according to Milner, is already part of "a moment later"; no less than pity, fascination, or even pleasure. All of these events supervene on the impact of the Real, the point of horror that we strive to associate with the beneficial depersonalization that emerges in analysis. Immediately, necessarily, things are "corked." The author next offers some extremely interesting illustrations. In this context, we might say that attention is focused on the beautiful. If one is working with the knot-chain, the moment that horror arises is an index of its unknotting; consequently, such an instant, as such, is (of the) Real. This can be given a "declension" in a series of clinical figures, including four points of great interest; as we will see, they allow us to understand that the Real is not only something dreamt up by "Lacan-the-Real." The first of these points is that of the spewing forth of meaning, which fits in with a variety of points we have touched on in our study. Concerning this, Milner adds: ". . . .where the bound tissue of signification comes undone." If this tissue of sense breaks up, there is an explosion of its fragments. It is as if a bomb were to be exploded within meaning: the tissue, weave, or chain is blown apart.

The second aspect referred to is the following: ". . . the radical gap of awakening between two series of representations that are equally imaginary, the dream and wakefulness. . . ." Waking up is a signifier referred to by many analysands in the course of a beneficial analysis: they claim now to be considered more "awake," literally. This is why, between these two imaginary suppositions—the dream and wakefulness—we find the experience of awakening. Lacan taught that when we sleep, we are at our most wakeful, given that we are open to the power of dreams (or nightmares). He also emphasized repeatedly that when we have our eyes open we often let ourselves slip into sleep. Being awake, then, does not entail being wakeful. Hence Macedonio Fernández's title *No toda es vigilia la de los ojos abiertos* ["Not everyone with eyes open is awake"]. Waking up, in short, designates a moment when we encounter the Real, which is far from being bound up with biological notions of sleep, rest, or awakening. Lacan is aiming, in nodal fashion, at moments that *arrive* in the analytic session. Having said that, there is no reason why awakening should indicate some kind of illumination whereby the analysand would be possessed by some mystical ecstasy or other. It could perfectly well correspond to the nihilation we have discussed. And thus we designate it as a deferred effect, in *Nachträglichkeit*.

Milner's third point is characterized as follows: ". . . the shock of the encounter, which the analytic session amounts to. . . ." Although written in a somewhat cryptic fashion, this is linked to the nonfinality of the analytic session in terms of a chronometric halt. If the end of the session is not chronological, the encounter collides, shocks, like an incision into the calm emptiness given by the standardized session. It is a shock to imaginary anticipation, to the "control" that the analysand can easily attain in "his" fifty minutes; it is a shock to the sedate somnolence produced by a session commandeered in this way.

Thus we reach the fourth and final of Milner's points, which is also considered by Lacan: Milner calls it "the scansion of interpretation." What he means by this is that interpretation ". . . has nothing to do with a symbolic translation, but everything to do with the impact of the real naming of a desire." Thus, interpretation is far from being a hermeneu-

tic, a decoding. It is an interpretation insofar as it constitutes the utterance of a real naming. In other words, it is the
act of giving a name in a "faunetic" manner, by foreclosing
meaning. It is in this that the *praxis* of the analyst resides:
in the real naming of a desire (*a* desire, in the sense of one-
by-one). The consequence of this is that analytic *praxis* is
defined not only in relation to the unconscious structured
like a language. Lacan had already seen this in, for instance,
Position of the Unconscious (1966). In that *Écrit*, he indicated
a way of working with the Real: it was a question of the
analyst splitting off certain terms from the discourse of analysis, as one modality of interpretation. We would thus be able
to work with *lalangue*, rather than undertake a symbolic
decoding. At the same time, this procedure relates to the
working of an operation constitutive of the subject, which
Lacan calls separation. The latter does not strictly entail
structure, but rather an act of destructuration, and on the
part of the subject. There is no doubt that it subsequently
restores its structure, but what is crucial for Lacan's point
here resides in the effect of disarticulation. Even at the date
of this text, 1966, there is already a clear indication of a
different way to understand interpretation. We should also
link this to Lacan's explorations on the question of the act
in psychoanalysis. Concerning this, we must adopt a series
of precautions, given the risks imposed by the topic. To begin
to tackle that topic, we will work on one of the many paradoxical aphorisms uttered by Lacan during his long years
of teaching: that is, the famous "Do as I do, do not imitate
me." Perhaps there are many readings of this aphorism, but
in our view it can be paraphrased as follows: "Do not copy
the character I embody. Do as I did with Freud: I re-questioned,
reformulated, thought through, critiqued what Freud said."

What Lacan said, we should add, goes very well with the spirit of such a statement. It is thus clear that Lacan did not put himself forward as a reproduction of Freud. Why repeat, then, the behavior of Lacan the character, the individual? Let us note that the term "character" [*personnage*] is not accidental here. We should be aware of the dangers entailed by emulating aspects of Lacan's methods, sheltering behind an "if he had done it himself." There are many who, as they finish at the university and begin their analyses, consider it appropriate to "do what Lacan used to do": in other words, to imitate him. And of course we can imagine what this leads to. For there can be no question of doubling the imaginary, novelistic character; this would be to engage in a practice of the Imaginary, to *believe* in the image of the image. A practice of semblance, in other words, with all the dangers comprised by "believing in it." It is a matter, by contrast, of making use of the Name-of-the-Father on the condition that one does without it (and also making use of the pun). With a view to such a process, let us propose the following proper names: *Freud-the-unconscious, Lacan-the-Real*. It is up to us to see how, without eternalizing a blinding love for the father, to put his teaching to work. There is thus absolutely no value in "adopting" the quirks of an analytic treatment, such as opening and closing windows, banging desk drawers, leaving the consulting room in silence, and so on. This kind of behavior is linked to a specific context and to a character who was authorized to carry it out by the symbolic network supporting it, which, there can be no doubt, is not ours. This is not a question of cultural relativism; by becoming victim to imaginary mimesis, we lend support to the Viconian myth of the inevitable reproduction of the identical. We might call the tendency that defends such behavior as an analytic act, borrowing a term from Elisabeth Roudinesco, neo-Lacanianism.[8] The prefix "neo" points to the condition of those who paradoxically, by wishing to imitate Lacan's character, betray his teaching and repeat the deviation of the neo-Freudians *vis a vis* Freud's teaching. Has the moment come, then, for a *return to* (*the meaning of the work of*) *Lacan*?

The imaginary emulation in question here, however, is nothing but another way of avoiding the horror of our act. As we have indicated elsewhere, the analyst prefers to begin in the manner of a decoder who, sheltering behind a supposedly general knowledge, speaks but without saying anything, without naming in the analytic sense. We can thus grasp the importance of the concept of naming [*nomination*], as presented by Milner, and how it is a consequence—in a compressed form, but not without act, as we will show in the next chapter —of Seminar 23 itself. How, then, does the linguist Milner conclude? As follows: "Now, analysis . . . is precisely the unknotting

---

8. One day there will have to be a serious study of the relations between this singular metaphysics of the act and the subtle fascist philosophy of Giovanni Gentile, theoretician of *atto in atto* and *atto puro*. As Paolo Casini rightly indicates, Gentile's statements were characterized equally "by the—voluntarist—elimination of error as by the abandonment of any normative ethics." Likewise, neo-Lacanianism, in the same tradition, has distorted in a regressive manner Lacan's notion of "decisive desire," which he held to be a suitable definition of the beginning of analysis. Thus, only someone driven by a desire of this kind would be—or "will have been"— in Lacan's view, his analysand. By contrast, neo-Lacanianism positions this notion as the cornerstone of the end of analysis. Yet in the golden age of identification with the *sinthome*, but which is very close to today, "decisive desire" was illustrated in a surprising way: by Adolf Hitler. (Cf. P. Casini, "Gentile, Croce e la prima crisi del'atto puro," *Lettera dall'Italia*, 35. Roma: Istituto della Enciclopedia Italiana, July–September 1994, p. 53.)

which constitutes the Borromean real."[9] What does this mean? As we have established, to ascertain whether or not a chain is Borromean, one must try to unknot it in order to confirm its structure. It is in this operation that the instant of the Real surges up. In other words, it occurs during unknotting or *dénouement*, rather than the reverse. Of course, knotting—if we pursue this way of presenting things—will immediately follow.[10] However, what is striking here is unknotting, which is Real. A clear and differentiated clinical program results from this statement, on the basis of the privilege accorded to what is Real. As can be guessed, such a program has little to do with "therapeutic" goals such as the rewriting of the analysand's history, the forging of new symbolic articulations, the expansion of the field of the ego, and so on. This is why, in our view, the incidence, inflexion, declension, and lastly the privilege of R amount to one of the fundamental points of Seminar 23.

---

9. J. C. Milner, *Les noms indistincts*, op cit., pp. 7–14 [Translations: LT].

10. In reading the *Wake* we see a similar process at work: the masses of vocables there seem at first to be dismembered, only to be subsequently reconstituted in unimagined, enigmatic, multilingual ways.

10

A Table of Joycean Nomination

In this final chapter, we put forward a reading that will seek to sum up and reorder the different questions formulated by Lacan in the course of his seminar. In particular, we will take account of the disparity of knots and chains, an aspect that, as our reading will seek to show, is more coherent than it appears at first sight.

But before embarking on this, we must illuminate little by little certain preliminary questions that form an integral part of the final session of Seminar 23. That session is focused fundamentally on a decisive theme that we have addressed in earlier chapters: that of writing. The theme is decisive, in the sense that it allows a Lacanian "pass" [*passe*] from the classical question of what Lacan terms signifying—that is, as he puts it, "that which is modulated by the voice"—to another problematic. To introduce this, we will use another of our didactic oppositions, from which we can draw comparative tables. The advantage of the latter, to counterbalance their possible schematism, is that they clarify certain points by giving them logical structure.

Let us therefore place on one side the signifier, on the other, writing. Lacan claims that these are not made of the same stuff, that they do not identify the same substance, as it were. The signifier, as he puts it, "has nothing to do with writing." Now, writing is obviously a certain concept here; it thus has nothing to do, let us stress, with the imaginary scene that amounts to picking up a pen and writing. This is because its distinct quality is encapsulated by the Borromean knot (chain). According to Lacan, the Borromean knot implies a total subversion, for it has changed—and he uses the term rigorously, without cancelling its effect—"the *meaning*[1] [*sens*] of writing." Thus, referring to writing entails taking into account "his" Borromean chain. The latter, as writing, is able to brush against the Real. Here Lacan makes a direct allusion to a philosopher whose relation to his teaching—as we saw in Chapter 3—is at least conflictual. Undoubtedly, this thinker has adopted, whether or not explicitly, many points from Lacan; which has not prevented him from sometimes launching scathing critiques that are usually based on misunderstandings of Lacan's work, when they are not driven by questions relating to the originality or priority of ideas. Lacan's mention of the brilliant Jacques Derrida (for it is he) in Seminar 23 relies on his correct insistence on the difference between signifier and writing. Derrida's work, of course, takes into account the precedence of writing over speech. Such a conception evidently implies an epistemological rupture, for our own experience as speakers tells us that we speak first, and then learn to write afterward. If we let ourselves be captured by the Imaginary, if we are evolving psychologists, we will only be able to support such a position, and conceive of writing as nothing more than speech written down.

---

1. Emphasis ours.

In an extremely lucid and intricate reading of Freud, Derrida shows that the psychical apparatus in Freud is a system of writings, beginning from the explicit theme of inscription.[2] The latter theme already appears in Freud's letter to Fliess of December 6, 1896, and continues in the notion of psychical systems, as we read in *The Interpretation of Dreams*. Here, we cannot dwell on this work that has given rise to very many responses, although we note its importance. Derrida argues for a psychical apparatus made up of inscriptions, structured like a form of writing, or more exactly, like a system of writings. Lacan notes in the final session of Seminar 23 that for the philosopher, writing amounts to "a precipitation of the signifier." Lacan's apparently amiable tone here should not mislead us; having ostensibly recognized his erstwhile detractor, his final comment is that, whatever Derrida has highlighted, "it is quite clear that I showed him the way." Once the leading figure of deconstruction has been relegated to the status of disciple, Lacan indicates that the "writing" of the Borromean consists, incontrovertibly, in the act of tying it: *it must be tied* [*il faut le faire*], to be understood in a literal sense. It is not to be drawn, then, but actively tied or "made" [*faire*]; this recalls the know-how-with [*savoir-y-faire-avec*] mentioned above. Concerning this action or *faire*, we recall that Lacan had warned us not to confuse it with the homonym *fer* ["iron"]. Surely Lacan meant us to read this warning, according to analytic technique, as an ironic negation: in other words, by removing the particle "not" and leaving the bald statement. Why, then, should we confuse *faire* with *fer*, "doing" with "iron"? The answer is linked to popular wisdom, as shown when something is described as "as

---

2. J. Derrida, "Freud and the Scene of Writing" (1966), in *Writing and Difference*, trans. A. Bass. London: Routledge, 1978.

tough as iron" [*dur comme fer*]. Such a thing might be, it is implied, wholly serious, extremely robust, self-supporting, without duplicity or concessions. The phrase can even be applied to certain speakers. If we return to "it must be done" [*il faut le faire*], we can see that a pun on *fer* is also possible: the *doing* of something is a kind of vaccination against Imaginary thinking, which tends to wander off unless provided with a support of *fer/faire*. Thought gives onto a dimension where everything is possible. As is well known, it is possible to argue forcefully in favor of something at the same time as one performs an action that contradicts the argument. Where, then, does truth reside? What is the famous truth criterion that the scientists, logicians, and epistemologists shout themselves hoarse about? As we have shown, Lacan—having been alerted by the *Ment* ["lie"]—replaces truth with the Real in his final seminars.

The act of tying the knot (or chain) has the following property: if, in "writing" it, we make a mistake, it is inevitably wrong [*faux*]; the "slip" catches our eye. In attempting to tie it, whether we manage to or we fail, we have a support, a prop for thinking. Thought, in other words, does not "rest" on empty air— in the Imaginary, that is: if I do it, I am given some prop, a piece of the Real. In order to extend his discursive range, Lacan insistently uses Joycean wordplay. He thus seeks to express the aforementioned prop [*appui*] for thinking [*la pensée*] by displacing the "ap" of *appui* onto *pensée*, producing the neologism *appensé*. The latter term would thus designate a thought that operates with a certain prop, obtained according to the following principle: "one props oneself against a signifier in order to think." What this new term teaches is that we should abandon Symbolic-Imaginary thinking and adopt the path of tying the Borromean. Once again, writing does not entail the simple act of using a pen, but rather working with the Borromean, and with all that results from the act of tying it [*la faire*].

We have just dealt with the *n*th bit of Lacan's wordplay; but, not content with that, he is about to introduce another *jeu de mots*. In what he does, he proceeds like Joyce: he forges equivocations, but the aim of these is to reason something out, to explain a problem, to mark a pathway. By contrast, with Joyce something different happens: we do not know where he is going, we lose track. Yet for a first-time reader of Lacan—particularly if she picks up a seminar like this one—he will not appear far from the Joycean world. To put it differently, Lacan's manifest statements are set apart, so to speak; what his teaching achieved is another story. It is for this reason that we must engage with the whole of Lacan's work with particular attentiveness—and especially regarding the "final" Lacan—in order to unravel those points that often appear to be riddles rather than equivocations.

The new *jeu de mots* takes the form of a neologism, *mensionge*. The "I" added to *mensonge* ["lie"] makes it almost rhyme with the *dit-mention* in which Lacan situates the signifier. On another occasion, he writes that "dimension" as *dit-mansion*, making it a place where speech resides or defends itself. But the crucial point is that, in that dimension, we tell lies [*nous mentons*]. This is what constitutes the core of the argument, its iron part. Conversely, with the knot or the chain we cannot lie; if we did so, there would be a fault, a "slip." With the word *said* [*dit*] we lie, beyond any desire "in good faith" not to do so. We should note that in the dimension of *Ment*, what is at stake is *le dit*, that which is said or the statement, and not *dire*, speech itself or the enunciation. The *dit* relates to the place where we recognize the ego; and *dire* to the subject. To sum up, then, the metaplastic term *mensionge* identifies, through condensation and homophony, the context we have explored, turning decisively around *mensonge* or the lie and its spoken dimension.

But Lacan will introduce yet another element: namely, that the Borromean chain contains—or is able to harbor, to support—a *bone* [*os*]. We will develop a reading below that will attempt to gloss the reason for that introduction. But let us first explore the significance of this "bone." In popular usage— "down to the bone," "close to the bone," and so on—the term designates what is most radical or most intimate about an issue or a subject. But Lacan writes *bone* into another word-game: as an *os-bjet* ["object" punning on *os*, "bone"]. This amounts to an object that constitutes the "bone" or deepest level of our psychical experience: in other words, of course, the object *a*. As we saw in Figure 8 above, that object is located in the central zone of the diagram of the triple Borromean chain. The conclusion is obvious: if the Borromean supports the *os-bjet*, Lacan claims that on this basis he himself brings about the first philosophy—or, as we recall, the first *sophy*[3]—that is able to support itself.

The following table of oppositions results from this:

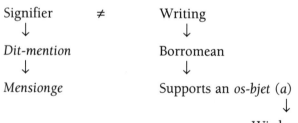

3. See Chapter 8 above.

Why have we presented these neologisms in a series? In order to show how Lacan carries out a mimesis of Joycean technique; how, once again, he is in a *process of verbal action*—which is what he claims takes place in his *Ecrits*—the enactment, precisely, of his teaching. Lacan does not make this explicit; he simply does it, because "it must be done." If he stated it—through explanation, allusion, or whatever—this would in no way be equivalent to the act of *doing it* through these verbal games, which are sometimes elucidated and at other times not.

To come back to the dichotomy signifier/writing, it is important to stress that Lacan claims to have been interested in such a question very early in his career. In our view, the "prop" Lacan chooses to support his point here leads to an ungrounded restriction. He refers back to his exemplary reading of Chapter 7 of *Group Psychology and the Analysis of the Ego*, where Freud distinguishes between three types of identification. Lacan is thus returning to a conceptual site on which he had reflected very often. There can be no doubt that it is his achievement to have highlighted the theory of identification that emerges there. Without pausing for too long on this, let us nonetheless note that with his second type of identification Freud emphasizes something that supports Lacan's conception. We are referring to the claim that identification is produced through a single trait, which we call *unary*. The latter term, which properly speaking belongs to mathematics, was borrowed by Lacan as a translation of Freud's *einziger*, which means "unique." *Einziger Zug* is thus "unary trait." Freud insisted on the fact that it was enough to identify with a single trait, as he put it, of the object, for the identification with it to be fully realized. Thus, this second type of identification is not mimetic, massive, or absolute. On this basis, then, Lacan claims to have "promoted" the question of writing: "the first time that I spoke of the unary trait in Freud." Yet with the knot (or chain), he ascribes another "support" to this unary trait: the straight line. In our view this new writing is not an equivalent of the notion of mark, mortise, scriptural trace in a sense that would bring Lacan close to Derrida. If, moreover, the straight line is equivalent to the circle, what would be the support of the unary trait of each circle, given that it stands for the registers? Would there be a unary trait for R, S, and I? This line of thinking, as we can see, seems more enigmatic than simply equivocal, as there is no simple bridge between two separate moments in Lacan's teaching.

Now we reach one of the crucial points of the seminar, which has given rise to endless debates. It concerns the understanding of the fourth order in the chain (which is not necessarily Borromean); that is, whether or not Lacan claims that it refers to what certain other analysts have termed "psychotic stabilization" (in Joyce). Lacan brings in here a fundamental concept that is strikingly different from his usual set of ideas: nothing less than the *ego*. And how does Lacan bring this in? We have examined several *possible* faults in various forms of knot. Now Lacan proposes another: in this fault, the Real and what he terms the unconscious—in fact the Symbolic—seem to be incorrectly knotted. As we indicated in the opening chapter, one register must be situated beneath the other—in other words, they should be simply superimposed—to allow the possibility of a third register bringing about a Borromean form of knot. Thus, as follows (Figure 48):

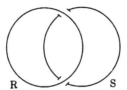

Figure 48

In the case indicated here, the Borromean condition is not satisfied, is not effective, for the two registers are interlinked, forming the Hopf chain mentioned above (cf. Figure 3). Each register passes through the hole of the other, indicating that the false hole is not at issue here. In fact, a false hole can be obtained without cutting, by transposing and folding, starting with the superimposed rings mentioned above. This leads to a crucial stage, as it entails an "appeal" to a third register in order to consolidate a chain, the false hole thus becoming a real one. By contrast, here R and S are themselves sufficient to form a chain (Figure 49):

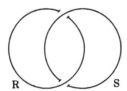

Figure 49

This situation leads to I remaining isolated, as it does not form part of the knot; thus the triple Borromean chain does not emerge. Lacan's guess is now, in this new proposal, that this is what happens with Joyce. Where does this idea "come from"? Lacan begins, as we have seen, with *A Portrait of the Artist as a Young Man*. But before we examine this reference,

let us continue with our topological exploration. What occurs when the "slip" takes place? The fourth term is necessarily included: the reparation that comes into effect is Joyce's
ego. This ego, which is quite singular, allows the Borromean
chain to be imitated, by connecting I to R and S, the last two
being bound together from the outset, as we have seen.[4]

Writing, says Lacan, is "completely essential" to Joyce's
ego. It is an ego that cannot live, that cannot support itself,
without its writing. Below, we illustrate the chain repaired by
Joyce's ego as the fourth term; we can confirm, by *tying* the
chain ourselves, the deceptive effect produced by the apparent crossings of I, before it is repaired by the ego. Thus, the
course of I follows the well-known alternate sequence of over
and under; yet it remains isolated, despite its visual illusion
(*Ment*). We can grasp this situation better if we examine Figures 50, 51, which show the sequence necessary to the workings of Joyce's ego:

---

4. Given this faulty knotting, it is clearly a mistake for Lacan's official transcription to record that the "slip" would reside in the *non*-knotting
of R and S (the unconscious), which is then given emphasis by an added
phrase, which appears in no other transcription. (And the diagram alongside shows something contradictory.) We read there: "*The I simply buggers
off, it slips away . . . , the imaginary relation does not occur, and the real does
not knot together with the unconscious*" (*Ornicar? 11*, pp. 2, 7–8). This gross
distortion—which begins with the words "and the real . . ."—is repeated
by those who, loyal disciples of the transcriber, take his text to be the
Authorized Version, without bothering to engage with any of the other
transcriptions available or even consider the basic topological reading at
stake. On the basis of this error, they put together their commentaries and
interpretations, which are thus rendered invalid from the outset. Let there
be no doubt: the myth of the murder of the father is not the equivalent of
being able to do without the Name-of-the-Father on condition that one
makes use of it. . . .

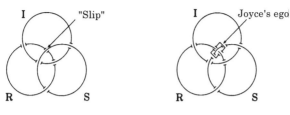

Figure 50   **Figure 51**

Thus, moving on to a reading of *A Portrait* according to the guiding principle of Stephen Dedalus being "Joyce insofar as he has deciphered his own riddle," Lacan formulates the latter's experience in terms of the knot. There are therefore two questions for us to resolve here. First, where does this ego come from? Why does Lacan use that term to describe the reparation of the chain? Why does he not use, for instance, a term he uses frequently elsewhere, *le moi*?[5] "Ego" is a Latin term, but one cannot ignore the fact that it has been largely adopted by Anglo-Saxon analysts, following in particular James Strachey's translation of Freud, where we find the second topography rendered as "The ego, the id, and the super-ego." This trinity has persisted as a kind of psychoanalytic password in English, to the extent of naming the well-known school *Ego* Psychology. Along these lines, we might nimbly gloss the reference to the ego as "Lacanian"—an ironic joke meant to show how a "strong ego" would end up. For that is the goal set by ego psychology to achieve a cure: building up in the analysand a strong ego. And it was Lacan who took on the task of showing that someone who suffers mentally is not

---

5. Translator's note: Lacan chooses to use the Latin *ego* instead of the standard French *moi*, normally translated as "ego." Harari comments on this choice in his next remarks.

suffering from a weak ego but from a kind of essentialism due to the force of the ego. This is possibly a very elementary and straightforward understanding of Lacan's critique of "egoism"; but it has led many to claim that what we read in Seminar 23 can only be a parody, amounting to a new and more corrosive attack on ego psychology. For our part, we incline *literally* to another reading, drawing equally on Joyce's letters as on the *Wake*. Let us begin with a letter: one sent to Joyce's brother Stanislaus on January 10, 1907. To give the letter some context, one of the recurrent themes of Joyce's correspondence at this point is his "financial distress," as he puts it. Almost at the beginning of his letter, he tells his brother: "You appear to be exasperated at my financial distress. No wonder. . . . All men are dolls or puppets, I think, except the English. My hatred of Italy and Italians is on the increase." Further on, he adds: "Anyhow I shall never be a model bank clerk."[6] This raises once again the problematic of a subject supposedly placed under the government of the Other. This connects up with *père-version*, according to which whoever conforms to the discourse of the Master, thus attaining the ideal model, will manage to conquer economic anxiety. Joyce, by contrast, insists on his craft as artificer, as he continues in the letter:

> I suppose, after all, there must be some merit in my writing. . . . If I knew Ireland as well as R.K. [Kipling] seems to know India, I fancy I could write something good. But it is becoming a mist in my brain rapidly. I have the idea of three or four immortal stories in my head but I am *too cold* to write them.

6. *The Selected Letters of James Joyce*, ed. R. Ellmann. London: Faber, 1975, pp. 141–143.

Our first reflection on this passage goes back to our discussion of the country, the fatherland. Joyce is famous for having written *Ulysses* with a strict precision concerning the names, the map, and the characters of Dublin. The book is obviously the product of someone with an extraordinarily intimate knowledge of Dublin and its urban geography. When, in his *Lectures on Literature*, Vladimir Nabokov reads Joyce, he traces lines on the map of that city in order to be able to follow the movements of the characters—Leopold Bloom and Stephen Dedalus, no less than the blind stripling and Farrell—and thus isolates the various encounters and missed encounters of the travelers.[7] This is therefore decisive for Joyce: if he is able to know in a detailed and exhaustive way every corner of his city, he will be able "to write something good." But, of course, he is in Italy, and his memories are becoming misty. Is the integrity and the consistency of the "patriotic" memory therefore a way to make up for paternal "shortcomings"? Joyce's letter continues: "Besides, where's the good. Ibsen, of course, may have liked that kind of sport." The editor Richard Ellmann (also Joyce's biographer, of course) glosses this last remark: "That is, total absorption in his work regardless of his environment." That may have been a valid position for someone like Ibsen, whom Joyce admired very early in his career, to the extent of learning Norwegian in order to be able to read him, and subsequently to write to him. Let us therefore abandon for a moment our reading of the letter and turn to the first text published by Joyce, at the age of 18 in 1900, that indeed deals with Ibsen. We read there the following:

---

7. V. Nabokov, *Lectures on Literature*. London: Weidenfeld and Nicolson, 1980, pp. 209–287.

Ibsen's power over two generations has been enhanced by his own reticence. Seldom, if at all, has he condescended to join battle with his enemies. It would appear as if the storm of fierce debate rarely broke in upon his wonderful calm.[8]

It is clear that Joyce thinks this attitude admirable. Regarding Ibsen's work, we should also recall that Freud himself had hailed him as a great dramatist, given that he had undertaken extensive psychological research in constructing his characters and due to the way he put together the scenarios and conflicts explored in his work.[9] But let us continue examining Joyce's youthful article; later on, he refers to the way in which Ibsen deals with a fact:

Ibsen treats it, as indeed he treats all things, with large insight, artistic restraint, and sympathy. He sees it steadily and whole, as from a great height, with perfect vision and an angelic dispassionateness, with the sight of one who may look on the sun with open eyes. Ibsen is different from the clever purveyor.[10]

This is clearly an idealized image! Another of Ellmann's footnotes reads: "This image of artistic detachment was to grow, with some assistance from Flaubert, into Stephen Dedalus' picture of the artist 'like the God of creation, . . . within or behind or beyond or above his handiwork, invisible, refined out

8. "Ibsen's New Drama," *The Critical Writings of James Joyce*, ed. E. Mason and R. Ellmann. London: Viking, 1959, p. 48.

9. S. Freud, "Some Character-Types Met with in Psychoanalytic Work" (1916), *Standard Edition* 14.

10. "Ibsen's New Drama," op. cit., p. 65.

of existence, indifferent, paring his fingernails.'" All of this would seem to indicate that Joyce was an artist 'in the mode of' Ibsen. Let us return to the letter to Stanislaus, written seven years after the publication of the high-flown article: "Ibsen . . . may have liked that kind of sport. But then he never broke with his set. I mean, imagine Roberts or Fay, with an allowance from the Irish Republic moving around Europe with correspondence tied at his heels like a goat's tether and you have H. I. [Ibsen]." What does Joyce mean by this? He is alluding to one of his crucial goals, which he sometimes achieved in part and for a time, in the course of a long history of "financial distress": namely, finding a patron. Such a person could be a prop—the very theme of his *père-version*—allowing him to pursue his work. And what name does he give to one who has attained that goal? "In the same circumstances perhaps I too would be an *egoarch*."[11] We emphasize this last word, for in our reading it is here, in Joyce's letter, that we should locate the basis of Lacan's use of the concept of "ego" in his effort to grasp the writer's structure as *sinthome*. Egoarch: the suffix, like that of monarch or patriarch, denotes command or government, while the prefix defines whoever possesses that condition. Thus, "egoarch" designates government, rule, or power belonging to the ego; it therefore names what is manifest of Joyce's ego ideal, embodying his explicit ambitions. Yet he, who claims to have broken with everything, says that unlike Ibsen he has torn himself away from his "set" at the cost of suffering permanent "financial distress"; and despite all this, he allows himself to mourn nostalgically the lost chances to obtain a patron to support his labors, a loyal

---

11. *Selected Letters*, op. cit., p. 142.

lieutenant of his *père-version*. But in fact Joyce fails to see that he has reached the position of egoarch, as a nominal suppletion (a point that we will return to).

To sum up, then: this emphasis on writing—essential for this ego—reveals itself, in our reading, to be derived from Joyce's thrust to attain the position of egoarch, as part of his *père-version*. We might imagine that this is only a single, precocious instance of Joyce using the term, but we would be wrong. If we turn to page 188 of *Finnegans Wake*, we read: "condemned fool, anarch, egoarch, hiresiarch, you have reared your disunited kingdom on the vacuum of your own most intensely doubtful soul." This passage, full of evocations and associations—where moreover the question of heresy reappears, linked metonymically with egoarch—might give rise to a long digression, but it would lead us astray.

We would ask, in the end, two questions. The first concerns Lacan's characterization of Joyce's ego; while the second is to ask why the register that remains unknotted in this new chain is I and not another. Regarding the latter, we have already indicated how Lacan takes a section from *A Portrait* as a prop. The episode in question has Stephen discussing with some schoolmates who is the best writer, the best poet, and so on. Stephen comes to be beaten up by Heron, the leader of the little band, whose name recalls *Hero*, close to Stephen in the book's original title. They are discussing Byron, whom Stephen puts forward as the greatest poet. Heron disagrees and repeatedly demands that Stephen retract his remark, but without success. Suddenly he yells "Behave yourself!," cutting at Stephen's legs with his cane. This, writes Joyce

> was the signal for their onset. Nash pinioned his arms behind while Boland seized a long cabbage stump which was

> lying in the gutter. Struggling and kicking under the cuts
> of the cane and the blows of the knotty stump Stephen was
> borne back against a barbedwire fence.[12]

Obviously, Stephen's experience is not a pleasant one. He receives a beating in a passive position, and Lacan thinks that anyone who endures this could only feel a sense of violation, be filled with rancor and hatred. In a strange way, Lacan seems to react to what has happened to Stephen with a certain intensity of affect. He notes in passing that there are obviously some subjects who undergo this kind of experience with enjoyment. Thus, he is able to launch the hypothesis that this crucial episode may have been enjoyable for Stephen, so that we might describe it as a masochistic act. In the light of psychoanalysis, we must note that on Stephen's part there is a certain amount of provocation, its unavowed aim being for him to end up against the barbed wire, suffering the kicks and blows of his three "friends." So far, we recognize a common, even classic form of psychoanalytic reasoning. However, Lacan goes forward to stress what happens after the episode itself:

> At last after a fury of plunges he wrenched himself free.
> His tormentors set off towards Jones's Road, laughing and
> jeering at him, while he, half blinded with tears, stumbled
> on, clenching his fists madly and sobbing.

This does not seem to indicate anything unusual, as it describes a "natural" reaction. But what is singular comes immediately afterward:

---

12. J. Joyce, *A Portrait of the Artist as a Young Man*, op. cit., p. 82.

> While . . . the scenes of that malignant episode were still passing sharply and swiftly before his mind he wondered why he bore no malice now to those who had tormented him. He had not forgotten a whit of their cowardice and cruelty but the memory of it called forth no anger from him. All the descriptions of fierce love and hatred which he had met in books had seemed to him therefore unreal.

In other words, the character is becoming passionless. Any extreme suffering can unexpectedly leave us perplexed, displaced, by the fact that we do not feel any anger, a reaction which might however be desirable to "correspond" to such aggression. We might ask whether Stephen is showing forgiveness toward his attackers. The text goes on to explain: "he had felt that some power was divesting him of that sudden-woven anger as easily as a fruit is divested of its soft ripe peel."[13] It is this that Lacan takes up: something falls away, and this falling-away is *imposed* on Stephen, in the same automatic manner that, according to Lacan, speech is imposed. What slips away from Stephen like "a soft ripe peel" is of course I, something that is confirmed by the fact that his memory, his imagination of the beating loses its determining power. Once the "peel" has come away completely, a certain type of reparation becomes imperative due to Stephen suddenly relating to the body as alien, with a reaction of disgust.[14] And it is at this point that the ego appears to recapture the I—or body—once the "peel" has come away. This ego is none other than the Ideal of "egoarchic" *élan* or verve. This episode from *A Portrait*, of such decisive significance for Lacan's

---

13. Ibid., pp. 82–83.
14. On this subject, see Chapter 8 above.

understanding of Joyce, allows us to distance ourselves from any psychological approach to the writer. In a brief digression, Lacan strongly criticizes psychology, describing it as the muddled image each one of us has of his own body. If psychology is such, it is inscribed in the register of the Imaginary; and consequently, due to psychological notions, it has not hitherto been possible to study the episode in question and give it its true importance. It is thus here that Lacan brings in the fourth register as reparation. At any rate, Lacan specifies the effect of this fourth ring now defined as ego with the following striking statement, given in the final session of his seminar: "Through this artifice of writing, I will claim that the Borromean knot is restored." A little further on, at almost the end of his presentation, he emphasizes the point: due to Joyce's ego, "we are in a position to see the Borromean knot reconstituted." However, this nodal *appensé*[15] is false, for no Borromean knot (or chain) is restored or reconstituted. According to Lacan, "it must be made"; and indeed, made according to the Borromean criteria, any unknotting at all—even a single one—would undo the chain. But in that case, if we untie the reparation brought about by the ego, then I—which it supports—remains isolated, but R and S are still chained together, as they were before the introduction of the ring marked "ego." Nothing is therefore restored, for no Borromean chain is "written." What, then, is "written," what is obtained? A quadruple chain that is *non*-Borromean, that we might call a "Joycean-ego" chain. The next question, then, is obvious: Is this simply an error, not noticed by Lacan? Did he not know what he was talking about? Let us leave aside

---

15. See above, p. 324.

any hypothetical interpretations as to why Lacan *literally* "shows" his error in understanding this new quadruple chain (which he calls a new knot). In our view, beyond any intention of Lacan's, a solid effect of teaching arises from this "slip": that is, one aspect is the question of reparation, which refers—as with Joyce's ego—to the reinforcement of a non-Borromean quadruple chain; while another aspect is that of writing the "normal," nonreparatory structure of the quadruple Borromean chain (we will shortly return to this below).

The Joycean episode we have referred to seems in Lacan's eyes to have been "evacuated." What does he mean by this? That the episode has not been repressed; for if it had, it would return as a formation of the unconscious, bearing the imprint of a process without weight in *Finnegans Wake*: that of metaphor. The episode has been directly excluded; a massive eradication has taken place around it. In our view, this would indicate that a foreclosure has taken place. In Joyce's case, foreclosure will determine the very "bone" or kernel, by what its occurrence leaves behind. We can thus see why, in the same session, Lacan calls the object *a* a "bone." When the peel or skin slips away from someone who, like those who starve, is "all skin and bones," the bone is all that remains. And if that takes place, it implies that in I, in the "muddled" (or psychological) relation to the image of the body—in other words, to the specular image identified with the ego: i (a)—in I, then, what falls or is evacuated is the "i" of "i(a)." And what endures is the bone: the *a*. The loss of this image, this fruit peel, is what takes place for Joyce in I, which itself also falls. We might describe this structural event as the foreclosure of the specular image, the support of the ego [*moi*]. Hence, in Joyce's case, the "ego" [*ego*] repairs the foreclosive fault of (what is normally termed) the ego [*moi*].

On this topic, we have already mentioned Lacan's reflections about the possibility of conceiving of other kinds of foreclosure than that of the Name-of-the-Father. According to the transcriptions, he stated: "It is quite certain that foreclosure has something more radical about it, since the Name-of-the-Father is ultimately something rather lightweight." In other words, the latter instance, because it is precarious, is structurally deficient and cannot account with sufficient rigor for the status of foreclosure. How are we to account for it, then? If we turn to Claude Rabant's latest book, *Inventer le Réel*, we will find that author giving another version of what Lacan argued, based on his own notes from the seminar. As he puts it, "The orientation of the Real forecloses meaning. This foreclosure is more radical than that of the Name-of-the-Father."[16] And it is due to this crucial statement, full of clinical consequences, that we are in a position to draw up a final table in our journey, where we will be able to articulate the diverse kinds of foreclosure; and moreover, we will consider at the same time there the various knots and chains presented in Seminar 23.

There is an additional point here. Concerning the slipping away of fruit peels, Lacan introduces the expression "to let fall," *laissez-tomber*. In Lacan's work this phrase becomes a concept, for it refers to the workings of *a*, especially as set forth in Seminar 10, on *Anxiety*. In this instance, the *a* remains and the "i" is lost, taking with it the I. Subsequently, the ego attempts to salvage what has been lost, an attempt that occurs in the body, for the ego is inscribed in I. Stephen's experience is an event in the body, a certain manner of not feeling

---

16. C. Rabant, *Inventer le Réel. Le déni entre perversion et psychose.* Paris: Denoel, 1992, p. 165 [translation: LT].

it, of "letting it fall" like a superfluous peel. In what context are we to understand this evacuation as foreclosure? On this point, there has been a stereotypical mode of explaining the concept of foreclosure in juridical terms. In other words, it is stated as a notion that derives entirely from that domain, from which it simply passed over into psychoanalysis. Rigorously speaking, a trial is "pre-closed" (foreclosure is located, according to this reading, as "pre-closure") or prescribed after some time during which a judicial action should have been undertaken and has not taken place. For instance, a period of time elapses during which it has not been possible, for various reasons, to carry out the sanction corresponding to an alleged misdeed. Hence, when the preestablished time limit has expired, the following juridical fiction comes into effect: that the accused has already been judged, sentenced, and has carried out the set penalty. The trial pre-closes, sidestepping the various stages that should have taken place; this is obviously equivalent, in legal terms, to "nothing took place." There were—and perhaps still are—a number of psychoanalytic supporters of this juridical illustration, by which forclosure would designate the omission of a trial, a precise equivalent of the dismissal of some instance of cardinal significance. But if the imaginary analogy is always fascinating, let us bear in mind that it is sustained in something that cancels out the explicit origin, as identified by Lacan, of the notion. In fact, Lacan did not conceal the sources of the term, which do not belong to the juridical domain but are strictly linguistic.[17] Let's say, first, that foreclosure is linked to

---

17. J. Lacan, Seminar 9, *Identification*, November 22, 1961 and January 17, 1962, unpublished; Seminar 18, *D'un discours qui ne serait pas du semblant*, May 18, 1971, unpublished.

grammatical negation, in a modality specific to the French language. The split or double condition of this modality has been discussed meticulously and with perspicacity by two analysts whom Lacan knew well, the authors of a famous book on grammar: J. Damourette and E. Pichon. In an article of 1928, they analyze the two terms that form the French negative as follows: first, they isolate the significance of *ne* by considering its function in subordinate clauses, where the particle "always expresses a discordance between the subordinate and the main clause." Their example comes from Molière's *Tartuffe*: "*Mettez-vous là, vous dis-je; et quand vous y serez, /Gardez qu'on* ne *vous voye, et qu'on* ne *vous entende.*" ["Sit there, I tell you; and once you're there /Make sure you are not seen or heard."] We see here the discordance between the efforts deployed by the subject and the danger that persists despite those efforts; this is why the particle *ne* is "usefully" termed *discordant*.

Let us now examine the second element of the French negative. All of the terms that can constitute that element relate, according to the authors, to "facts which the speaker does not envisage as forming part of reality. These facts are in a sense foreclosed, and so we give this second part of the negative the name *foreclusive*." Thus, they argue that the "ideas" connoted by *jamais* ["never"], *rien* ["nothing"], and the like are "expelled from the field of possibility perceived by the speaking subject." They take an example from Racine's *Iphigénie*: "*Argine, il me défend de lui parler* jamais." ["Argine, he forbids me to ever speak with."] They deftly link foreclosure to scotomization, the misguided conception of R. Laforgue that Freud himself had doubts about.[18] It was this conception that inspired Lacan, in adopt-

---

18. S. Freud, "Fetishism" (1927), *Standard Edition* 21.

ing and adapting foreclosure from Damourette and Pichon,[19] in order to read Freud's term *Verwerfung*.[20]

It is in this manner that Seminar 23 implicitly takes up the broad sense of what is proposed by these two analysts about forging the term "foreclosure," a term that now "extends" to experiences of which the judgment of existence appears directly excluded. This, then, is the conception of foreclosure that we have worked with, one that rules out both a juridical reference for the term and its flattening-out by being applied exclusively—and thus erroneously—to psychotic structures.

Let us now return to the examination of R and S. Two situations determined by knotting arise in Joyce with regard to these registers. First, his writing presents us with a riddle [*énigme*], as we have noted: it is a defect in the Imaginary, and its eventual reparation, that for Lacan gives the author of *Dubliners* the title of "the writer of the riddle *par excellence*." In other words, Joyce—as egoarch—is little concerned with whether or not he is understood; this is why his riddles give rise to decipherings. The riddle is now defined as a statement [*énoncé*] that cannot find its enunciation: the very reverse of the fomer definition, where a riddle was an enunciation that cannot find its statement. Despite this transformation, one trait persists: the discrepancy, the "cannot find," in a congruent manner (i.e., united by I) between enunciation and state-

---

19. J. Damourette and E. Pichon, "Sur la signification psychologique de la négation en français," *Grammaire et inconscient*, *L'UNEBEVUE*. Paris: EPEL, 1993, pp. 29–53.

20. On the basis of a strictly defined linguistics, it is once again J.-C. Milner who has taken up, with rigor and precision, the work of Damourette and Pichon. Cf. "Une anaphore non-référentielle: Le système de la négation en français et l'opacité du sujet," in *Orders et raisons de langue*. Paris: Seuil, 1982, pp. 186–223.

ment. Jean Paris, a writer close to Lacan's circle, presents this as follows: in his view, the consequences of the enigmas or riddles inscribed by Joyce "extend to infinity."[21] If we read this on the basis of the "Joycean ego" chain, we could theorize the riddle as the result of a fault in the Imaginary, given that R and S remain interlinked in a Höpf chain.

The missing point is where Lacan is in a position to claim—let us recall the question, officially censored, which he poses to Jacques Aubert, namely whether or not the term "epiphany" belongs to Joyce (see Chapter 2 above): "I must say a few more words, which I have prepared, about the 'Epiphany,' Joyce's famous Epiphany, which you find all over the place."[22] Lacan reports that his question springs from his work on the chain: the epiphany may be "the result of this error, namely that the unconscious [i.e., the Symbolic] is tied to the Real."[23] The unconscious tied to the Real: thus, the riddle as epiphany bound up with Joyce's ego. Or, to be more precise: bound up with the "slip"—through excess or absence—which occurs in the writing of the triple Borromean, a slip that calls for the reparation to be carried out by the ego.

With what we have so far established, we are in a position to undertake the final table of our study, which will of course

21. J. Paris, *James Joyce par lui-même*. Paris: Le Seuil, 1957.

22. There is no doubt, though it is worth signaling, that the term "epiphany" itself—which we have located in *Stephen Hero*, published post-humously in 1944—no longer appears in *A Portrait*. Of course, the writerly experience that we associate with the term unfolds throughout the rest of Joyce's work, but he never again uses the term "epiphany."

23. The official transcriber of the seminar once again rebuts the attachment of R and S (unconscious), and writes instead: "Epiphanies are always linked to the real, a fantastic thing." *Ornicar?* 11, op. cit., p. 9.

involve scanning again the points we have already explored. The table will certainly center on the question of the father: not on the lack, but on the sheer absence [*carence*] of one. In other words, this absence of the father is not only a symbolic lack, it entails something actually missing. Such an absence of the father results in the Name-of-the-Father failing to operate as a substitute, a point to be grasped in terms of an appeal with no response. This is fundamental for understanding the absence [*carence*] here: someone is invoked, and does not appear. This is what determines the series of suppletions, which are efforts to "supply," make up for, that absence. Such suppletions, of course, are not metaphorical—as Joyce's prose can show us;[24] in particular, they do not engage with the paternal metaphor. That is, they do not substitute, they are not "in place of" anything, for the terms co-exist *in praesentia*, like a portmanteau word. If we follow this strand, we come back to what was presented in the opening chapters: that is, *nomination*, which as a fourth element completes the knot. We explored this question in Mark Twain's *The Diary of Adam and Eve* in Chapter 2, where we were able to specify what naming, as opposed to nomination, consisted in. We distinguished between a new Lacan and the Lacan of old, insofar as the latter was a creationist. In the earlier work, it was enough to name something, and it would emerge: this amounted to a creationism of the signifier. By contrast, Lacan's later position splits off "so-called divine" creation—which is an act—from what is entailed by symbolic nomination. Thus, on one side is the *Fiat lux!*, the act of naming something and founding it, making the Real emerge on the basis of the Symbolic; and on another, quite distinct side we

---

24. See Chapter 3 above.

have the invention of a name—both the proper name and the common noun—that attains its real through the abrogation of the identity authorized by the code. Symbolic nomination is therefore alone capable of making a hole in the Real, determining it as not-all, as "fragmented." It is thus the concept that makes up for the sheer absence [*carence*] of the Name-of-the-Father: nomination, as a generic term that, as we saw, can be "declined," rendered adjectival in each of the registers. And in terms of a new conceptuality, it is nomination that allows Lacan to read Joyce as an analyst—not as a literary critic, nor as a naive "applied" psychoanalyst, but in order to bring grist to his mill. Nomination therefore encapsulates what we can posit as an alternative to what Lacan reminds us of again, and not uncritically: namely, that for Freud everything is sustained by the function of the father; in fact, by precisely an eternal love for the father. By contrast, what Lacan advances—as we have presented it—aims to do without the Name-of-the-Father on condition that it is put to use. This is what makes nomination possible.

To sum up, then: we will undertake drawing up our final table on Joyce by taking nomination as the foundation, as it takes adjectival forms in each of the registers. Thus, under real nomination we will put the *Verwerfung* [foreclosure] of meaning as pathognomic. Why do we do this? As will be recalled, in the layout of the triple Borromean chain meaning ex-sists outside the Real. Rabant works on precisely this idea, but in a different sense than ours. For him, this foreclosure of meaning implies being able to extricate oneself from the multiple meanings entailed by any particular word. Effectively, if one were to hear all the reverberations of a word, one could no longer speak. It is thus necessary to foreclose meaning, given the plurality or polysemy involved. This is precisely what did not occur in the case of Joyce, insofar as his writing exploits that polysemy. But the ordinary speaker cannot do this—were he to do so, there would be a breakdown of understanding that would block the communicative function of language. If something can be transmitted, concludes Rabant, it is because other meanings have been foreclosed. Thus, what a term denotes becomes definable because the whole range of other connotations has been put to one side. The majority of linguists claim, by contrast, that a term has first of all a denotation, a proper sense, and that subsequently other connotations are added to this. And these connotations, it is usually claimed, merely confuse or disturb communication. Well, Rabant argues for the opposite case: the abolition of connotations, their foreclosure, is a necessary condition for any term to be able to manifest a certain univocity. This is his understanding of the foreclosure of meaning, which comes to be slightly restricted each time that a speaker "gives language a little nudge"—through invention—in Lacan's formulation.

Without wishing to denigrate Rabant's argument, our own has a different reference: the conception of the death drive as a force of unbinding. This unbinding has a double sense, as we have shown, following Milner's work: it also refers, of course, to the coming-apart of the knot. Having said that, the knot that touches the Real due to paranoia is the trefoil knot; yet this is not to be written on Joyce. In his case, unknotting is repaired, allowing for the writing we are familiar with (Figure 52):

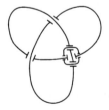

Figure 52

This is one of the writings through which a recurrent theme of Seminar 23 emerges: the question of repairing knots and chains. If what we show above is, in our view, *equivalent* to a repaired trefoil knot, what does it give rise to? To something that we can link to the foreclosure of meaning: that is, work with phonetics, which Lacan renames *faunetics*. The faun in question exists only in what is heard. This process of punning, of using glossolalia, forfeits meaning because it works with the letter, with the material through which phonation is put to work as *ph-onation* (using the *ph* of *Phallus*), obtaining what Joyce calls "a music of ideas," which is in no way an ethical offshoot of the principle of contradiction, for it operates in the domain of the undecidable. What, then, should be stressed in terms of the dominance of R? Working with imposed speech: with Joyce, what is imposed is made into voices that do not, however, lead to deliria or to hallucinations, but to writing. At the same time, this Joycean process is the origin of what Lacan names "exiled writing": exiled from meaning, that is. Moreover, we confront the *eaubscene* here: for one possibility indicated by the falling-away of the body like ripe fruit peel is also that Joyce is overwhelmed by disgust at his own body. Disgust, as we have shown, is very closely linked to the *eaubscene*. These characteristics mean that, as with psychosis, the result lies outside of discourse; yet there is no question of this "outside of discourse" being psychotic. It is different because, as the example given by this kind of nomination shows, the "outside" here consists in not seeking the social bond. For Lacan, we recall, a discourse is what produces a social bond; and in such nomination, this is prevented in the way we have described. This is why the result in question appears to us enigmatic and barely sympathetic: by cultivating ab-sense or non-meaning, it consecrates the opaque jouissance of *lalangue*.

Let us now consider symbolic nomination. Here, our argument leads toward a *Verwerfung* or foreclosure that is *de facto* or "actual." Which knot or chain should we consider here? We recall that in the seventh session of his seminar Lacan presents a triple Borromean chain with two slips that, he claims, cause S to remain isolated; that is, two points where the knotting of S comes undone. And this is the context where he introduces *de facto* foreclosure. But as we argued in Chapter 6 concerning an isolated Symbolic, if the chain were "made" in this way, it would not only be S but all three elements that would become isolated. Thus, a fourth element comes to knot everything together, producing a quadruple Borromean chain. To sum up, *our argument relies on giving the name "sinthome" to this nodal writing alone*. Once again, we can include the writing of the quadruple Borromean, but with a displacement—in relation to Figure 11—regarding the layout of the registers, brought about by a first step in turning anti-clockwise. What is the cause of this? The fact that the following writing transcends the conception of what we have argued, in this sense: the *sinthome*, disinvested from S, crosses the latter register four times, while R and I cross it barely twice each. Without doubt, this predominance gives a fitting account of symbolic nomination (Figure 53):

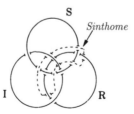

Figure 53

Astonishingly, the word *sinthome* does not appear in the final session of Seminar 23, as a cross-reference for the notion of Joyce's ego that Lacan brings in there. It seems to us that this might be due to the fact that imaginary, and not symbolic, nomination is what Lacan is taking as his context here. And in the former, of course, we do not find the *sinthome*.

The fourth element that knots together the three separate registers, the *sinthome* in its strict sense, leads Joyce to seek to make a (proper) name for himself through symbolic nomination. This is a separate level that Lacan consistently emphasizes as not to be confused with Joyce's *ph-onation*. The emblem of this level of Joyce's work is not to be found in *faunetics*; rather, Lacan sees it as a question of what drives him to make a proper name for himself. How is this to be understood? In the very first session of Seminar 23, and insistently throughout it, Lacan claims that making a proper name for oneself involves an artifice of pure, mental jouissance and a belief in being. There is One, a singular beyond any context: a *sinthomatic* identification with the "Old artificer" whom we read about in the closing lines of *A Portrait*.

Our thesis is therefore that to every type of foreclosure there corresponds a *type of unknotting* occurring in a specific knot or chain. Thus, with real nomination, we have the trefoil; with symbolic nomination, the triple Borromean chain with S detached. As we have shown, the following cannot be inscribed in Borromean terms: I remaining detached, amounting of course to imaginary nomination. It is in the latter that we encounter the above-mentioned *Verwerfung* of the specular image, with which the ego identifies [i(a)]. It strips naked, masochistically, the bone [*os*] of the object, as well as the object as bone. We can take as one sign of the value of this *os-bjet*, the letting-fall that characterizes it, as we saw in the episode from *A Portrait* with the excess jouissance of ripe fruit peel and so on. This is equivalent, furthermore, to R and S knotted together and the ego "saving" I: the Joycean ego, that is. The latter's sought, and frequently attained, ideal is to be an egoarch. Conversely, this condition is transcended in Joyce's riddles and epiphanies—especially when they take effect by means of broken phrases.

We integrate all of these conclusions in the following table:

Absence of Name-of-the-Father ⟶	Suppletion (nonmetaphorical substitution:
Nomination (not the creationism of *Fiat lux!*)	r: *Verwerfung* of meaning—unbinding death drive ≈ repaired trefoil → ph-onation, *faunetics*, imposed speech, opaque jouissance of *lalangue*, exiled writing (outside of discourse and the social bond), the *eaubscene*.
	s: *Verwerfung* "de facto"—discernment ≈ S detached from the triple Borromean chain, the origin of the quadruple chain, the *sinthome* → making a (proper) name for oneself by artifice with pure (mental) jouissance, belief in "being," singular identification with the One of the *sinthome*.
	i: *Verwerfung* of i(a)—masochistic baring of *os-bjet*, letting-fall, excess jouissance ≈ R and S knotted together, the ego knotting I → egoarchic verve: riddles and epiphanies (in particular broken phrases).

What is clear, beyond the case of Joyce, is that *nomination* is a concept that takes over from the Name-of-the-Father. The latter notion entails for Lacan an eternal love for the father, if that dimension cannot be surpassed. He argues that Freud made this situation explicit in *Totem and Taboo*, a text on which he carries out a surprising, insightful reading. Lacan emphasizes that love for the father ultimately entails giving up women. According to the Freudian myth, the brothers unite to kill the father of jouissance who possesses all of the women. After they have killed him, their retroactive obedience of his interdiction relating to women means that, in order to love the father—and of course to be loved by him in turn—in order to maintain this dimension of eternal love and thus be beyond the death drive, they must abandon women. And here, of course, we see a *père-version* (or "turning to the father"). At this point, in our view Lacan implies a sticking-point in his theorization of Freud, for if this *père-version* remains static as the law of love, then the unavoidable condition of maintaining the father as "guarantee" of castration consists in renouncing ~~The~~ woman. Hence that other aphoristic formulation condensing Lacan's thinking: to do without the Name-of-the-Father on condition of making use of it. In other words: to choose, ultimately, to make one's choice, but only if that choice finds its heretical real. We might perhaps posit this as a "good" form of heresy. As Joyce put it, "anarch, egoarch, hiresiarch": an "unconditioned" Name-of-the-Father, then, not secondary, not subordinate—subordinating.

In order to bring our study to a conclusion, we will add a personal reflection that derives from the Lacanian explorations we have traced; we trust that it will be revealed as both clinically relevant and topologically coherent. It is a question of Lacan's oscillation between the triple and the quadruple Borromean chain, which we stressed in our first chapter; or better still, of his movement from the triple to the quadruple, clearly revealed in the course of the seminar. This movement of Lacan's is not only revolutionary but also subversive: its revolution relating to the stars (to complete it is to return to the point of departure), its subversion by contrast consisting in a change of discourse. For us, this is what occurs in Seminar 23. In our view, both the oscillation and the subversion are nothing but different ways of writing moments that can occur in analytic treatment. We might consider, in this sense, the beginning of analysis, the establishment and maintenance of the transference situation—in other words, the trajectory of analysis—and its bringing-to-conclusion. This singular argument forms part of a text we have published, *No hay desenlace sin reanudacion*, in a volume entitled *¿De que trata la clinica lacaniana?* Thus, at the outset, an analysand who is "blocked" (in Lacan's phrase) is located in the R.S.I. written around a central ring, which can account for any one of the three registers in turn. But with a difference: the central register is doubled. This way of writing the knot is surely partly inspired by the non-Borromean quadruple chain. The chain of the symptom, then, proper to the beginning of analysis, can be presented as follows (Figure 54):

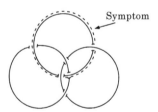

Figure 54

This duplication allows us to conceive of the symptom as a new kind of "product," but also as a formation that is excessive, incongruous, that does not function in the Real and is thus condemned by the analysand. Yet why do we not write in the letters to identify the registers? Because that which occupies the middle can write, according to each analysand, his or her suffering, in terms of the dominance of and through the Real, the Symbolic, or the Imaginary. And in this way, the ring in the center can be written in any register, with its appropriate double.

In the transference, which is not by accident called an "artificial neurosis" by Freud (note the recurrence of *artifice*), the artifice that lies in analysis transforms the non-Borromean quadruple chain into a triple, and Borromean chain. How should one proceed to reach such a result? The answer is relatively simple: one must cut the two central rings and attach them to one another, tying them top to bottom. Thus, two links are transformed into a single one. This operation, known as "making continuous," emerges as a radical inscription of Lacan's aphorism that claims that psychoanalysis is a matter of suture and splicing. Now, once this circle has been produced, one can proceed to attach the other two in order to make up the triple Borromean chain. We have thus carried out an un-knotting in order to re-knot. This is why we have proposed calling this the "chain of the paranoiac trinity," in which the stabilization proper to the transference prevails (Figure 55):

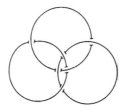

Figure 55

Why give it this name? Because it introduces the question of the continuity of the registers, given that they are all equivalent: there is no privileged term among them. This is why we describe this as a moment of stabilization. It thus emerges as a writing apt to account for the fact that analysis can perfectly well be interminable. Let us repeat what happens with Freud here, and on this basis with every analyst. The founder of psychoanalysis once said that at the beginning of his praxis, he did not know how to hold on to analysands, then later he did not know how to get rid of them. It is thus that arises the question of interminable analysis, as a hypnotic form of orthopedic comfort. For the jouissance triggered off by the analytic situation can be limitless in the temporal dimension, since it puts into effect an ever-renewed mythical promise of the recovery of the jouissance lost because of castration.

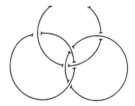

Figure 56

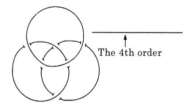

The 4th order

Figure 57

In order for things not to occur in this way, it becomes indispensable to bring about another effect bearing on the central circle—we emphasize this, for any kind of transformation depends on it—in the following way: the first cut to the circle frees the chain, allowing us to confirm its truly Borromean status (Figure 56). But the two other registers remain rings, each supported by a trivial knot. The central register, by contrast, not only does not form a trivial knot but is again cut; thus, from one we obtain two (Figure 57). We knot one of these two cords into a ring—a trivial knot—while, due to the fourth element thus obtained, it now becomes possible to write a quadruple Borromean chain, accounting for the *sinthome* (Figure 58):

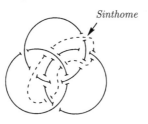

Figure 58

We thus have an unbalanced chain; it can therefore represent the chain of the end of analysis, because a formation of its subjective position is imposed on the subject with this quite specific condition: that which is "imposed" (like words). This is not a delirium but a know-how-with. But in that case, with what and how? By purifying that which lay at the origin of the symptom. We have always been working on the same order [*consistance*]: when we have transformed it into a triple chain, by making it continuous; and then, in the last move, by means of making it discontinuous. Either, in one case, through stitching-together, or in the other through unstitching. These are of course processes apt to be carried out with chains.

We thus have a quadruple Borromean chain that goes beyond the transference. And, let us repeat again, this makes it astonishing for a good number of those who follow Lacan's teaching to claim emphatically that the triple Borromean chain embodies Lacan's final position. Does this mistake not once again correspond to the Ideal of the balanced analyst and the adapted analysand? With shared horror these would view the mark of a dominant presence in the chain, as shown by the crossing-points of the fourth order: it crosses four times over only one of the three other elements. As we have noted, there are in total fourteen crossing-points, and four of these thus show the privileged relation that exists between the fourth order and the one it crosses. These two orders are not on a par with the others: they manifest a privilege, embody an imbalance. And this imbalance is a characteristic quite unlike that indicated by adaptation, the latter usually being defined by analysts in terms of the capacity to move freely between different vital spaces, attaining a certain flexibility of behavior by means of various defense mechanisms adapted to the occasions they are required. This kind of chameleon-like procedure is very often reckoned to be a "good end" of analysis, a good Ideal coming into effect. Yet since ideals cannot be reconciled—for to launch an imperative that an ideal should be abandoned is to fall into a logical trap, since that also implies an Ideal—we will advance an Ideal different from that of the adaptive chameleon: the privileging, for each analysand, of his or her know-how-with. It is clear that this emphasis implies inventing something in an analysis, working with bits of Real. This is why it denotes a process other than that characterized by the interpretation of symptoms, and likewise that marked by traversing the fantasy; it amounts, in fact, to the identification with the *sinthome*. And what does identification mean in this context? Here, Lacan is aiming at a formation with no division or fault, a formation with which there can finally be a mode of understanding and which thus is not indicative of the division of the subject. Hence our argument about the subversive implications of the *sinthome*. The subject of the symptom, by contrast, is a barred or divided subject, one who says: "I do not wish to be like this," "I do not wish to have that," or, indeed, "I cannot go on living like this." Conversely, one is sure that "one cannot live without" the *sinthome*. This, then, is the function Lacan attributes to Joyce's writing: he devotes his life to it, because it *is* his life. The consequence of this for analysis is not the chimerical goal of attempting to produce doubles of Joyce; but rather an effort to bring about in the analysand an inventiveness. Or even better: poetry and inventiveness. And, once again, these metaphors do not evoke some utopian production line of poets or great inventors, but aim to realize a change of discourse to allow access to a new perception of what is implied by letters and invention, thus to new signifiers. This point is crucial; and because of it the objective relies on a traversal of fantasy, insofar as that latter is what constructs reality, implying further stagnation. But it is not simply a matter of traversing this, for in the reality that depends on fantasy we confront a real: that of the identification with the *sinthome*. And the latter is of the Real, of course, as it always returns to the same place. Thus, in contrast with what occurs in psychotic wandering, in the hole of aimless drifting signifiers, it is easy to confirm that Joyce kept on his pathway.

To conclude, then, that pathway allows us to give psychoanalysis a new name: to call it, now that Lacan has swept the way clear, a *post-Joycean* psychoanalysis. Since this kind of psychoanalysis is of course our own, we should specify that its *wake* did not begin very long ago. And it would be truly gratifying if our book, composed in "*the cuidad of Buellas Arias*" (FW, 435), could contribute to its "*rire-vers l'un*."[25] In fact, to its *riverrun*.

---

25. Translator's note: Harari alludes to Philippe Sollers' "Joyce & Co," where the opening of *Finnegans Wake*—"riverrun"—is made to rhyme with the French for "to laugh-toward-the one."

Index

Freud, S., 86, 103, 125, 149, 164, 166, 211, 225, 323
  3 vs. 4 registers of, 13–15, 17, 19, 60, 62, 294–295
  on analysis, 108–109, 184, 356
  on anxiety, 257–258
  on art, 26, 81–82
  and Freudians, 153
  highlighting oral and anal drives, 55–56
  on identification, 327–328
    influence on Joyce's work, 193–194
  Lacan comparing work to, 296–297
  Lacan distancing self from, 294–296, 300
  Lacan's critiques of, 17–18, 118, 271
  Lacan's relation to, 106, 316–317
  on love of father, 347, 353
  and melancholy, 179–180
  self-analysis of, 303–304
  on symptoms, 15–16
  on woman, 29–30, 165
Freudian slips, 73, 75, 175, 324
Fromm, E., 89

gaze, 56–59
Gentile, G., 318n8
Genuss (jouissance), 108–110
God, 84, 91, 149
  jouissance of, 125–126
  naming, 27–28, 38
Godin, J.-G., 134
Gracián, Baltasar, 18
Gradiva (Jensen), 26
Gross, J., 142–143, 148, 199

Group Psychology and the Analysis of the Ego (Freud), 327
Guilbaud, G. Th., 7

harmony. See consonantia
Hayman, D., 46
Head, 152–154
hearing. See listening/hearing
Heidegger, M., 74
hellenization, 27
heresy, 353
heretics, 84
  Lacan and Joyce as, 8, 34, 280
heterogeneity, 206–208, 213, 297
history, Joyce's criticism of, 268–271
Hoffmann, E.T.A., 101–102
holes, 127, 148, 329. See also false holes
  and circles, 91–92, 212–213
  role of, 144–145
  and the Symbolic, 100, 222
  honoring, 146–147, 194–195
hope, 271, 277–278
Hopf chain, 10, 69, 212, 329
horror, from encounter with Real, 312–314
hysteria, 63, 223–224, 232–233, 259

Ibsen, H., 333–334
identification, 4, 191
  hysterical, 232–233
  with sinthome, 119–120, 145, 151, 170, 232–233, 358–359
  sinthome as, 211
  types of, 327–328
identity, 13, 161
il n'y a pas formulas, 285–286, 288